From
HEAVEN TO EARTH

From HEAVEN TO EARTH

THE REORDERING OF CASTILIAN SOCIETY, 1150–1350

Teofilo F. Ruiz

PRINCETON UNIVERSITY PRESS
PRINCETON AND OXFORD

COPYRIGHT © 2004 BY PRINCETON UNIVERSITY PRESS
PUBLISHED BY PRINCETON UNIVERSITY PRESS, 41 WILLIAM STREET,
PRINCETON, NEW JERSEY 08540
IN THE UNITED KINGDOM: PRINCETON UNIVERSITY PRESS, 3 MARKET PLACE,
WOODSTOCK, OXFORDSHIRE OX20 1SY
ALL RIGHTS RESERVED

LIBRARY OF CONGRESS CATALOGING-IN-PUBLICATION DATA
RUIZ, TEOFILO F., 1943–
FROM HEAVEN TO EARTH : THE REORDERING OF CASTILIAN SOCIETY, 1150–1350 /
TEOFILO F. RUIZ.
P. CM.
INCLUDES BIBLIOGRAPHICAL REFERENCES AND INDEX.
ISBN 0-691-00121-9 (CL : ACID-FREE PAPER)
1. CASTILE (SPAIN)—SOCIAL CONDITIONS. 2. CASTILE (SPAIN)—HISTORY. 3. LAND TENURE—SPAIN—CASTILE—HISTORY. I. TITLE.

HN590.C36R837 2004
306′.0946′3—DC21   2003045979

BRITISH LIBRARY CATALOGING-IN-PUBLICATION DATA IS AVAILABLE

THIS BOOK HAS BEEN COMPOSED IN GALLIARD

PRINTED ON ACID-FREE PAPER. ∞

WWW.PUPRESS.PRINCETON.EDU

PRINTED IN THE UNITED STATES OF AMERICA

1 3 5 7 9 10 8 6 4 2

To Jacques Le Goff

MAÎTRE ET AMI

CONTENTS

Preface and Acknowledgments ix

INTRODUCTION
From Heaven to Earth 1

CHAPTER ONE
A Taste for the New: Commerce, Property, and Language 12

CHAPTER TWO
The Evidence of Wills 37

CHAPTER THREE
Property: Wills and the Law in Medieval Castile 54

CHAPTER FOUR
Itemizing the World: Boundaries, Consolidation of Property, and Rights of Way 67

CHAPTER FIVE
Family and Property: Lineages and Primogeniture 87

CHAPTER SIX
Heavenly Concerns: Charity and Salvation 110

CHAPTER SEVEN
Toward a New Concept of Power: Unsacred Monarchy 133

Conclusion 151

Appendix 155

Notes 163

Bibliography 199

Index 215

PREFACE AND ACKNOWLEDGMENTS

I HAVE BEEN thinking about the topics in this book for a long time. More than two decades ago, I published an article titled, "The Transformation of the Castilian Municipalities: The Case of Burgos, 1248–1350." This was followed, shortly afterward, by another article, "Expansion et changement: La conquête de Séville et la société castillane, 1248–1350."[1] In both pieces, I sought to describe and explain changes in the social, political, and economic structures of Castile from the mid-thirteenth century onward. These changes, I argued then, stemmed from the conquest of most of western Andalusia by the Castilian Crown between the 1230s and 1260s, the ensuing expulsion of the Mudejar population, and the settlement of Christians in the region.

I continued to elaborate on these themes, with forays into other topics in Castilian history (the history of festivals, rituals of monarchy, popular culture). In the summer of 1996, I began to think of the conquest of Seville and the Christian settlement of the region not as markers of political and social shifts in late medieval Castilian history, but as part of a wider and pervasive reordering of Castilian society and culture; not as catalysts for change, but as manifestations of these changes.[2]

This awareness of the interconnectedness of seemingly unrelated aspects of Castilian history has forced me to think of the transformations of Castilian society in new ways. I was led to my reconceptualization of Castilian history in part by Peter Linehan's provocative insights into the period but most forcefully by his article "Religion, Nationalism, and National Identity in Medieval Spain and Portugal," which raises crucial questions about the construction of a Castilian identity in the late twelfth century.[3] Jacques Le Goff's works on the emergence of new systems of values—a notion from which I have unabashedly borrowed—and the concept of changing *mentalités* in western medieval Europe have also been important in providing me with a methodological framework. Most pointedly, *The Birth of Purgatory* proved an initial interpretative tool with which to explain broad cultural changes.[4]

Two things became evident as I began to work on this material. First, I would have to leave the comfortable confines of the post–mid-thirteenth-century period, where I had done most of my research and writing for almost thirty years, and focus most of my inquiries on the late twelfth and early thirteenth centuries. Second, in order to trace Castilian social and cultural changes, I would have to use different sources from those historians have deployed to explain value shifts elsewhere in Europe. Finally, I would have to find an alternative way to conceptualize these changes and place them in the broader context of mental transformations occurring in other parts of the medieval West and Iberia.

More than a decade ago, I had the great pleasure and intellectual benefit of attending a lecture by Jacques Le Goff at Columbia University's Society of Fellows. The suggestive title of Le Goff's conference, "Du ciel à la terre," provided me with the title for this book. In the 1980s, I was working on a different book and was able to explore the topic of cultural change only in monographic articles. In undertaking this new task, I ran into difficulties. Le Goff's work, like that of other historians of the twelfth century, seldom addresses Iberia's social and cultural life.[5] Although many of these studies mention Toledo's role in fostering the translation of ancient learning and cite the Jewish, Muslim, and Christian intermediaries who promoted the transmission of classical texts, they focus primarily on the role northern European scholars played in rescuing ancient texts and expound on their bold travels to and from the isolated islands of learning in the Iberian Peninsula, Sicily, and the East.[6] In many respects, the term *orientalism* is not inappropriate to describe a history that features intellectual colonialism as its most distinguishing attribute and derives its perspective almost exclusively from a small number of learned centers—Paris, Chartres, Cluny, Bologna, Oxford—with little or no regard to the so-called peripheries.

Within this historical tradition, the Iberian Peninsula, and Castile in particular, have appeared as exotic lands, at best, or as havens of cultural backwardness mired in endless wars of reconquest. The Castilian concern with martial pursuits left little room for cultural development—or so the explanation went. All noteworthy achievements in architecture, literature, and the arts were assumed to be imports from France or elsewhere. Iberian scholarship, when taken into account at all, was deemed borrowed from Bologna, Paris, or some other center of learning.[7]

In the last three decades, Hispanists seeking to illuminate and reconstruct aspects of Spanish and Castilian culture have produced a voluminous amount of research, but their endeavor has not helped much. These works, written mostly in Spanish or appearing in obscure journals with little circulation outside the world of Iberian medievalists, have had little or no impact on the general historiography of medieval culture or on the broadly published syntheses of cultural changes affecting western Europe between the late eleventh century and the end of the thirteenth century.[8] Although this is certainly not a book about scholasticism, historiography, or intellectual history, it is pertinent to note here that cultural production—the act of writing books, creating art, setting up philosophical disputations—always occurs within an intersection of social, economic, and political dynamics. Cultural transformations, shifts in value systems, "renaissances," if we wish to call them that, follow along fractures created by deeper structural changes. Vital for us to examine, then, are the changes that lead to new cultural production; these are often revealed and articulated not by artifacts but by social and economic transactions. Our discussion here and in the subsequent chapters thus focuses on specific changes in Castile's social context rather than on comparisons between Castile's cultural revival and that of its northern neighbors.

As does every other work I have published, this book owes a great deal to the publications of other scholars and to the insights of many loyal friends and colleagues. Their suggestions and criticism have prevented numerous infelicitous errors and mistaken conclusions. I remain conscious of the cooperative nature of intellectual production and am indeed very fortunate in the support and guidance I have received over the years. In truth, this is as much the work of others as it is mine, except, of course, for my unavoidable mistakes and limitations. Those, I claim all for myself. Manolo González Jiménez has thoughtfully and generously critiqued my work in his published books and articles for the last two decades. I have gained much from his insights and friendship. Adeline Rucquoi, Hilario Casado, John H. Elliott, Xavier Gil Pujol, Ariel Guiance, Denis Menjot, Charles Radding, Joseph F. O'Callaghan, Christoph Kimmich, Inga Clendinnen, and William and Carla Phillips have made important contributions to my understanding of the topics presented here.

Many of the ideas found in this book were presented as papers at Princeton's Shelby Cullom Davis Center. I greatly benefited from the comments and suggestions of the late Lawrence Stone, whose uncompromising commitment to history inspired generations of historians. I also profited enormously from the comments and friendship of William C. Jordan, Judith Herrin, Peter Brown, Giles Constable, and Natalie Davis. Portions of this book were also presented at Cornell, Stanford, Johns Hopkins, UCLA, and the California Medieval Seminar at the Huntington Library. Participants at these seminars provided vigorous critiques for which I am most grateful. I wish to acknowledge in particular Michael Steinberg, Richard Kagan, Maureen C. Miller, Carlo Ginzburg, Patrick Geary, John Dagenais, Ronald Mellor, Margaret Jacob, Lynn Hunt, Joan Cadden, Simon Teuscher, and David Ringrose. At Princeton University Press, Brigitta van Rheinberg has been most patient and generous with me and my work. She has been a true friend and supporter throughout this long process. Kim Hastings, who copyedited the manuscript, has done extraordinary work in rendering my text easier to read, in preventing unfortunate redundancies, and in correcting my numerous mistakes. I am most grateful for their help and support.

Paul Freedman read through the entire manuscript and provided generous comments and his abiding friendship. Our meetings and phone conversations have long been a source of pleasure and inspiration. David Nirenberg delivered a thorough critique of the whole manuscript. His was a labor of love and dedication to the making of history. The final organization of this book I owe to him. There are no words to express my gratitude for his support. Scarlett Freund, wife, sister soul, and cherished companion, placed her own pursuits aside, as always, and gave her wonderful editorial skills and sound scholarly understanding to making this a better book. More than ever, she is the reason for which I write, for which I am.

But the chief inspiration and intellectual presence behind this book has been Jacques Le Goff. I have had the privilege and pleasure of knowing the Le Goff family—Jacques, his wife, Hanka, his children, Barbara and Thomas—for a quarter of a century. Over the years, I have sat in the fabled Le Goff seminars at the Ecole des Hautes Etudes, and at his equally legendary, and deservedly so, dinner table. Jacques Le Goff's contributions to history are too well known for me to review here; far more important are his generosity and forthright friendship. His kindness and understanding as a friend, his wisdom and sensibility, have had an enduring impact on my life. It is to him and his family that I dedicate this book, a very small token of my gratitude and admiration.

Los Angeles, California
Summer 2002

From
HEAVEN TO EARTH

INTRODUCTION

FROM HEAVEN TO EARTH

IN AUGUST 1230, in the Rioja town of Logroño (Castile), Sebastián, a cleric of the collegiate church of Santa María la Redonda, drew up his testament and last will. Written in a Latin already badly corrupted by Castilian words and syntax, Sebastián's will was a modest affair. Altogether his monetary bequest, just a bit more than 80 *maravedíes* (*mrs.*), and gifts in kind—cloth, land, three vineyards, half a house, a silver chalice, and other items—did not exceed 200 *mrs*.[1] Part of his legacy, mostly small annual rents scattered among diverse ecclesiastical institutions and confraternities, was earmarked to feed and clothe the poor and to subsidize masses and prayers for his soul and the souls of relatives. The bulk of his lands, vineyards, and money, however, went to his immediate family and, in lesser amounts, to his friends.[2]

Sebastián's will is, at first glance, unremarkable. The property he left to the Church and his family was not substantial. The amounts in question suggest a well-to-do but by no means wealthy cleric. What makes his will important to us, as we read these records almost eight centuries later, is the novelty, at least for northern Castile, of its composition. Sebastián (or the lay scribe Dominicus de Ubago, drafting the will) was not only disposing of earthly possessions, he was also articulating new ideas about property, charity, and salvation, using his will as a tool to lobby for forgiveness and preserve his property within the family.

This will and similar testaments written in northern Castile from the early thirteenth century onward departed radically from the well-established formulas of donations and wills drafted in northern Castile between the ninth and the late twelfth century. In the pre-1200 documents, donors and testators bestowed their property indiscriminately to ecclesiastical establishments for the "salvation or remedy of one's soul" or for the "salvation of the souls of friends and relatives." With minor changes, the post-1200 patterns of scribal language and property distribution found in Sebastián's will became the norm for testaments in Castile and Spain until the modern period.[3]

Sebastian's last wishes, and those expressed in similar wills of the period, open a window onto a distant past. They allow us to capture, even if only partially, a moment when the way Castilians thought and wrote about property, salvation, charity, and themselves was radically transformed. Sebastián's will is, as noted, one of the earliest extant testaments that addressed these new concerns. In this respect, it serves as a useful guide and entry point to the change in northern Castilian mentality and values. Sebastián's last wishes expressed these different conceptions of the material world and the afterlife. His preoccupation with family, property, and salvation provides us with a first glance at what would eventually become a model for Castilian material and spiritual transactions, the drafting of new legislation, and other cultural and institutional practices. In order to trace these changes, we will look closely at the narrative structure of Sebastián's will, especially at its new form of scribal redaction, and examine the way it handles topics such as the fragmentation of property; property and the family; negotiating charity and salvation; language; and geographic location.

Sebastian's will differed greatly in organization, language, and structure from previously drafted documents. The scribe was different, too. No longer a clergyman who recorded donors' bequests in a highly formalized language and with the Church's interests at heart, he was often a municipal scribe, elected by fellow townsmen or named by the municipal council.

It may in fact be argued that what changed was not so much the values or attitudes toward salvation, property, and family, but the way documents were redacted. These new redaction formats allow us to perceive patterns of behavior that were obscured by ecclesiastical scribal discourse. New forms of writing and new ways of presenting texts—in this case, wills—were thus at the heart of the transformations of Castilian society. Unlike before 1200, most of the documentation written after the thirteenth century, especially in urban centers, was drafted by lay scribes. These scribes brought new secular sensibilities to the composition of wills and other recorded transactions; moreover, they conferred a smidgen of authority on those commissioning written testimonies. Sebastián's will and other documents of the period make this very clear. Testators in wills, sellers in transactions of property and rental agreements, and donors now had a hand in organizing their own documents, and they often dictated their wishes to the scribe in a confused and not too logical fashion. But these new methods of redaction were not unfounded. Following broad social and cultural shifts, they were but a manifestation of the sweeping changes taking place in Castilian society.

Sebastian's will, and almost every other will after 1230 (see appendix), showed a clear desire to divide legacies among as many clerical establishments as possible. This stood in sharp contrast to the almost universal tendency, in pre-thirteenth-century wills and donations, to bestow wealth on a single institution. This change did not occur gradually; it was remarkably swift. The speed with which this new practice took hold signals a watershed in the way people writing or dictating their wills thought about the distribution of their inheritances.

Legacies were not only fragmented among diverse ecclesiastical institutions; they were also divided among family members (whereby some received more than others), friends, and colleagues. Sebastián's will, like others I examine in succeeding chapters, also made sure that the family, not the Church, would be the main beneficiary of the deceased's wealth.

The dispersion of pious gifts and the requisition of masses in Sebastián's will evidences a hard-nosed bargaining for salvation. In these transactions aimed at securing a place in the life to come, charity came to play a significant role. Sebastián and his executors appropriated the act of charity and transformed it into a highly symbolic performance in which only a selected few of the poor were fed and clothed. The relationship between testators/donors and the poor—until now seen as an embodiment of Christ—became a direct one, no longer mediated by the Church.

In Sebastián's will, language also played a major role. Not only were the redactive forms new; the intrusive vernacular—the Castilian language—had supplanted the already considerably corrupted Latin of early thirteenth-century Castile. Sentence structure, word choice, idiomatic expressions—all point to new sensibilities now being articulated in a very different written form. Shortly after 1230, wills and all documents dealing with property were written in Castilian.

Sebastián's will was written in Logroño, an important stop on the pilgrimage road to Compostela and, as such, a site for commercial exchange between Castilians and foreigners from north of the Pyrenees. It is no accident that new forms of thinking about property, the family, and salvation first emerged along this route. Logroño and other cities on the road were among the first Castilian urban centers receptive to the new intellectual and cultural changes sweeping the rest of Christendom.

Between the late twelfth and the mid–fourteenth century, the mental world of most Castilians was radically transformed. This shift in *mentalités* or values constituted a reordering of mental, spiritual, and physical space; fresh ideas about sin and intercession coincided with emerging perceptions of property as tangible space and new ways of representing the self.[4] The evidence for this transformation comes from specific social groups whose mental outlook and values became normative for large segments of late medieval society: mercantile elites, well-to-do farmers, lower nobility, clerics, and literary figures, the people who, for lack of a better term, may be described as "middling sorts." This shift in values—which brought new attitudes toward the spiritual world and encouraged itemizing the physical world—was fairly rapid in northern Castile, transpiring over a period of fifty to seventy years, between the late twelfth and the mid–thirteenth century. Although precedents for many of these changes can be found in earlier centuries, the repercussions of these late medieval transformations would shape the tenor of Castilian social and cultural life into the early modern period.

A shift in values could be detected within a broad spectrum of social and cultural activity: (1) in the way Castilians (at least, at some levels of society) thought about property and family at a time when economic innovations and an emerging mercantile mentality were eroding the traditional relation between the two; (2) in the way Castilians thought about and acted on salvation and charity; (3) in the way Castilians related to their local communities and the rising notion of a unified realm; (4) in the way Castilians represented their collective and individual identities by rewriting history, refashioning themselves, and defining others, especially the religious minorities in their midst.[5]

This birth of new values, or reordering of mental and physical landscapes, formed part of what Le Goff has described as a transition "from heaven to earth"—from spiritual and religious beliefs to the quasi-secular pursuits of merchants and scholars, from "Church's time to merchants' time." But in Castile this shift cannot be traced as in other parts of the medieval West. Elsewhere in the twelfth and thirteenth centuries the shift in mentality can be followed in the lively intellectual debates that flourished in cathedral schools and universities, in the myriad literary works that were produced in both Latin and the vernacular, and in the rise of an urban and mercantile spirit (see chapter 1) with a distinctive perception of the self and its relation to the spiritual.

When we turn to medieval Castile in the twelfth century, we find no universities, at least not yet.[6] Gifted Castilians often traveled abroad for their learning (as other Europeans did to Iberia to study Arabic, Jewish, and classical—i.e., Greek—sources); only stirrings of the intellectual ferment and debate that were so central to western Europe's twelfth-century Renaissance reached the land of castles and lions.[7] Moreover, the great vernacular monuments of the Castilian Middle Ages—*The Poem of the Cid* (which Colin Smith has dated to the early thirteenth century), the anonymous *Poema de Fernán González* (mid–thirteenth century) and the work of Gonzalo de Berceo (c. 1250)—paralleled the dramatic transformations that are the subject of this book, or appeared shortly afterward. These literary works reflect the changing moods and attitudes of Castilians, but the supply of pre-1200 written testimonies (chronicles, learned treatises, and the like) is meager. Wills, and charters, for the period between 1150 and the early 1200s, however, provide useful entry points into the history of Castilian values.⁸

When Alfonso VII died in 1157, his lofty pretensions to be the "emperor of all the Spains" had come to little more than verbal claims. Despite his conquest of Almería in 1147, when the Castilian king led an international army to victory in southern Spain, Castile still faced the stiff opposition of the Almohads, a wave of North African invaders who had defeated the diverse Almoravid kingdoms in the south and established power there.⁹ The Almohads presented a seemingly unassailable obstacle to the Christian forces. Alfonso VII's coronation, anointment, and assumption of the imperial title in León in 1135—an event I discuss in greater detail later— were, in many respects, empty gestures. The new political realities of the peninsula—the rise of an independent Portugal, the union of the kingdom of Aragon and the county of Barcelona under Ramón Berenguer IV (1131–62)—gave the lie to Alfonso's hegemonic ambitions. Further complicating Castilian expansion, Alfonso VII's will partitioned the kingdom between his two surviving sons, as was traditional among Castilian and Leonese rulers. Sancho III (1157–58) received the kingdoms of Castile and Toledo, realms at the vanguard of the Reconquest and recipients of fabulous *parias* (tributes paid by the Muslim kingdoms of *taifas* to Christian rulers).¹⁰ Ferdinand II (1157–88) inherited the far less attractive ancestral kingdoms of León and Galicia.

Alfonso VII's demise and the division of the realms signaled an important watershed in peninsular history. The years after his death ushered in profound social, economic, and political changes. Constant civil wars, a restless nobility seeking to gain control of the throne, a rising mercantile society, and a growing monetary economy served as context and cause for the emergence of new mental attitudes in late twelfth- and early thirteenth-century Castile. At present, a brief outline of political events in the one hundred years or so following Sancho III's ascent to the Castilian throne and his untimely death will suffice. But what was Castile in the twelfth century?

Although this study makes incursions into the Leonese realm and touches on the newly conquered regions in Andalusia after the 1240s, the core of my sources deal with Old Castile—in this case, a political rather than a geographical unit, extending roughly from the Bay of Biscay in the north to the Central Sierras (north of Madrid) in the south. In the west, it reached the contested borders of the kingdom of Asturias-

León; and in the east, the political borders with Aragon. Geographically diverse (green mountains in the north, with abundant rain; high cereal lands on the plain, with little rain), this vast area was, already in the twelfth century, the heartland of Iberia; in time, it would become the center of Spain's imperial glory. Port cities, such as Santander, Castro-Urdiales, Laredo, Bilbao (after 1300), and Fuenterrabía on the northern coast; towns on the plain, such as Burgos, Logroño, Nájera (all three flanking the road to Compostela), and Soria; and military outposts on the forefront of the Reconquest—Avila, Segovia, Sepúlveda, and others—were islands of nascent urban life in a predominantly rural world.[11] It was hard land with thin soil, a harsh climate, and a proud, warlike population. A world of free peasants but increasingly large lordships, Old Castile stood poised, in the mid–twelfth century, between two contending axes.

Castile's short history—its origins dated only to the early ninth century—had in fact long flowed in two directions. One axis ran east-west along the road to Compostela, a site of great pilgrimages. The Milky Way, as the road was called by countless French pilgrims, traversed the northern part of Iberia, linking regions north of the Pyrenees (after the 930s) to the rising cities of northern Castile and, farther to the west, to the ancient kingdoms of León, Asturias, and Galicia (political life in these western regions dating back to the early eighth century). The road, and its innumerable secondary shrines and urban centers, reached a high point (in number of pilgrims, impact on the economy and social life of Castile) in the mid–twelfth century.[12] Religious devotion and commercial opportunities drew thousands of pilgrims and merchants to Iberia in this period. Some made their way to Compostela, fulfilled their vows, said their prayers, and went back to Frankland. Others stayed in Castile and, throughout the next century, were integrated into Castilian life. In 1157, this road, which collected traffic from other feeder roads north of the Pyrenees, was the central axis of Castilian society and culture. Along the road to Compostela and beyond, to Braga, Toledo, and other destinations, foreign and native scholars traveled to and from, as Adeline Rucquoi has shown, the intellectual centers of Europe.[13] Some went north in search of the new knowledge that was being offered at Bologna, Paris, Orleans, and Salerno in the fields of law, theology, and medicine; others came south, seeking, in Spain, the wisdom of Aristotle, Galen, other classical authors, and their incisive Arab and Jewish commentators.

By the second half of the twelfth century, the north-south axis began to overtake the pilgrimage route's central role. This new route, which led south to al-Andalus, produced increased commerce between Christians and Muslims, laying the foundation for the profitable extortion of Moorish kingdoms (the *parias*) later on. These were the roads of the so-called

Reconquest, though, in fact, Castile's history had run along this direction from its very inception. Castile, as both county and realm, had always defined itself—geographically, culturally, politically, and religiously—through its contest with al-Andalus. By the second half of the thirteenth century, the road to Compostela, although still attracting numerous pilgrims, started its slow decline and began to play a secondary part in Castilian and Spanish history. By then, Iberian history was firmly oriented in a north-south direction. The great Christian victories in the south from 1212 onward and the final conquests of Andalusia by Castile in the mid–thirteenth century sealed the fate and destiny of the realm.

In 1157, however, all that was still in the future. The new king of Castile, Sancho III, came to the throne with heightened expectations. He was a bold and promising young monarch, but his sudden death in 1158 left the kingdom in dire straits. His son and heir, Alfonso VIII (1158–1214), was just three years old. In Castile, as in most medieval realms, royal minorities were particularly wicked periods. This one was no exception. The young king became a focal point of contention between the two great Castilian noble houses, the Castro and the Lara. They fought for control of the young sovereign and royal revenues and sought to advance the influence, power, and territorial holdings of their respective families to the detriment of the realm. The endless civil wars that ensued allowed Sancho VI, king of Navarre, to usurp substantial territories in Castile's eastern borders. Ferdinand II of León, the young king's uncle, not only interfered often in the conflicts over the regency, but grasped Castilian territories on its western frontier as well. Ferdinand eventually held the regency for his nephew, maneuvering to consolidate León's gains, and his own.

When Alfonso VIII came of age and assumed the rule of Castile in 1170, he found a kingdom deeply divided by noble antagonism and diminished by foreign occupation. He was, perhaps, one of the best kings who ever ruled Castile. A pious, earnest man, the grandfather of two saintly kings, Louis IX of France and Ferdinand III of Castile-León, Alfonso VIII slowly recovered the territories that had been alienated during his minority and curtailed, by a combination of threats, military actions, and bribes, the ambitions of the high nobility. Once order was restored, Alfonso VIII cast his eyes on the south and on its rich financial and territorial rewards.

In 1179, the Treaty of Cazola between the Crown of Aragon and Castile established various spheres of influence in the south. Castile received the choice share, but its newly gained ascendancy was not without shortcomings. Its growing power prompted all the other peninsular kingdoms, including the Almohads, to band together against Alfonso VIII.

The 1190s were an uncertain decade, punctuated by conflicts and shifting alliances between the different Iberian kingdoms, and by the growing menace of the Almohads. The latter's strength triggered new actions. Alfonso VIII's most significant achievement was his ability to forge a broad international alliance of peninsular and northern rulers (the Crown of Aragon, France, and England) against the Almohad threat—an alliance that his English connection through marriage to Eleanor, Henry II and Eleanor of Aquitaine's daughter, helped consolidate. After extended negotiations and bickering among the allies, a mighty Iberian and northern European army (except for León, which refused to join the alliance because of its conflict with Castile) delivered a crushing defeat to the Almohad army at Las Navas de Tolosa in 1212.[14]

After 1212, who held the upper hand in the peninsula was no longer in dispute. The Christians did. The battle of Las Navas changed the status of Christian-Muslim relations forever, leading ultimately to the mistreatment of the Moors and their banishment from al-Andalus. It opened the way for Christian expansion and secured Castile's hegemony within the peninsula. After a short unstable period following the death of Alfonso VIII in 1214 and the minority—and then untimely death (1217)—of his son, Henry I, Ferdinand III, Alfonso VIII's grandson, claimed the Castilian throne. He did so as heir to his mother, Berenguela, queen of Castile, who relinquished the throne on his behalf; when his father, Alfonso IX of Asturias-León, died thirteen years later, Ferdinand assumed rule of both realms. The two kingdoms, Castile and León, finally united in 1230, were never to be divided again.[15] The great conquests of Córdoba (1236) and Seville (1248) were just around the corner. Victory brought new patterns of occupation to Muslim lands and surges of repopulation to the newly conquered territories; more tragically, it introduced the defeated Muslims to an unprecedented era of punitive treatment. Commanding the historical spotlight, these dramatic changes have often obscured other, more structural but equally enduring transformations of Castilian society.[16]

Contrary to the trajectory suggested by my title, "From Heaven to Earth," I have chosen to address the material world first. In attempting to explain how and why changes took place, chapter 1 suggests a connection between the transformation in values and the linguistic shift from Latin to the vernacular. It also provides a social and cultural context for the interrelated topics of property, family, and perceptions of the material world explored in succeeding chapters. Chapter 2 investigates the formulaic nature of pre-1220s wills and demonstrates how wills evolved, in the late twelfth and early thirteenth centuries, from unrestricted donations to structured, restrictive testaments in tandem with shifting values. The evidence presented in this chapter is deployed throughout the book to trace similar shifts in northern Castile. Chapter 3 expands on this discussion by examining the legal codes of inheritance rights and property transfers. Chapter 4 deals with shifts in the perception and representation of property. From the late twelfth century, a significant change occurred in the way northern Castilians conceived of property. Rather than perceiving it as a matter of rights and jurisdiction, Castilians began to think of property as physical space and set out to map and itemize by installing landmarks, initiating litigation over boundaries, and commissioning carefully drawn inventories. This new awareness of the physical (as opposed to the jurisdictional) attributes of property transformed the mental landscape of Castilians in the late twelfth and early thirteenth centuries. Continuing to explicate the interests linking power, family, and property, chapter 5 focuses on the emergence of bourgeois and noble lineages and the eventual triumph of primogeniture among the upper classes.

In the next two chapters, the narrative takes us from concerns with the here and now to more cultural and politically bound affairs. Chapter 6 reexamines wills as strategic devotional devices. Charitable donations were carefully scripted and designed to enhance the social and spiritual status of donors and their families. Chapter 7 expands on some of my earlier research and revisits the rapidly changing political culture of Castile. The establishment of a nonsacral kingship articulated new concepts of royal power. The use of the vernacular, the implementation of a new, Roman-based law, and the advent of institutional reforms led to the laicization of the bureaucracy, which proved an additional incentive in changing the way Castilians thought of power. A conclusion summarizes the book's salient arguments, threading these different strands into what I hope is a clear and comprehensive picture.

My presentation contains gaps, conscious choices I have made about what to include and what to omit. For example, I treat political developments or transitions only as context for the cultural shifts I wish to examine in this book. We already have excellent summaries (in English, French, and Spanish) of Castile's emergence as a kingdom and of its subsequent political life.[17] Similarly, I abstain from any prolonged discussion of the Church or of the way these mental changes affected Castile's religious life; instead, I take on ecclesiastical questions as they intersect with the changes my research has uncovered. Partial omission, however, does not mean a lack of understanding of the Church's, or of religion's, central role in constructing a new mentality. Several first-rate works allow us to trace the general outline of Castile's religious culture in the period.[18] The absence of a thorough examination of the ecclesiastical order does not, therefore, constitute a significant lacuna. The main thrust of this book is, after all, that in late twelfth- and early thirteenth-century northern Castile, a shift took place "from heaven to earth," from a society in which values were to a large extent formulated and guided by a spiritual authority to a society in which, without abandoning religion or a religious vocabulary, new values emerged from the earthly concerns of the middling sorts (including churchmen).

It may be argued, however, that even these material transactions were guided by an ecclesiastical agenda, one that steered bequests to ecclesiastical establishments and placed the business of salvation at the core of Castilian life. Ecclesiastics drafted and recorded most property exchanges before 1200 and couched those exchanges in a formulaic language of piety. The move from ecclesiastical concerns to those grounded in the material world—signaled by the appearance of lay scribes and new patterns of will-writing—marked a radical shift in culture and values. This shift may be called secularization (though religion continued to play a signal role in the production of new values), or it may be viewed as an early manifestation of secular attitudes in the medieval West. I contend that in late twelfth- and early thirteenth-century Castile, we gaze on the barest beginnings of a process that would eventually sweep across western Europe—without fully overthrowing Christian culture—and lead to the emergence of the "rational" state in the early modern period.[19] Another term that may help shed light on this transformation was used long ago by my late and much missed master, Joseph R. Strayer: *laicization*. Strayer and others employed this more ambiguous term to explain shifts in the political and institutional structures of France and England.[20] But laicization, of course, went far beyond political or administrative changes. The new laic spirit affected, as has already been noted, the language of material transactions and narrative strategies. It affected political organization and privileged new forms of ritual and symbolic political language. It transformed the relationship between Church and Crown, and the role of royal agents in running the realm. One can also posit, as I do here, that broad changes in values preceded shifts in the political realm and led to more formal and visible transformations of Castile and other medieval societies. In many respects, the new attitudes toward property, salvation, and power discussed in the next seven chapters represented novel ways of seeing and experiencing the world.

This book serves as a corrective and companion volume to my previous work, above all, *Crisis and Continuity*, in which I sought to account for various kinds of economic and social change. Using those findings as a backdrop, I seek to tell a very different story here. Though still focused on social history, I am interested in another kind of social history this time. My aim is not so much to describe and explain social relations, antagonisms, and power struggles. The story I am about to embark on concerns the construction of new values and the impact of these new outlooks on the status and relations of different groups within a society of orders. With these caveats, let us travel back more than eight centuries to a world that still lives, albeit hazily and in half-shadows, in the written records of late twelfth- and early thirteenth-century Castilians.

CHAPTER ONE

A TASTE FOR THE NEW:

COMMERCE, PROPERTY, AND LANGUAGE

IN HIS STUDY of Ferdinand III's reign, the great Spanish medieval historian Julio González provides an engaging description of the first half of the thirteenth century.[1] It was, in González's words, "a new time of great reforms." Although the transformations he describes were far more visible than the ones I focus on in the following chapters, they were intimately linked. After Las Navas de Tolosa, a new generation of rulers replaced the older kings who had dominated the political landscape of Iberia during the second half of the twelfth century. These new rulers—Ferdinand III (1217–52) in Castile-León, James I (1213–76) in the Crown of Aragon, and Afonso II (1211–23) in Portugal, set new political agendas for their respective realms. The young kings marched at the vanguard of an entire generational renewal, bringing to Castile and other Iberian kingdoms youthful new tastes and fashions. Parallel to this, the moral reforms that swept Christendom after the Fourth Lateran Council (1215) also found echoes in Castile. As González has shown and as Peter Linehan demonstrated thirty years ago, although the Castilian Church resisted many of the reforms dictated by the Council, Innocent III's anti-Semitic and crusading programs found a warm reception in Castile.[2]

Culture in general, and education in particular, experienced a similar dramatic renewal, as cathedral schools and universities began to dot the Castilian landscape. Educational developments had their counterpart in the emergence of new poetical and musical forms. This, in turn, was accompanied by the reception and spread of new architectural forms (the Gothic), an active building program (mostly cathedrals and monasteries, but also great bourgeois houses), and the introduction of new dress fashions in Castile. Architecture and literature, above all, exemplified this taste for the new.

The Gothic style made its way into Castile along the pilgrimage road to Compostela; from there it spread to other areas of the realm. In the late twelfth century, the Cistercian monastery of Las Huelgas in the outskirts of Burgos began to be built at the expense of the Crown in a pure and beautiful Gothic style. Mass was celebrated in the new and unfinished Gothic cathedral of Burgos in the 1210s to give thanks for the Christian victory at Las Navas de Tolosa. In León, the construction of an imposing Gothic cathedral with exuberant stained glass began shortly after that of Burgos. Avila added its fortresslike Gothic cathedral in the early thirteenth century, as did Segovia; and Salamanca's Old Cathedral (with the first iconographic depiction of purgatory in Castile, c. 1300) rose in what was until then a sea of Romanesque architecture. With the Cistercians and the Gothic came a new devotion to the Virgin. Mary stood as a counterpart to St. James and became, by the mid–thirteenth century, the central inspiration for active architectural (at Villasirga and elsewhere) and literary (the *Cantigas de Santa María* and the work of Berceo) production.[3]

In literature, the thirteenth century witnessed an explosion of philosophical and political treatises in Latin, chronicles (in Latin and Castilian), and lyrical and epic poetry in the vernacular. These works reflected new intellectual interests and cultural concerns. From the Galaic-Portuguese *cantigas de amigo* and *cantigas de escarnio* (love and satirical troubadour poetry) to the great historical chronicles of the early thirteenth century—those by Lucas de Tuy and Ximénez de Rada as well as the vernacular and royally sponsored chronicles of the mid–thirteenth century—to the lyric poetry of Gonzalo de Berceo (c. 1195–c. 1265), the so-called *mester de clerecía*, to such political treatises as Diego García de Campos's *Planeta* (c. 1218), a long discussion and commentary on the hymn *Christus vincit, Christus regnat, Christus imperat*, to the composition of the great epic poem about the deeds of Ruy Díaz de Vivar, the Cid (1206), and, finally, to Alfonso X's *Cantigas de Santa María* and his entire promotion of scientific and historical works, Castile experienced an extraordinary burst of creativity. These works differed in style and content from those of preceding decades, marking a great intellectual shift in Castilian culture.[4] In architecture and literature, and in a broad range of other social and cultural developments, a "taste for novelty" (*gusto de novedades*), in González's felicitous phrase, captured the sense of newness sweeping Castile in this period.[5]

Although González locates these transformations in the years after Las Navas de Tolosa, this taste for new things rested squarely on new notions of property, salvation, and political power that were already evolving in the last decades of the twelfth century, spurred by the transition from written Latin to Castilian. Even though this shift in values predated Ferdinand III's reign, González's description of the "liking for new things" brilliantly limns the reordering of Castilian society in the late twelfth and

Fig. 1 Cathedral of Burgos (spire)
Building of the cathedral of Burgos' in the new Gothic style began in the early thirteenth century. The pilgrimage road to Compostela, which played an important role in the development of mercantile life in northern Castile, ran alongside the cathedral. (Photo by Scarlett Freund)

Fig. 2 Cathedral of León

Built in the new Gothic style in the early thirteenth century, the cathedral of León was adjacent to the famous church of St. Isidore of León, a sacral center for the Asturian-Leonese monarchy. The cathedral was one of the important stopping points on the road to the tomb of St. James. (Photo by Scarlett Freund) early thirteenth centuries. But what was the underlying structure of this reordering?

The Rise of Commercial Life and a Monetary Economy in Castile

Many decades ago, the distinguished and insightful historian Luis García de Valdeavellano described the emergence of the northern Castilian bourgeoisie along the road to Compostela in the twelfth century. The rise of a new social group, the bourgeoisie, the proliferation of stores (*tiendas*) in the urban centers along the pilgrimage road, and the awakening of trade stemmed, according to García de Valdeavellano, from the torrent of pilgrims traveling from north of the Pyrenees into northern Castile on the way to the tomb of the Apostle St. James in faraway Galicia.[6] The general characteristics and route of the pilgrimage road became fairly fixed by the eleventh century, and both the route and the pilgrimage itself began to be heavily promoted by Cluniac monks through the establishment of monastic foundations in strategic locations on or near the road (Sahagún, Silos, San Zoilo of Carrión, and others). The production of the famous guide (the *Liber Sancti Jacobi* or fifth book of the *Codex Calixtinus*), mistakenly attributed to Ameryc Picard, served as a launching pad for the success of the pilgrimage.[7] Many pilgrims, most of them French (*francos*), settled in the bourgeoning towns along the Milky Way, as the pilgrimage route was also known, and came to play a signal role in the development of urban society and commercial life in northern Castile. As in Burgos, the most commercially oriented city in the region, they were joined in their commercial pursuits by locals. The latter, although not always joining in the commercial ventures of French settlers—or at least not in the same degree—left their rural origins for the towns. In the twelfth and early thirteenth centuries, these northern Castilians often derived their income and power from the land or from municipal or ecclesiastical offices, not from commerce. Nonetheless, they came to share fully in the values and lifestyle of the bourgeoisie. The Sarracín, to be discussed in detail in chapter 5, are a good example of these local families who, through marriage, education, clerical pursuits, and land purchases, joined with those recently settled *francos* in promoting new ways of perceiving property and the afterlife.[8]

The Bonifaz, a family that according to Robert Lopez originated in Genoa, settled in Burgos probably in the very late twelfth or early thirteenth century. They represented the other component of the nascent middling sorts, the foreign merchant, whose activities and mental out-

Fig. 3 South side of the cathedral of Santiago of Compostela

The Portal of the Platerías. Built in the Romanesque style but adorned with later Plateresque accretions, the square in front of the cathedral's southern façade was a center for silversmiths. Most of them had settled in the city as a result of the commercial activity generated by the pilgrimage trade. (Photo by Scarlett Freund)

Fig. 4 Image of St. James as a pilgrim from the cathedral of Santiago de Compostela. This shows the iconographic importance of the pilgrimage in northern Castilian life. This image is reproduced in almost all the churches along the pilgrimage road from France to Galicia. (Photo by Scarlett Freund)

Fig. 5 Sculpture from the cathedral of Compostela
The new sensibilities of the twelfth and early thirteenth centuries are displayed in this sculpture from the cathedral of St. James of Compostela. (Photo by Scarlett Freund)

look would transform Castilian society. The founding father of the Bonifaz family, already a man of great substance in the 1220s, as revealed by his real estate holdings and the building (with his cousin) of a big and expensive house on one of the most important streets of Burgos, rose to a prominent place in the kingdom. Ramón Bonifaz led the fleet from the Bay of Biscay port towns at the siege of Seville in 1248. In Burgos, members of the Bonifaz family held the position of *alcalde*, or mayor, throughout most of the late thirteenth and early fourteenth centuries, served in the *regimiento* of the city in 1348 (disproportionately, controlling four of the sixteen seats), and held the deanship of the cathedral chapter for most of the first half of the fourteenth century.[9]

The experiences of the Sarracín and Bonifaz families were replicated in other important cities along the road to Compostela and in the emerging towns on the eleventh- and twelfth-century moving frontier (Valladolid, Sepúlveda, Avila, Segovia, and others).[10] This crucial period also witnessed the resettling of urban centers on the shores of the Bay of Biscay. Towns such as Santander, San Vicente de la Barquera, Castro-Urdiales, Laredo, and the Basque maritime localities of Fuenterrabía, Bermeo, San Sebastián, and Bilbao (after 1300) figured prominently in the commercial ventures of the nascent northern Castilian bourgeoisie. The Castilian presence on the northern coast led to the beginnings of maritime commercial links with Flanders, England, and France. Less than a century after the resettlement of Basque and Cantabrian towns under Castilian rule, the new direction of trade (from transactions with al-Andalus to exchanges with Flanders and England) dramatically altered the realm's economic and political life.[11]

One should not exaggerate, of course, the magnitude of mercantile life in northern Castile in this period. Unlike in certain areas of Flanders, Brabant, and Italy, the development of the bourgeoisie in Castile was a truncated phenomenon. Those who lived by commerce and craftsmanship shared political power and mental outlooks with those whose economic well-being derived from the land or the transhumance. Many of the towns in northern Castile were essentially large rural settlements, agro-towns. Places such as Avila, Sepúlveda, Soria, Riaza, and others were dominated by urban elites with little or no ties to trade. In Avila, to give just one example, petty mercantile activity and artisan crafts were almost exclusively in the hands of religious minorities in the thirteenth century.[12] Yet, whether their source of income was trade or land, those who ruled the cities sought to build significant landed estates and, with notable exceptions, aspired to become landholders and even nobles.

Nonetheless, in the critical period between the 1170s and the 1250s, a sea change took place in the social and economic structures of northern

Castile. Even earlier, in the first quarter of the twelfth century, an emerging bourgeoisie had flexed its muscle in a series of "bourgeois" rebellions in the towns along the road to Compostela. Urban uprisings in Sahagún, Compostela, and other localities along the pilgrimage route (and thus places with large settlements of *francos*) echoed similar and earlier communal revolts in other parts of Europe.[13] By the second half of the twelfth century, which coincided with the restoration of order, rebellions were no longer necessary. By then, the middling sorts were solidly entrenched in their respective towns. Through service in the incipient royal bureaucracy and participation in the cortes (the representative assemblies), the Castilian bourgeois, had gained an important foothold in the political life of the realm.[14] More significantly, the middling sorts came to exercise a larger role in the kingdom's military affairs. Urban militias—those of Avila seem to have been especially prominent—assumed greater importance in realmwide conflicts around the late twelfth century, and they proved to be a superb and reliable force not only against the Muslims but, far more significantly for the well-being of the Crown, against unruly noblemen.[15]

This dynamic social group, already beginning to monopolize political and ecclesiastical power in their respective cities and towns at the turn of the twelfth century, developed new attitudes toward the material and spiritual worlds that were grounded in their own experiences and specific social and economic contexts. Some of these new ideas were borrowed or imported from abroad, as shall be seen later, and derived from constant contact with pilgrims and merchants from other parts of Europe. Some emerged from the new material and political conditions in which this evolving social group lived. One reinforced the other, and in not so subtle ways led to a broad shift in mental outlook and behavior. These mental transformations were sometimes paralleled and often prompted by structural changes. In this respect, the reorientation of northern Castilian trade from almost exclusive dealings with al-Andalus to binding economic and commercial ties with northern Europe—changes already noted by Francisco Hernández and described in detail by Olivia Constable—played a significant role in the transformations taking place in this period. That the middling sorts frequented the royal court; that urban militias were led and manned by merchants, artisans, and city dwellers; that important ecclesiastical positions began to be dominated by these same social groups; that as merchants they traveled abroad and transacted business in the great textile and financial centers of northern Europe; that their children began to attend universities from the late twelfth century onward—these are only some of the most obvious changes that took place. The middling sorts served as powerful locomotives for shifts in values. Without merchants and trade there would not have been cities, at least no cities on the new northern models; there would not have been a bourgeoisie standing apart from the well-defined world of lords and peasants; there would not have been a shift in values.

Thanks to Jacques Le Goff's works, we already know the critical effect that the rise of a mercantile culture had on the development of new spiritual values. These changes not only concerned the famously sharp distinctions between Church's time and merchants' time. They also involved the way western medieval men and women, Castilians most certainly among them, grasped the implications of the material world, as opposed to heavenly considerations.

It may be useful to summarize briefly some of the points to be elaborated in the next five chapters and to link them with the preliminary explanations I am seeking to provide here. Although I hope what follows will provide substantial evidence for the shift in attitudes toward salvation, charity, and political culture in the late twelfth and early thirteenth centuries, evidence is not always as solid for the link between new perceptions of property and the pursuit of spiritual redemption.[16] As shall be seen, from the early thirteenth century onward, extant wills reflected testators' desire to retain property (lands, houses, cash) within the family and to spell out in great detail who was to get what and when. Ecclesiastical institutions received mostly rents or income, but even these donations remained restricted. This is not to say that the Church in Castile and elsewhere did not continue to benefit from large donations of actual property. It did, mostly from great lords and the Crown, but also from members of the bourgeoisie and well-to-do farmers, the same social group from which I draw most of my evidence. Yet these new players brought with them a new way of seeing things, one derived from mercantile experiences, a monetary economy, and life in the cities.

Legal codes, rights of way, the creation of contiguous estates, and concerns with boundaries are also found in an earlier age as part of a symbolic code and an oral culture, which established jurisdiction over land, rents to be paid, terms for the actual occupation of the soil. These practices included ritual gestures such as throwing a stone against a fence to indicate a boundary, or passing on to a purchaser a handful of earth to indicate possession. In other parts of Iberia, Old Catalonia, for example, where records are far more detailed than in Castile, some of the developments outlined here took place earlier, even though, to my knowledge, no one has called attention to them as evidence for the change in values or *mentalité*. If we tentatively accept that these shifts occurred, the question remains: why?

The formation of mercantile elites along the road to Compostela, the emergence of a bourgeoisie in northern Castile in the cities associated with the pilgrimage to Santiago—that is, those areas in which changes in values happened first—point to the link between commercial pursuits, a money economy, and the genesis of new ways of thinking about property, salvation, charity, and power.[17] These connections, which have already been illustrated for the rest of the West, transformed notions of time and the sacred in the new commercial culture emerging throughout western Europe from the eleventh century onward.

Money, Numbers, and Changes in the Value System

Intimately tied to the development of commercial life and the birth of a bourgeois culture in northern Castile was the new importance of money and a new understanding of commercial arithmetic. Increased trade and commercial transactions required increased circulation of coins and new ways of counting and calculating prices and goods. Although money circulated in Castile throughout the ninth, tenth, and eleventh centuries— after all, trading with al-Andalus required species—there was little or no minting of coins in Castile before the twelfth century. By then, however, the changing political relationship with Andalusi kingdoms (which placed Christians on top), the influx of bullion and coins as tribute (the *parias*), and changing economic realities led to the wider circulation of money throughout the Christian realms.

During the late twelfth and early thirteenth centuries, Castile experienced a marked increase in its monetary supply. Alfonso VIII's (1158–1214) aggressive minting policies greatly expanded the amount of coins available in Castile. Not coincidentally, these new issues, mostly the *burgalés* and the first gold coin minted in Castile by a Castilian king, the *alfonsí*, were identified by vernacular words. This stands in sharp contrast to previous coins, which were identified by terms that derived from the Arabic (the *morabetino*) or from Latin (*denarius, solidus*).[18]

Coins are, of course, another significant way to conceive the material world and to see and feel its presence in a very tangible manner. Rents, what we may call "feudal" rents, continued to be paid, at least in part, in kind well beyond the mid–fourteenth century, but following the beginning of widespread use of coinage in northern Castile, payment in kind came to be replaced more and more by payment in money. This also applied to labor, as the same social groups that engaged in the aggressive consolidation of land and the defining of boundaries began to hire day laborers (*jornaleros*) to tend their fields. This occurred not only in northern Castile but in the newly conquered lands in Andalusia after the 1230s.

Fom the mid–thirteenth century onward, the ordinances of the Castilian cortes show a preoccupation with rural workers' salary, which was always set in monetary terms. One of the first gatherings of the cortes in Castile, in 1207, signaled the presence of merchants in the royal court and addressed, almost exclusively, the question of what could and should be traded, and at what price.[19] Some scholars have traced the gathering of these representative assemblies—the first in the medieval West—to the townspeople's desire to prevent the alteration of the coinage. In 1202, at the curia of Benavente, all the men of León (magnates, high ecclesiastics, and representatives from selected towns) agreed to pay an extraordinary subsidy, *moneda forera*, to the king, Alfonso IX, in return for his promise to maintain the integrity of the coin of the realm.[20] One must also remember money's role money in the *Poema de mío Cid* (c. 1206). The Cid's gains may have been territorial, but the tribute sent to his king, the donations made to the Church of Burgos and the monastery of Cardeña, and his borrowing from the Jewish moneylenders, Rachel and Vidas, were articulated in monetary terms. These allusions would have been clearly understood by the rising middling sorts and lower aristocracy, the main target of the *Poema*'s propagandistic intent, and the harbingers of cultural change.

By the early thirteenth century, books on commercial arithmetic such as the *Liber abbaci* (1202) began to replace an older mathematical tradition of Muslim provenance and centered in Toledo and southern Spain. These new texts became widely used in the expanding mercantile transactions of the period. Arabic numbers (in reality Hindu numbers), which greatly facilitated commercial exchange, also began to appear throughout the western Mediterranean. Though many of these developments were centered in Italian commercial centers, Castile benefited from them. There was, after all, a long acquaintance with such knowledge through the economic exchanges and relations between Muslim and Christian Spain. The first treatise on commercial arithmetic written in Castile has been dated to the late fourteenth century, but, clearly, knowledge of these techniques was practiced before that. Indeed, Arabic numbers began to creep into Castilian documentation in the thirteenth century and, by the next century, dates (especially days) were often rendered in Arabic numerals. New awareness of the importance of commercial arithmetic also paralleled novel concerns with calendars and with what Alain Boreau has called "the instrumentalization of time." In the thirteenth century, scholars, among them Robert Kilwardby, Peter of John Olivi, and others, began to develop new ideas about time and its measurement throughout the medieval West. In the case of Olivi's *On contracts*, this meant allowing merchants and bankers to charge for time.[21]

A New Spirituality and the Discovery of Purgatory
The Mendicant Orders

If changing social and economic conditions served as cause and context for the shift in attitudes toward the material world, these new ways of perceiving and counting property, money, and material goods led to new forms of spirituality and piety. Three or four years ago, when I began to present some of these ideas in seminars across the country and abroad, the most frequent response was to suggest a link between the rise of the Mendicant orders (Franciscans and Dominicans) and their new spiritual concerns and the transformation of values I was positing. I have, of course, always been aware of the strong connections between bourgeois culture and the novel preaching of Franciscans and, to a lesser extent, Dominican friars. The pioneer works of Lester Little and Jacques Le Goff (discussed further in chapter 6) provide an excellent entry into this topic. But, in reality, even before these two orders began their work in the early thirteenth century, spiritual sensibilities were already changing. The appeal of such movements as that of the Poor Men of Lyons (the Waldensians) and the popularity of heretical movements in the western Mediterranean (the Cathars above all) point to the inescapable tie between urban commercial life and religious restlessness.

The Mendicant orders settled early in northern Castile. Between 1213 and 1215, St. Francis himself traveled to Compostela, following the traditional pilgrimage route and visiting the same towns (Logroño, Nájera, Burgos, and others) that figure prominently in this story. According to tradition, he even performed some miraculous cures in Logroño.[22] Chronologically, this occurred almost at the same time as the clerk Sebastián was preparing the will with which this book begins. Santo Domingo de Guzmán, the founder of the Dominican order, hailed from northern Castile, from a small town in the shadows of the great monastery of Santo Domingo de Silos, one of the offshoots of the pilgrimage road.

The Mendicants came into northern Castile with a vengeance. From the very start, they held a significant role in urban life, attracting the largesse of the urban middling sorts and their requests for burial. These were the same people who generated the overwhelming majority of the wills considered in this book.[23] Mendicant preaching to urban dwellers provided the middling sorts with access to new types of spirituality. This new religiosity, which sought to sanctify everyday life and show that property also had a religious purpose, differed sharply from the hegemonic religion successfully articulated by rural and small town Benedictine monasteries (Sahagún, Silos, Cardeña, San Millán, and others) until the middle of the twelfth century. Engaged in bitter rivalry with older monasteries and, above all, with the secular Church (cathedral and collegial chapters), the Mendicants, mostly the Dominicans in northern Castile before the 1250s, climbed easily into the most intimate circles of the royal court and, to the consternation of their clerical rivals, even captured important bishoprics throughout the peninsula. Thus the Mendicants significantly shaped the mental outlook of Castilians through their effective preaching, confession, example, and writings.[24]

But the Mendicant orders succeeded so spectacularly precisely because the appropriate social, economic, and mental contexts were already in place when they arrived in northern Castile. Nor was their success predicated on their role in combating heresy. There is no evidence that Catharism or Waldensianism prospered in northern Castile in the late twelfth century. One finds sporadic references to heretics, but their work and preaching was not widespread. The mental climate, specifically the rise of an urban culture, the awareness of the importance of wealth as a means to bargain for or purchase salvation, the new perceptions of the material world were already established, providing a fertile ground for Mendicant preaching. Thus, in Castile the Mendicant orders (mostly the Dominicans) did not usher in new values; rather, their presence and new spiritual practices strengthened the appeal of novel ways of thinking about salvation, charity, and the afterlife among an eager and dynamic new social group. The Mendicants' redefinition of poverty as a religious and willing choice, for instance, gave solace to the middling sorts and confirmed their growing disdain for the involuntarily poor, for the numberless "undeserving" poor in their midst. The middling sorts' new strategies of salvation and charity were thus abetted and reinforced by Mendicant ideology.

Purgatory

There were other ways in which the new spiritual climate and theological adaptations of the Mendicants' message to everyday life connected with new perceptions of the material world and with the middling sorts' preoccupations with the afterlife. One of the most intriguing answers to why these changes took place can be found in Jacques Le Goff's formidable book *The Birth of Purgatory*. The birth of the notion of purgatory, which Le Goff dates to the latter half of the twelfth century, arguably spread to northern Castile by the following century. Documentary evidence clearly shows that the bourgeois and petty-nobility of Castile began consistently to demand pious services—masses, anniversaries, candles in churches, feeding and clothing of the poor, and the like—in return for their donations in the early thirteenth century. Ideally, these offerings were best suited to reduce time in purgatory. Support for this link between the discovery and acceptance of an intermediate place between heaven and hell and the new concerns with property, as well as the emergence of different types of wills, comes from iconography and from the geographical distribution of donations and wills. One of the earliest pictorial representations of purgatory in Castile-León (c. 1300) comes from Salamanca, and there are strong indications that wills drawn in towns along the road to Compostela (and thus more open to French influences) were among the first to contain donations to more than one ecclesiastical institution, to express concern with the preservation of property within the family, and to abandon the formula "for the remedy of my soul."[25]

As attractive as this formulation is—its chronological symmetry and elegance are very appealing—one must still exercise caution. In truth, although none of the wills I have examined used the term *purgatory* before 1350, the absence of the word does not necessarily imply that people did not know about it. As Le Goff himself has pointed out, in earlier centuries unrestricted donations for the salvation of one's soul and the souls of others already held an expectation of redemption and forgiveness beyond death.[26]

Le Goff's ideas on the emergence of purgatory have not gone unchallenged. Scholars in France and elsewhere have questioned his chronology and his emphasis on the spatiality of purgatory.[27] Recently, Ariel Guiance has studied purgatory's role in the writings of Julian of Toledo (d. 690)—a role Le Goff himself had already noted in *The Birth of Purgatory*. Julian, in his *Prognosticon futuri saeculi libri tres*, discussed in some detail the *ignis purgatorium*. Guiance also reports other sources that mentioned purgatory in the seventh century (contemporary with Julian's writings) as well as in the late eleventh or early twelfth century.[28]

Regardless of the fact that purgatory, or something like purgatory, was obviously known in Iberia before the twelfth century, purgatory as a place (in Le Goff's sense) appears prominently only in the works of Lucas de Tuy (first half of the thirteenth century) and Gonzalo de Berceo (mid–thirteenth century).[29] The writings of Lucas de Tuy (see chapter 7) and Berceo (chapters 4 and 6) reflected the shift in values outlined in previous pages. It is therefore no coincidence that they contributed prominently to the formulation of a new and clear idea of purgatory in northern Castile. And Berceo presented this idea in a new language: the vernacular.

In Lucas de Tuy's *Milagros de San Isidoro*, a homicidal monk returns from the dead to recount his experiences in the underworld to a fellow monk in the monastery of St. Isidore of León. The dead monk tells of being in "purgatory's fire, where the cruelty and harshness of the punishments are so great that no human tongue can describe it." "For those who are there," the monk continues, "every day seems like a year." Concluding his story, the monk describes how the punishment visited on the souls in purgatory was lessened on Sundays and other main religious holidays, or when a mass was offered for those doing penance there.[30]

In Berceo's *Milagros de Nuestra Señora,* miracle 10 tells the story of two brothers—Pedro, an avaricious cardinal, and his equally greedy and shifty sibling, Esteban, a senator in early Christian Rome. Esteban's actions—he took by deception houses from St. Lawrence and a garden from St. Inés (the latter's worth is described by Berceo in monetary terms[31])—lead him, after his death, directly to hell. His brother, who had predeceased him, had, deservedly, already been sent to purgatory ("y se fue al purgatorio como lo había ganado" [as he had earned]). As he descends into Hell, Esteban sees his brother burning in pain and inquires whether there is a way he can lessen his brother's suffering. Pedro informs him that if the "pope and his clerics would sing a mass for his soul, he was confident that the Virgin would intercede with God for some relief." Through the intercession of St. Proyecto, Esteban is given a second chance, returned to the world of the living, and given thirty days in which to make amends. On his knees, he asks the pope to sing a mass for his brother, gives his wealth to the needy, amply confesses his sins, takes communion, and, in a state of grace, his thirty days concluded, gives his life to God. One supposes that his brother was also released from purgatory and joined him in heaven.[32]

Whether or not the idea of purgatory predated the twelfth century, and whether or not it was thought of as a space before that date, the important development for our purpose is the nexus of death, purgatory, wills, the notion of defined space, and property. By the early thirteenth century, the middling sorts in northern Castile grasped the meaning of purgatory in their lives and the implication of purchasing ways to reduce one's time in that liminal place between heaven and hell with masses, charities, and pious gifts. Berceo, whose work faithfully reflected the shift in values in northern Castile, tells us as much in miracle 10. But since masses and charity cost money, purgatory also legitimized the middling sorts' pursuit of material possessions. Property could now be "sanctified" in the negotiation for salvation.

To reiterate, the swift transformation in the format of pious donations and legacies, occurring over several decades, and the novel desire to fragment pious legacies and accumulate "good deeds" clearly point to a new awareness of how salvation had to be negotiated or, better yet, how the chances of reducing one's time in purgatory could be increased. This line of explanation remains attractive, although no will ever directly addressed the issue of purgatory. Even later, when its existence was a well-established theological category, wills did not mention purgatory.[33] For no one would ever admit, even at the edge of death, the possibility of going to purgatory—certainly not in writing. As far as wills were concerned, there were only two choices: the fear of hell or the hope for heaven.

From Latin to Castilian: The Absence of a Notarial Culture

Language

Another possible explanation for the shift in values is that the change from Latin to Castilian as the language of royal administration and private affairs, which coincided with the changing patterns of the wills and donations, transferred the drawing of such instruments from ecclesiastical to lay hands. Simply put, as already noted in the introduction, the methods of redaction had changed. Donors and testators now enjoyed greater control and had more say over how their property was to be divided and what kind of returns they might expect for their gifts or investment in salvation. A change from one language to another, especially one as swift and widespread as that which occurred in Castile in the first half of the thirteenth century, had to be accompanied by various other transformations. Along with linguistic change came religious, psychological, economic, and political shifts of deep and lasting impact. Not the least of these changes was the growing literacy of the petty-nobility and the bourgeoisie, which, as Marc Bloch once pointed out, put an end to the clergy's ability to mask its selfish actions under a veneer of "simple piety."

The origins of the Castilian language can be traced back to the early Middle Ages. The Visigoths and later on the Muslims never fully conquered the mountainous northern regions of Iberia. There, in the eighth century, and by the early ninth century in the northern plains, new political entities were in the making. Each of these fledgling kingdoms (in the case of Castile, a county) developed their own distinct dialects (Galician-Portuguese, Leonese, Castilian, and Navarrese-Aragonese). Most of these early vernacular languages or dialects derived from the vulgar Latin of the late Visigothic period. Of these, Castilian, owing to complex political and geographical factors still in operation into the early modern period, proved the most dynamic. By the eleventh century, the Castilian language had acquired a remarkable uniformity and maturity. Unlike medieval French or English, which are almost incomprehensible to the modern lay reader, medieval Castilian, like medieval Catalan, can be read by most people who read what we call Spanish today, without great difficulty. In many respects, neither Castilian syntax nor vocabulary has undergone dramatic changes from the early thirteenth century to the present, and Castilian's intrusive character is most evident in late twelfth-century Latin documents that became more and more "corrupted" by the interpolation of vernacular syntax and words.[34]

My purpose here is not to trace the history, origins, or development of Castilian from its first use as a written language to the late twelfth century. Rather, my aim is to see how the transition from Latin to Castilian, from the early thirteenth century to its official adoption midcentury, stimulated the transformation of values and worked as a catalyst for the reordering of Castilian society. Despite some scholars' contention that Castile was a cultural backwater and that its acceptance of twelfth-century intellectual currents was a "belated" phenomenon (to use Deyermond's description), Castile's embracing of the vernacular as the official language of the realm was precocious indeed, predating similar developments in other parts of the West by centuries.[35]

The linguistic shift from written Latin to written Castilian helps explain the changing patterns not only of wills but also of property exchanges, boundary definitions, rights of way, and other spatial markers. The use of the vernacular for material transactions and testamentary negotiations empowered the middling sorts to articulate their new spiritual and economic interests in a language that was their own. In a very real sense, the shift in written language also marked an important victory of one language community over another—of the discourse of lay scribes, merchants and, eventually, the nascent more centralized realm over that of canons and the Church. Elsewhere in Europe, notaries were a powerful group. Because of their corporate nature and formal knowledge of Latin, they were able to monopolize the drawing of all significant legal instruments and material transactions. Because northern Castile lacked notaries, local scribes, writing in Castilian and themselves members of the burgeoning urban elites, became the vehicle through which these distinct economic aspirations and latent spirituality could be expressed.

Notarial Culture

Notaries were not unknown in northern Castile. There was a vibrant and ancient notarial culture in the Crown of Aragon, just over Castile's eastern borders. Shortly after its conquest in 1248, Seville also had a thriving notarial culture. Nonetheless, notaries did not begin to appear in northern Castile until the first half of the fourteenth century, and regular notarial activities did not gain a foothold in northern Castilian legal and documentary life until much later. There are, in fact, no rich notarial holdings for northern Castile until after 1400. Transactions, wills, and other legal contracts remained the work of scribes (the *escribano público*). One might think that scribes, whatever the name we give them, were notaries in practice, performing the same duties and functions, but this was not fully the case.

Unlike notaries in other parts of western Europe, scribes in northern Castile did not create notarial dynasties or parlay their craft into a traditional family occupation. Scribes were, after all, often municipal officials in search of promotion to higher offices: that of *alcalde*, a position in the royal bureaucracy, and similar high-ranking appointments.[36] Moreover, unlike notaries elsewhere who kept their own records of legal transactions, scribes were not the repositories of documentary holdings. Churches, municipal councils, and the individuals directly involved in the transactions in question were the keepers of legal documents. But why were there no notaries in northern Castile? The simplest and most logical answer is that the *fueros* (the tradition of granting individual royal charters to localities instead of an overarching Roman legal tradition) served as an effective deterrent to the emergence of a notarial culture. When Alfonso X sought to impose a Roman-based legal system in the realm in the mid–thirteenth century (the *Siete partidas*), he met with stiff resistance and had to abandon his reforms.[37] By then, Castilian reigned supreme, and that which had heretofore accorded notaries their unique place in society (their monopoly of a formulaic legal language, written and read by the few) was no longer acceptable.

In many respects, the triumph of Castilian as the language of material and spiritual transactions "democratized" the relationship of the middling sorts (those who had property) with the world around them and, far more important, with royal and ecclesiastical authorities. When notaries came to Castile as a corporate group in the late Middle Ages and at the onset of the early modern period, they wrote in Castilian. Not even the influence of Renaissance learning and the widespread university training of bureaucrats and notaries could defeat the overwhelming power of the vernacular.

Language and the Change in Values

Did this shift in mentality, the rise of a money economy, the birth of purgatory, and the absence of notaries lead to linguistic change? If so, why did it not happen elsewhere in the West? The written language of administration and of business, of wills and of material transactions, with occasional exceptions, continued to be Latin throughout the medieval

West. Why not in Castile? Was it the presence or absence of notaries that made all the difference?

In Castile, the use of the written vernacular served as a distinct boundary between one type of discourse (ecclesiastic) and another (lay, bourgeois, commercial); and the recording of property transactions, wills, and the like in Castilian, even by clerics, marked the victory of the latter discourse over the former. The advantages of the vernacular were not limited to the creation of a lay discourse vis-à-vis a spiritual one—and here I hesitate to call this new discourse secular, for it also articulated new and distinct spiritual concerns. The written vernacular also defined a new relationship between the Crown and urban elites. From the late twelfth century onward, the kings of Castile had come to rely more and more on the cities for financial and military support against the Muslims, as well as against unruly and ambitious nobles. These ties were formalized in the extensive privileges granted to the nonnoble knights (most of them merchants), culminating in the charters to urban knights of 1255 and 1256.[38] Articulating a growing alliance between Crown and urban elites, these charters, drawn mostly in Castilian after 1200, point to the connection between language and power.

Moreover, there is ample evidence that the pressure to write in Castilian came from below. A few decades before the royal chancery and its scribes began to draw charters in Castilian regularly, local scribes in monasteries and municipalities registered land transactions, donations, and other legally binding agreements in Castilian. Table 1.1 traces the chronological shift from Latin to Castilian in northern Castile, showing that Castilian had become the local language before the royal chancery adopted it as the language of administration in the 1240s.

But why look for a shift in language as an explanation for the emergence of a new system of values? Is not this shift in language itself a consequence of a new *mentalité*? And could they not be concomitant phenomena, each feeding the other? Although one can ascribe the decline of Latin to the cultural backwardness and poor education of the clergy in Castile, the fact remains that royal and local scribes, who were eminently qualified to write Latin, switched to Castilian from one day to the next without missing a beat. Such is the example of a royal inquest, undertaken on 23 May 1231, of a dispute over the use of grazing lands. The royal scribe began the document in Latin, then switched to Castilian, and concluded with Latin. Most of the Castilian text recorded the testimony of several inhabitants of the villages of Planiello, Muniella, San Andrés, Fumada, Pedrosa, Villadiego, and other small localities. The witnesses testified as to their recollections of who held the rights to the lands of Lama. One may assume that the testimony given in the vernacular was

TABLE 1.1
Change from Latin to Castilian in Sample Documentary Collections
(Northern Castile)

Origin of the Documents (Region)	Date of First Castilian Document[1]	Documents Are Written Solely in Castilian[2]	On or Near the Road to Compostela[3]
San Salvador de Oña	1237	1241	No
Las Huelgas Burgos	1210	1223	Yes
Hospital del Rey, Burgos	1221	1228	Yes
La Trinidad Burgos	1223	1223	Yes
Cathedral of Burgos	1209	1228	Yes
San Juan Burgos	c. 1200	1221	Yes
San Zoilo de Carrión	1228	1235	Yes
Silos Burgos	1228	1230	Yes
Cathedral of Segovia	1257	1257	No
Cathedral of Palencia	1214	1225	Yes
Cathedral of Salamanca	1236	1255	No
Santo Toribio de Liébana	1233	1241	No
Cathedral of Avila	1260[4]	1260	No
Santa María de Aguilar de Campoo	1214	1214	No
Chancery of Ferdinand III	1237	1246–47	No

1. This is the date of the first document written entirely in Castilian found in these different documentary collections. Before the date indicated, one may find documents, usually transactions of land or litigations over boundaries, with a Latin opening and conclusion and the main text in Castilian.

2. All private documents, that is, documents dealing with daily life and material transactions, were written exclusively in Castilian by the date indicated. Ecclesiastical visitations and letters from or to foreigners were still written in Latin.

3. There seems to be a correlation between proximity to the road to Compostela and change to Castilian. Similarly, the eastern regions of Castile, that is, those closest to the entry point of the road, seem to have adopted Castilian as the language of everyday transactions earlier.

4. No private documents exist before this date.

copied down verbatim: "De Sant Andrés, Migael Rollo juró et dixo que uiera levar a su padre yerua de la Lama . . ."[39]

Similarly, Petrus Roderici, a royal scribe, wrote a report of an inquest that sought to determine whether or not the monastery of Valbuena had jurisdiction over Froililla. Following a long introduction in Latin, the testimony of several witnesses appears in Castilian, after which the document returns to a formulaic Latin conclusion.[40] Clearly, by the 1230s royal scribes were often competent in both languages and able to shift from one to the other in the same document. In Salamanca, where the change to Castilian came later than in the northern and central regions of the realm, the scribes Petrus Carus and Johan Pascal recorded land transactions, donations, and other documents dealing with the material world in a combination of corrupted Latin and embryonic Castilian in the late 1240s and early 1250s.[41]

Besides the obvious fact that Latin was not understood by most people and thus was useless in the transaction of business at the local level, the majority of the population in Castile had probably used the vernacular orally long before the shift in writing from one language to another. Moreover, a partial answer to why the shift in written language occurred in Castile, and tangentially to the issues of changing attitudes toward salvation and property, may be the growing distance between Church and Crown from the late twelfth century onward, which is most evident in the diminished role of Church scribes and the predominance of lay scribes (municipal or royal) in the writing of private documents. Although almost all the documents I have examined come from ecclesiastical archives, most were drawn by municipal scribes. These were town or village officials elected or named by the citizens of the town, the municipal or village council, or the king.[42]

Representing Castile: The Land and Its People

A shift in values and in the social and political culture of Castile is also evident in the deployment of new ways of representing Castile and the relationship to foreigners and religious minorities in its midst after 1200. I have explored this topic elsewhere; here the briefest summary will suffice. The first half of the thirteenth century witnessed significant historical and literary activity. Most relevant for our purpose in this section are two chronicles (examined further in chapter 7), written in Latin, that shaped historical discourse for the next century: *Chronicon mundi* by Lucas de Tuy and *De rebus Hispanie* by Rodrigo Ximénez de Rada, the archbishop of Toledo. The first work dates from the late 1230s, whereas *De rebus* (which borrowed extensively from the *Chronicon mundi*) may have been completed in the early 1240s.[43] Both works followed a narrative tradition dating back to the chronicles of early medieval Asturias-León, but the rhetorical strategies deployed in these two texts also borrowed freely from classical sources—made more accessible and relevant by the cultural revival of the twelfth century and the frequent contacts of Castile with centers of learning north of the Pyrenees—and from Isidore of Seville's evocative depiction of Spain. Both chronicles exalted Castile and its mission against Islam, giving a heroic rendering of its history. As important as Lucas de Tuy's and Ximénez de Rada's chronicles were—and a great deal of chronicle-writing over the next two and a half centuries cannot be explained without reference to these two works—they were written in Latin and, as such, directed to a cultured readership of ecclesiastics and a few magnates, and wedded to the ideological aims of the royal court. In fact, both authors, particularly Ximénez de Rada, held positions in the highest circles of power. We do not know for sure who read Latin in Castile during the first half of the thirteenth century, but one must assume few did. These histories thus preached to the converted.

My focus here is on vernacular "official histories" and literary texts that, from the early thirteenth century, carried the history of Castile and its idealized construction to a broader and, socially, more middling audience. The aggressive development of Castilian as a language for writing history and the selective highlighting of certain episodes in the nascent "national history" point to the conscious manner in which certain political programs (the conquest of most of western Andalusia, Alfonso X's legislative and administrative reforms, and similar initiatives) were advanced in the mid–thirteenth century. These programs required a new imagining of Castile as a place and a new conception of how its people related to other religious groups within the newly constituted realm.

Although representations of the land, of Castile's wealth or lack of it, of its fertility or aridity were directly linked to the making of a collective identity, for the sake of clarity and brevity these can be grouped into two distinct categories: representations of Castile as a geographical entity and homeland; and representations of Castilians in terms of their physical, moral, and cultural attributes. In these depictions two texts stand out in their vernacular reconstruction of the past. In the thirteenth century, the *Primera crónica general* and the anonymous *Poema de Fernán González* provide a normative vision of the Castilian landscape. This vision already enjoyed a long history and was part of a well-established tradition. In the early to mid–thirteenth century, this official view of Castile as a whole (but most importantly of northern Castile in particular) became idealized and fully formulated in the vernacular (the *Primera crónica general* was written under the aegis of the Castilian Crown, and the *Poema de Fernán González* comes from one of the most important ecclesiastical establishments of northern Castile, the monastery of San Pedro de Arlanza).[44] Not coincidentally, as these representational strategies reached a broader audience, they conflated with the well-articulated political programs of Ferdinand III and, later, with those of Alfonso X, with Castilian expansion into al-Andalus, and with the final union of Castile and León in 1230. In the first half of the thirteenth century and afterward, representations of Castile as a "holy land" and the linking of Castilians to a noble Visigothic ancestry were accompanied by increasingly more virulent pejorative representations of Muslims and Jews in literary texts, law codes, chronicles, and the cortes' legislation. The shift in values, one must sadly note, also produced long-term nefarious consequences for the history of Castile and its religious others.[45]

The Laicization of Daily Life: From Heaven to Earth

New representations of the land and its people also affected the institutional life of the realm. Castile's political life in this period seems to have been governed by two distinct agendas. One represented the dominant and quasi-secular program of the king, his agents, and the cities; the other concerned the less important goals of the Church (less important in terms of the relative power of each institution by the late twelfth century, at which time the Church became subordinated to the Crown).[46] Elsewhere in my work and below, in chapter 7, I show how, in the late twelfth century, the Castilian monarchy abandoned crowning and annointing with holy oil as symbolic rituals in the making of a king. Instead, martial and popular ceremonies marked a new monarch's ascent to power and legitimized his or her rule. The Church was, for all practical purposes, excluded from this self-fashioning of the monarch.[47]

These different policies overlapped most vividly with the shift in language in the epitaph placed on the tomb of Ferdinand III (d. 1252) in the cathedral of Seville. Written in four languages—Castilian, Hebrew, Arabic, and Latin—the first three versions addressed Ferdinand's human qualities, wisdom as a ruler, tolerance of other religions, and valor in the battlefield. The Latin version, a clerical production, concerned itself with religious matters and retained the combative crusading ideal advanced by the Church.[48] Alfonso X's reign (1252–1284), with its emphasis on Arabic science and magic, its ambitious program of Roman-based legal reform and political centralization, even if failed, further advanced the boundaries of a laic spirit. This was not so simple, of course. Alfonso X wrote poems to the Virgin and, through his building program, demonstrated his devotion to Mary. Laicization was never a clear-cut development; it was a heady mixture of religious beliefs, a search for pagan forms of knowledge, and political expediency.[49]

In the previous pages, I have sought to provide a context for the discussion that follows and preliminary explanations for the mental and political reordering of Castilian society. Nonetheless, this remains a broad depiction of these changes. In the subsequent chapters, I undertake closer examination of what I mean by a shift in values and how this came about.

CHAPTER TWO

THE EVIDENCE OF WILLS

IN EARLY September 1347, Martín Ortiz de Agonçiello, a merchant and citizen of Logroño, lay sick in bed, awaiting death. He was probably still quite young, for his children had not yet come of age, and his mother, Elvira Jiménez, was alive and active. Wishing to put his affairs in order, Martín sent for the royal scribe of Logroño, Ruy García, and for witnesses and relatives. In their presence, "being of good memory and good understanding and *cobdiciando* (greedy for, coveting) the glory of Paradise," Martín dictated his will.

In this impromptu testament obviously dictated from the bedside, he moved from one concern to another in no apparent order, trying to make certain that nothing would be left out. Yet, Martín had clearly given thought to the matter. Half of his earthly goods were to go to his wife, but solely on the condition that she not remarry and that for the next fifteen years she care for their children. If she married before the established period, María would have to relinquish both the property and the children to Martín's relatives. Once the children came of age, most of the property was to be settled on them. On the day of his burial, funds were also to be provided to churches and monasteries with the express purpose of distributing bread, wine, and meat (or fish, if required by the liturgical calendar) to thirty *envergoñados* (literally meaning ashamed, but more accurately connoting worthy or deserving), poor citizens of Logroño. Moreover, Martín donated one hundred *varas* (about 85 yards) of *sayal* (sackcloth) to dress the poor "for the love of God (and) for [his] soul," but, undoubtedly, also to reinforce the memory of his name, to reaffirm his social standing.[1]

Greedy for (*cobdiciando*) paradise—the use of the word *codicia* (greed) as a prelude to paradise is in itself significant—Martín secured the salvation of his soul in a businesslike manner, with donations to a sprinkling of churches and monasteries in return for numerous masses, pilgrimages to famous shrines, and a ceremonial funeral feast. All in all, this was a shrewd yet financially minuscule investment in eternity. In his final hour, with one eye on the afterlife and another firmly set on this world, Martín's driving wish was the preservation and rational distribution of his fortune among his kin.

Drawn more than a century after the will of Sebastián, the cleric of Santa María la Redonda (1230), that opened the introduction to this book, Martín's will differs only in the amount of his legacy and in the language. His testament reflects the prosperous merchant's larger income and social concerns as well as the official and final transition of the written word from Latin to Castilian after the mid–thirteenth century. From the early thirteenth century into the modern period, most wills in northern Castile followed the format of these two testaments.[2] Most wills divided the testator's income and property into three broad but well-defined categories: (1) pious donations—that is, money or property to pay for masses, candles, chaplaincies, and the like—to ensure the salvation of one's soul and/or the souls of relatives; (2) testamentary dispositions to ensure the transfer of one's property to relatives and friends; and, less often, (3) charitable bequests to feed, clothe, and care for the poor.[3]

Although medieval testaments varied little in how they were written or what they sought to accomplish after the 1220s, they differed sharply from the donations and wills of an earlier age, drawn "for the remedy of my soul." What do these changes in will-writing between the late twelfth and the early thirteenth century tell us about Castilian society? What prompted these transformations?

The Meaning of Wills

New testamentary forms and the language shift from Latin to Castilian constitute important sources of evidence for the social and cultural changes that became manifest in Castile after 1200. I draw on this evidence from multiple perspectives to show how the drafting of wills evolved over time, dovetailed with Castilian attitudes toward property, family, salvation, and charity, and reflected a wide-ranging overhaul in the region's value system.

As indicated earlier, we have no notarial records in northern Castile for the period before 1350. In southern Castile (Seville, Toledo, and respective environs) and in the eastern Spanish kingdoms that comprised the Crown of Aragon (Aragon proper, Catalonia, and Valencia), a vigorous notarial culture developed in the second half of the thirteenth century. Notaries appeared in Seville, for example, right after the city's conquest in 1248. Seville became an important outpost for Genoese and other Italian mercantile and banking houses (although, under Islamic rule, the Genoese had been active in the city's commercial life since the mid–

twelfth century). Clearly, Seville's lively commercial life, far-flung trade interests, and Genoese-inspired notarial procedures influenced the formation of a notarial culture on the banks of the Guadalquivir.[4] Moreover, Seville's public scribes "followed the protocols set out in the *Siete Partidas* (*Partida* III, xviii, xix)," functioning as notaries in drafting documents. Although the great legal code composed under Alfonso X's direction in the second half of the thirteenth century was rejected in toto elsewhere in the realm (see below), it retained a great deal of authority in Seville and its hinterland. Seville was, after all, Alfonso X's favorite city, frequent residence, and one of the few places in Castile that remained faithful to the king during the noble rebellions of the early 1270s and the civil war against his own son, the Infante Don Sancho, in the late 1270s and early 1280s. In Catalonia as well, even small localities like Santa Coloma de Queralt (a town of around one thousand inhabitants in the thirteenth century and located sixty kilometers from Tarragona) had extensive notarial registers for the period after 1276, in contrast to the lack of such practices or documentary collections in northern Castile.[5]

In northern Castile, different legal traditions (the *fueros*), the dynamics of early land settlement, and an idiosyncratic political culture (the strong power of the counts in the ninth and tenth centuries and a fairly centralized monarchy afterward) delayed the emergence of notarial practices and their rational drive to standardize legal and property transactions (wills included). Although there were no notaries or notarial archives before the mid–fourteenth century, something approaching a notarial culture could be found in pre-1350 northern Castile. Ecclesiastical and lay scribes fulfilled many notarial functions, drawing documents and establishing the formulaic language that provided the legal context and precedent for all transactions. But ecclesiastical and lay scribes, because of their opposing agendas and conflicting interests, often worked against each other. Moreover, because of the haphazard character of scribal activity and the difficulty of keeping permanent manuscript collections or registers (except for monastic archives) in northern Castile before the Black Death, only fragments of what must have been a much larger documentary evidence have survived (unlike the formidable notarial archives available for most of the western Mediterranean region).[6] This brings up the inevitable question of why the western Mediterranean developed a strong notarial tradition while northern Castile did not. I attempted to provide some tentative explanations in the previous chapter, which may be useful to reiterate and expand here.

In the Mediterranean a possible answer can be found in the region's adherence to the Roman legal tradition and the significant, Italian-led, legal revival of the late eleventh and twelfth centuries. Moreover, in Italian and southern French urban centers, which came to life much earlier than their counterparts elsewhere in Europe, the legalization of material transactions became an engine for notarial activity.

To return to northern Castile, most of the extant pre-1350 documents were preserved in ecclesiastical archives because they included some provision, donation, or legacy that benefited that particular monastery or church at one time or another. The trove of archival evidence, therefore, offers only skewed glimpses into the past, with a strong bias toward ecclesiastical interests and concerns. Although we do not have actual notarial records to provide us with a clear view of shifts in values and mental attitudes, thousands of donations and testaments extant in Castilian archives or published in documentary collections provide a rich source for our inquiry.[7] The wills and living gifts examined throughout this book can be divided into two overlapping chronological sets. The first runs from the early ninth century, when Castile emerged as a political entity, to the period between the late twelfth century and the first half of the thirteenth, when the cultural shift I am exploring took place. The second set begins with these changes and extends into the mid–fourteenth century, concluding with the Plague.

Table 2.1 shows a detailed breakdown of donations and wills in northern Castile from the ninth to the mid–fourteenth century, indicating the donors' and testators' purposes in drawing these legal instruments. A close examination of this table, and an even closer reading of the sources, reveals specific patterns. Living gifts and wills up to the early 1200s were overwhelmingly uniform. They were mostly straightforward settlements of property and, to a lesser extent, income on a single ecclesiastical institution for the "remedy of souls" or "remission of sins" of the donor, his or her parents, and other close relatives. All of these documents were written in Latin, and almost always by ecclesiastical scribes.

These donations and the handful of wills (or what I call protowills) one finds before the thirteenth century followed well-established formulaic patterns. Linguistically and textually, there is little or no difference between a late ninth-century donation and its late eleventh- or even early twelfth-century counterpart, even though sweeping political and economic changes took place in the intervening years. For example, around 884 Sisnando gave his lands and other possessions to the church of St. Emeterius and Celedonius "pro remedio anima mee." Almost two hundred years afterward, in 1076, Beila Beilaz, his wife, Anderazu, and three other members of the family "pro anime nostre remedio" donated houses and lands to the monastery of San Millán de la Cogolla. Except for the fact that the latter document was a bit longer, reflecting the properties and individuals involved in the donation, there were few differences.

More than one hundred years later, when Diego López made a donation to the monastery of San Salvador de Oña in 1198, apparently very little had changed, except that the Latin therein was already well on its way to becoming Castilian, and the donor requested prayers for the health of his king, Alfonso VIII: "In Dei nomine, Ego Didacus Lupi, pro salute domini mei, regis Aldefonsi, et pro remedio anime mee et parentum meorum, da al monasterio de Oña omnem hereditatem quam adquisiui a domno rege Aldefonso in alfoz de Pedralada. Obligase el abbad y conuento de decir vnas misas."[8]

These donations, however, differed from other documents that began to be drawn in the twelfth century. Protowills established various conditions in the managing of donated property, requested some privilege or grant from the monastery or church beyond the usual appeal for masses or prayers, and set aside some of the donor's wealth for the family. In 1137, Elvira Téllez donated her property (*heredad*, an allod or land owned outright) in the village of San Felices to the monastery of San Zoilo de Carrión "pro remedium anima mee et animas parentum meorum," except lands she planned to keep for the rest of her life and transfer to the monastery only after her death.[9] Similarly, in March 1225, in a text still written in Latin, Don Alvaro and his wife, Doña Rosa, made an agreement with the prior of San Zoilo. The couple donated their property in Vezdemarván, while the monastery agreed to grant them use of the lands for as long as they lived.[10]

The latter transaction marked the advent of agreements in which the middling sorts donated property to monasteries and churches in return for burial, an annuity, some guarantee of support until death, or a combination of these. As we shall see in chapter 3, these types of exchanges reveal a growing concern with restricting donations, retaining use of donated property, and garnering an income or maintenance in old age that would protect against the loss of one's land to violent neighbors or to the vagaries of weather and poor cropyields.

The Nature of Donations: Toward a Typology

Besides making donations for the remedy of one's soul, many testators and donors requested burial in the church or monastery to which the donation was being made. Specific requests for anniversaries, lighting of candles, chantries, or similar pious services were far less frequent in this earlier period, and gifts were rarely settled on the needy. More significantly, these early donations or wills seldom specified monetary terms; nor did they define property spatially. The descriptions of donated land,

TABLE 2.1
Pious and Charitable Dispositions in Wills and Donations in Northern Castile

	807–999	900–999	1000–1099	1100–1199	Total (807–1199)	1200–1250	1250–1350	Total (1200–1350)
donations	9	137	231	189	566	102	191	293
wills[1]	1	29	39	16	85	12	91	103
TOTAL	10	166	270	205	651	114	282	396
to redeem donator's soul[2]	10	147	323	160	640	51	82	133
burial	4	41	63	11	119	9	50	59
anniversaries	—	—	—	12	12	13	67	80
chantries/chaplaincy	—	—	1	3	4	4	51	55
candles/oil for lamps	—	2	3	4	9	3	29	32
food for the clergy	—	7	2	—	9	3	21	24
to feed/clothe the poor	—	2	1	4	7	5	36	41
alms to hospitals	—	—	2	—	2	3	18	21
to more than one institution[3]	—	—	—	5	5	15	91	106
masses/prayers for the soul[4]	—	6	1	37	44	2	32	34

sponsorship of pilgrims	—	—	—	—	4	11	15
aid for the crusades	—	—	—	—	6	13	19
to found hospital/monastery	2	—	—	0	1	8	9
to maintain self or kin	2	5	4	2	3	11	14
other	—	1	3	11	—	10	10
donations by king or counts	—	—	—	4	—	—	—
	43	58	59	160	29	24	53

Sources: Archivo de la Catedral de Burgos, Archivo Histórico Nacional (Clero and Códices collections), Archivo Municipal de Burgos, and published collections in *Cartulario de San Millán de la Cogolla; Cartulario de Santo Toribio de Liébana; Colección diplomática calceatense; Colección diplomática de las colegiatas de Albelda y Logroño; Colección diplomática de San Salvador de Oña; Documentación medieval de la catedral de Avila; Fuentes medievales castellano-leonesas; Fuentes para la historia de Castilla; El real monasterio de las Huelgas y el Hospital del Rey; Recueil des chartes de l'abbaye de Silos.*

[1] Wills or protowills before 1200 were donations in which the donor restricted in some manner what was donated (almost exclusively land). Mostly this meant a donation to one single monastery or church with the property to be given after the donor's death. In reality, these protowills are very different from the ones found in the Castilian documentation after 1200.

[2] After 1200, a good number of donations included the formula "for my soul," which corresponded to the "pro remedio anima mee" of an earlier period. By 1300, the formulaic language disappeared, above all, in royal donations to monasteries.

[3] All the wills after 1200 gave legacies to more than one ecclesiastical institution.

[4] Prayers for the soul should not really be considered a different category. Donations for the "remedy of one's soul" already implied prayers and inscription in the memorial books of the monastery or church.

with notable exceptions, were vague, reflecting jurisdictional rights rather than clearly spelled-out territories.

Although I have drawn a distinction between donations and testaments using the documents' wording as criteria, most living gifts before the 1220s—excepting those made by kings and counts—were bestowed late in the donor's life or following the death of close relatives. Most of the donations in the early period were, in fact if not in name, wills, and they expressed the donors' wishes to settle their goods on a monastery or church in exchange for forgiveness of their sins. Donors felt no need to specify how the gifts were to be used, and the reciprocal aspects of the act of giving (the hope of gaining entry to heaven's gate in the afterlife), though only implied, were clear. What mattered was the giving, and the brokers between the secular and the divine—the priests and monks—chose the most efficacious ways (prayers, food for the poor, inscription in the liturgical calendar, votive candles, etc.) to bring the donor's gift to the designated church or monastery and, thus, to God.[11]

I do not wish to imply, however, that this pattern of pre-1220 wills and donations, so predominant in northern Castile, was atypical in Iberia or other parts of the medieval West. In fact, donations were quite similar in all regions; what set Castile apart was the sparse number of actual wills and the scarce use of the word *testamentum* before the 1220s.[12] In northern Aragon, just east of northern Castile, wills, or at least donations that identified themselves as such and were rare in Castilian documentation before 1200, were not uncommon. Even donation patterns and the formulaic language differed from Castilian practices. The archives of Leire, Huesca, and other Aragonese localities show a number of early testaments, clearly identified as such in the texts.[13] In contrast, in certain northern regions of Castile (specifically Liébana), where Asturian influences were considerable and Visigothic legal practices remained somewhat alive, the word *testamentum* was not uncommon into the late eleventh century, at which time, with the area coming under Castilian rule, it disappeared from the documentation. Thus, Froila made his "donationem vel testamento," giving his lands to the church of St. Stephen in 826, and Sindino "facio regulam vel testamentum," donating his property to the monasteries of Santa María de Lebanza and San Martín de Turieno.[14]

With this caveat in mind, it may be useful to look closely again at some of these early Castilian donations. Around 947, García Ciclero, "pro remedio anima mee," donated salt wells in the village of Ganiz (Geniz) to the abbot Dulquito and the friars of the monastery of Albelda (in the Rioja region). He did this inspired by the "fear [of] and love [for]" the majesty of the Lord. The donation, a meager one, indicates the individual was not a prominent or powerful member of the community.[15] On 1 December 1053, a certain Tello Muñoz and his wife, Apalla, most probably members of the lesser nobility, made four donations to the monastery of San Quirce in the diocese of Burgos. The formulaic language of all five donations or living gifts (whether of well-to-do or lowly provenance) was exactly the same; only the location and size of the donated property changed. "Knowing that their lives were drawing to a close and aware of the eternal life to come," Tello and Apalla donated their (*divisa*) cereal lands, woods, pastures, and other properties, with rights of entrance and exit, to San Quirce. The properties were given without restrictions and, although the sources do not state so explicitly, with full *dominium* and forever.[16] That donations and testaments retained a uniform structure and language for almost four centuries regardless of the donors' social filiation or type of bequest reflected the tight grip ecclesiastical scribes had on these early negotiations for redemption.

Although regularly couched in pious formulations, the donations fulfilled a variety of purposes. In some instances, they were clearly intended as rewards for services rendered in the past, for a monastery's proven loyalty to and support of the counts' or royal interests—such as having served the Crown in times of crisis or having provided havens for royal children.[17] In others, there was an implicit expectation of reciprocal services: a donation in exchange for protection, a gift for a prayer or an anniversary. These exchanges could involve matters of grace, salvation, and charismatic protection; or they could be hard-nosed deals relating to material life in which specific provisions were laid out for feeding, care, and burial of the donor in return for an offer of property.[18] These types of negotiations were only implied before 1200, but they were clearly and quite boldly stated afterward. What the Castilian documents fail to show—because of the fragmentary nature of the evidence or, as I argue below, because of Castile's early political development—is a pattern of gift-giving to monasteries by great lordly families. I refer here to models of gift exchange commonly found in northern Europe, whereby royal and great noble houses associated themselves with particular monasteries and ecclesiastical foundations. As studied by Barbara Rosenwein, Stephen White, and others, pious gifts formed part of a complex political process and were an intrinsic component of lordly power.[19] Although Castilian great noble houses had much to gain, politically and economically, from a sustained policy of donations to important monasteries and shrines, conditions in northern Castile were diametrically different from those in northern Europe in the ninth and tenth centuries. This is worth emphasizing: there is no evidence of extended lordly kin networks associated with monastic foundation. As shall be seen in chapter 5, there were no great territorial lordships in León-Castile until the late twelfth century. Until then, the great noble houses depended on royal largesse for their wellbeing. The kind of relationship between secular lords and great religious houses found in Germany and France in the central Middle Ages was fairly restricted to the royal family (or the count of Castile) before the twelfth century. Great lords did not command the prestige of association with ritual sites until much later.

While the Carolingian lands were slowly disintegrating into separate political entities, undergoing political fragmentation and privatization in the ninth century, Castile was just beginning to be settled, barely emerging as a fledgling autonomous region. Furthermore, few, if any, monasteries in northern Castile (certainly not south of the Peaks of Europe, a mountain spur of the Pyrenees) predate the early ninth century. Preceding lordly power into the region, monasteries had, in fact, established their jurisdiction and territorial domains before they could be effectively challenged by lords.[20] Finally, the power of the Castilian counts in the ninth and tenth centuries, and royal power afterward, was far more centralized and effective than that of regions north of the Pyrenees. Although powerful noble houses emerged in northern Castile, they could never claim the autonomy their counterparts enjoyed in the post-Carolingian world.[21]

In short, we cannot document a rational policy of donations aimed at establishing strong familial, political, or ritual ties between individual families and monastic institutions in northern Castile from the ninth century onward (except for the counts' and royal families). The donations and few wills of this period fail to indicate any long-term policy of donations; rather, surviving sources show that donations to ecclesiastical institutions were made by high nobles and even lesser people for no other purpose, as far as one can determine, than to vouchsafe the "remedy of their souls." The only exception to this approach to donations by the great and the humble were, as already noted, the gifts given by the counts and, later, the kings of Castile. Yet, even though the rulers of Castile preferred certain monasteries over others, their donations were broadly distributed throughout the region.

Donations and, to a lesser extent, wills before 1200 can also be classified according to social groupings. Clearly, social class determined not only the type and extent of donated property, but also the relationship between donor and recipient. Following Maureen C. Miller's work on medieval Verona, one can divide donors into specific categories: (1) that of counts (later, royal family) in Castile and the kings of nearby Asturias-León and Navarre; (2) powerful nobles; (3) clerics; (4) well-to-do farmers, low nobility, and city dwellers (the middling sorts).[22] As in Verona, fluctuating social and economic conditions changed the social filiation and number of donors, with prosperous farmers and urban residents playing a more significant role.[23] In Castile, however, members of this group did not become important actors until after 1200.

To summarize our discussion on donations: the extant documentation from the early ninth to the early thirteenth century depicts thousands of donations and a small number of wills in which men and women in the Castilian central Middle Ages bequeathed their lands to a single monastery or church for the remedy of their souls or the souls of others, the remission of sins, escape from hell's fire, or admittance into heaven.[24] Except for the hope for spiritual salvation, they did not impose restrictions or expect, at least on the surface, to gain any profit. But rather than merely bestowing property, these donations exchanged seignorial rights to rents and lands for prayers that might ease the soul's final passage to God.[25] In fact, almost without exception, testaments before the 1220s chose a single monastery or church as the recipient of private largesse, rather than spreading donations among diverse ecclesiastical institutions, as was the case later.[26] The shift from fairly uniform donations to a single ecclesiastical institution before the 1200s to the later fragmentation of gifts to multiple churches signaled a new way of bargaining for salvation.

To bolster their spiritual well-being, donors or testators began to order the posthumous delivery of prayers, masses, and charitable acts. Indeed, the rise of bequests to assorted urban ecclesiastical institutions (as opposed to the former practice of bestowing gifts to a single monastery in the countryside)—prompted by donors' desire to retain control over their donations and ensure that prayers and masses for their redemption would be widely performed—is the strongest sign of a transformation in values and a reordering of the spiritual and material landscape in Castile.[27]

Moreover, although donors before the early thirteenth century quite possibly made settlements—on relatives, friends, religious institutions, perhaps even the poor—that were concurrent with pious donations to a specific church, we seldom find documentary evidence to guide us on these matters. Whether these pre-1200 arrangements were ever put into writing or whether they inhabited a world of oral formulas and gestures, it is clear that a sharp distinction existed between what was offered to the Church, and therefore to Christ, and what was given to kin and friends. Rarely did the two worlds come together in donations and wills before the early thirteenth century. What the sources do reveal is the desire to deliver land or part of one's property, unfettered, into ecclesiastical hands. At most, some donors kept a life interest or retained use of the land for their children, but very infrequently did this extend beyond one generation.[28]

Donations and Wills after the 1220s

In the early to mid–thirteenth century a series of important events changed the way Castilians made charitable and pious donations and wrote their wills. First came a shift in language, from Latin to Castilian, as lay scribes replaced ecclesiastical ones. This was most evident in royal grants, where earlier Castilian expressions of piety—literal translations of the Latin expression "for the remedy of my soul"—began to disappear. By the 1260s and 1270s, such formulaic locutions had, with a few exceptions, vanished from the documentation.[29] Instead, royal donations to ecclesiastical institutions (a type of document whose continuity permits us to trace its linguistic permutations over the centuries) became simply instruments of royal policy and largesse.

At the same time, either because the economic prosperity of the twelfth and early thirteenth centuries had turned sour, or because attitudes toward the Church had changed, bringing about a breakdown of confidence in ecclesiastical institutions, the number of donations to the Church dropped dramatically.[30] Northern Castilians, especially members of the bourgeoisie and the petty-nobility who generated most of the wills found in the accompanying tables, still made donations after the 1220s, but the Church could no longer expect the unrestricted giving that had been the foundation of its early economic prosperity. Moreover, unlike previous donations and wills, those after the early thirteenth century exacted specific services in return. Money, or rental income, often in kind, now often replaced property as the donated item, and it was given to churches and monasteries under very strict guidelines.[31] Ecclesiastical institutions still served as intermediaries between donors and recipients, between humans and God, but priests and monks were now asked to perform specific rituals in return for gifts.

Furthermore, the conditions under which legacies were made were often so restricted that they allowed for little diversion of funds; and, as we move into the fourteenth century, the donor's relatives were the executors, secular overseers assigned to make sure that pious bequests and chaplaincies were reserved for kin and that the terms of the will were fulfilled. Just as often, property was passed on to family members, albeit with the obligation to set aside part of the income for pious and charitable ends—but the indiscriminate willing of property to the Church had clearly come to an end.[32] Finally, unlike before the early thirteenth century, ecclesiastical institutions faced increased competition for donations and gifts, not only from the donors' family and friends but also from a growing number of quasi-religious institutions and causes: brotherhoods, sponsored pilgrimages, crusades, ransoms, and other pious or philanthropic activities. Most testaments after the 1220s show an almost universal tendency to scatter donations as widely as possible. This was probably done to ensure every possible mode of salvation and reprieve from damnation.

The Case of Liébana

It may be useful to move from these general remarks and the broad statistical sample of donations and wills in northern Castile presented in table 2.1 to look at the transformation of donations and wills in one particular location. This brief case study—supplemented in later chapters with numerous individual examples—follows the shift in the extant documentation of the ancient Benedictine monastery of Santo Toribio de Liébana, an ecclesiastical institution perched on the mountains of Cantabria (northern Castile). The first document in Santo Toribio's archives dates from 790, and there is a fairly uninterrupted record of donations and wills into the early modern period.[33]

For the period between 790 and 1350, most of the documents of Santo Toribio record land transactions, rental agreements, inventories of the monastery's vast holdings and rights (the latter date mostly from around the early fourteenth century), royal charters, and confirmations of regal grants, donations, and wills. For the years 790–1200, I have found thirty-nine donations/wills. All describe giving land, houses, livestock, fruit trees, and other property to Santo Toribio or its earlier incarnation, the monastery of San Martín, for the "remedy or redemption of one's soul or the soul of relatives." In a florid, formulaic language, some donations state the donors' desire for paradise and fear of hell. Others petition for the remission of sins, remembrance through prayers, burial in the monastery, and candles to light the church. Table 2.2 provides a breakdown of the evidence.

Reflecting Liébana's relative geographical isolation, its early life under the jurisdiction of the Asturian kings, and the role Visigothic law thus played in the region, many of the wills specifically stated that the bequests represented only one-fifth of the donors' total assets.[34] As shall be seen in the next chapter, the *Lex visigothorum*, which did not come into full use in Castile proper until the first half of the thirteenth century, forbade legacies to the Church exceeding more than one-fifth of the entire estate. In the same vein, and evoking an early age, many of the donations were identified as *testamentum*, a word seldom used in Castile proper (that is, south of the mountain range) even in the vernacular doc-

Fig. 6 Façade of the collegiate church of Santillana del Mar
In Cantabria, the northern region of Old Castile, monasteries, such as that of Liébana, and collegiate churches, such as that of Santillana del Mar, retained their old Romanesque style and adhered to ancient Visigothic formulaic language in wills and transactions of property. (Photo by Scarlett Freund)

uments of the thirteenth century. Thus, on 23 January, Sindino made his will or testamentum, donating all the property he held in the jurisdiction of the church of Sant Fagunt in Tanarrio to the monastery of Santa María de Lebanza and the monastery of San Martín de Turieno. Four years later, a document describing the donation of property by a man named Arecio to the monastery of San Martín closed with the words "ego Arecius in oc meo testamentum manu mea."[35]

One should also note that the florid and formulaic language found in the opening paragraphs of donations and wills began to taper off by the early twelfth century. Introductory passages such as

> In Deo nomine, Ego Godestio Didace, una cum uxora mea Marina, placuit mihi bono animo et caro consilio et propia nostra uoluntate, scio quia mortale duco casum, scio quia dies ultimus euenit mihi, quia nascendi inicio nescire baleo termino, et ego dicto Godestio, una cum uxore mea Marina et scelerum meorum adeptus et onera pergrauatus, quia habundauerunt iniquitates nostre super numerum arena maris, et per ingencia peccata et iniquitates nostre . . .

TABLE 2.2
Donations and Wills in the Area of Liébana, 790–c. 1200

Number of donations	39
Donations of land, houses, other property	39
"for the remedy or redemption of one's or one's relatives' souls"	24
"wishing for paradise and fearing the Last Judgment or the fires of hell"	7
"alms extinguish sins"	1
"remission of sins"	6
"candles in the church"	1
"for prayers"	2
"for burial in the monastery"	2
Donations to more than one monastery	1
Donations by the count or ruler of the region	2

appear with little or no change in several of the thirty-nine donations/wills under consideration.[36] The expression "our sins are more numerous than the sands of the sea," probably the poetic flourish of a monastic scribe, may have given the right tone of contrition to those contemplating the end of their days. By the early twelfth century, however, this language had disappeared, often replaced by the simple catch-all phrase "pro remedium animarum nostrarum vel parentum nostrarum."[37]

An even more dramatic shift took place in the early thirteenth century. Over the next 150 years, the number of donations decreased markedly, from thirty-nine to seventeen in the post-1200 period, reflecting donors' migrating from the older ecclesiastical institutions such as Santo Toribio to the newer Mendicant orders or adopting other urban pious concerns. But not merely the quantity of donations changed. Throughout northern Castile, the way property was donated, and the rationale prompting donations, changed as well.

Although donations continued to be made for the remedy of one's soul or prayers—such formulaic language can be found in fourteen of the donations/wills after 1200—the written record reveals elaborate negotiations. The donors, with little exception, requested specific services for what they gave. Moreover, the property to be donated or willed was now clearly described, unveiling a new preoccupation with boundaries and inventorying and measuring one's material property (see chapter 4). These new donations were also written in Castilian, giving the testators and their executors a control over their legacies that was altogether lacking in an earlier period.

In 1204, García González gave lands in Tama, Armaño, Vierguas, and Liébana to the monastery of Santo Toribio "propter remedium anime mee." García requested that as long as there was a community in Santo Toribio, the monks pray for his soul in the altar of the monastery's patron saint. The very short document (fourteen lines in the printed edition) is neatly divided in two equal halves. The upper portion, which describes the extent and location of the donated property and the donor's request for continuous prayer for his soul at a specific site, was written in Castilian, except for the Latin formula "propter remedium anime mee." The rest of the document, a formulaic cursing of those who might violate the terms of the agreement, was written in Latin.[38]

García González's will marked the beginnings of a series of settlements on the monastery (no longer described in the vernacular as testaments—a word that harkened back to Latin and the Visigothic legal tradition) that carefully requested services such as burial and anniversaries, intended to expedite salvation, while placing restrictions on how the monastery was to use the property or income it received. In 1220, Diego Gutiérrez, in a document written in Latin, "pro remedio anima mee et parentum meorum," asked to be buried in the monastery. He donated twenty cows and a mare. What makes this donation/will interesting to us is the clear and unprecedented parceling of his livestock for different purposes. First, his livestock was not to be given to the monastery until after his death. Second, the mare and two cows were to provide income for Santo Toribio's charitable work; eight cows went to support eight anniversaries in Diego's memory. Similarly, in 1236, Pedro Díaz, on his way to campaign in the south (presumably in the siege of Córdoba), promised three pregnant mares to the monastery in case of his death in action. But, were he to return alive, he would give 30 *mrs.* to the monastery for the mule he had taken on campaign and take his mares back—the implication being that the mule belonged to the monastery and had been given to him as a pledge or in exchange for the promised, and obviously highly prized, pregnant mares.[39] This and other documents of the confirm that shrewd bargaining for salvation had become the norm in northern Castile. Ecclesiastical establishments such as the monastery of Santo Toribio de Liébana could no longer depend on the unrestricted giving of an earlier period and had to build or preserve their domains through purchases, exchanges, and other financial transactions.

In 1292, Gómez Pérez de la Lama and his wife donated vineyards and lands (carefully described as to location and boundaries) to the monastery, plus 1,000 *mrs.* to be rendered after Gómez's death. In return he was to be buried in the center of the monastery's church choir. This desirable location for burial was, of course, reserved for the very wealthy or the very pious. After his death, Gómez Pérez was duly buried in this place of honor and sanctity, his body, and one hopes his soul, regaled by the daily singing of the canonical hours. The problem with all of this is that in 1315, the monastery was still litigating to get the 1,000 *mrs.* from Gómez's heirs. As we shall see, promising and actually handing over property were two very different things.[40]

From the 1220s onward, wills became the most common form of property exchange between testators and the Church, between testators and their family and friends, their language, intent, and format differing completely from those of earlier bequests. The cultural and economic changes sweeping Castile in this period—later than similar developments in Italy, other parts of the northern medieval world, and even eastern Iberia—transformed the understanding of what wills did and how they were crafted. In looking at these documents, drawn almost eight centuries ago, we look over the shoulders of Castilians, poised at the dawn of a new age. The means and the language to articulate concerns about property, salvation, charity, and the self were new, and, in many ways, even revolutionary.

CHAPTER THREE

PROPERTY: WILLS AND THE LAW IN MEDIEVAL CASTILE

ON 23 APRIL 1225, Iohan (Juan) Peregrín (Peregrino), canon of the cathedral chapter of Santa María of Burgos, "being healthy and happy" (or is it happy of being healthy? *sano y alegre estando*) made his final will and testament. Providing a careful itemization of his property and rents, Juan donated a mill in the town of Oreiulo (Orejuelo)—worth 25 *mrs.*—to the cathedral (presumably to the chapter) to pay for *collaçio* (meals) to be given during the feast days of St. John and St. Luke, and for ten masses in his memory. Some gardens in Santa Gadea, worth 13 *mrs.* of rent annually, he distributed among clerics he knew so that they would celebrate masses for himself and for his uncle, Don Tostén, formerly a canon as well and now deceased. In addition, Don Juan Peregrino donated two vineyards to the cathedral of Burgos.

To his relatives and friends, however, he gave the bulk of his possessions. His brother, Don Gonçalvo, received houses in the neighborhood of San Gil in Burgos and all his vineyards there. His sister, Doña Melina, benefited from houses next to the ones in which Juan Peregrino had lived and vineyards. These legacies to Doña Melina were given with the condition that she was neither to sell nor to pawn them, and that, after her death, the properties were to pass undiminished to her daughters and grandchildren. To her nieces, Doña Viviana and Doña Constança, Juan Peregrino gave "houses in Sanctivannez with their gardens." A similar restriction as that placed on Melina's legacy forbade the sale of the property, which was to be left to Viviana and Constança's children. Juan's nephew, Petro Gonçalvet, received a vineyard, and Juan's servant, as well as other colleagues in the chapter, also received property, mostly vineyards and houses. These gifts were given with the condition that if the recipients died before Juan, the property would revert to his nieces and his nieces' children.[1] The most salient feature of this will, therefore, was Juan's attempt to retain his material goods within the family.

Two very long testaments, the first the will of Don Martín Ibáñez, prior of the cathedral of Burgos (1333), the second, that of Don Gonzalo Pérez, canon of the cathedral of Burgos and archpriest of Aguilar de Campoo (1349), show the same pattern in composition. They begin with some pious donation, requests for masses or burial in the church, but soon the testators engage in a hard-nosed inventory of their rather substantial properties and in the assignation of the bulk of their goods (lands, houses, vineyards, household goods, rents, etc.) to members of their respective families. The texts of these two wills are too extensive and the provisions too numerous and complex to summarize in detail. What is clear—and in almost every will written from the early thirteenth century onward—is their emphasis that the property they donated and the running of the philanthropies and ecclesiastical benefices they had set up remain in the hands of their relatives. Martín Ibáñez ordered in his testament "that [these chaplaincies] be given to men of his own lineage, or to those closest to his family . . . and as long as there are members of his family [alive] that these chaplaincies could not be given to anyone else." Only after his lineage had been extinguished could the chapter name other chaplains.[2]

When Don Gonzalo Pérez dictated his will, he bequeathed funds for a ten-bed hospital for the poor in his own hometown, Aguilar de Campoo, and enough money to clothe two hundred of them (one hundred with wool cloth, the other hundred with linen).[3] Besides a large number of masses, anniversaries, oil for church lamps, money for the Crusade, and other pious legacies, Gonzalo also provided enough income to feed one hundred poor men and women on the anniversary of his death. Yet, as with most wills in this period, settlements on relatives and friends took most of the estate. He also insisted that the chaplaincies he endowed were to be reserved for his kin as long as there were living relatives, and in their default, that the positions be given to citizens of Aguilar de Campoo.[4] Thus, Don Gonzalo Pérez selected fellow citizens in Aguilar de Campoo—where he remained an active player in the land market and in pious activities—as the final recipients of his wealth in the absence of relatives. In these three wills and in hundreds of similar documents, one witnesses a clear commitment to keeping one's property within a narrow circle of relatives, friends, and fellow citizens. It did not matter at all that most of Gonzalo's wealth had been obtained from his benefice in the cathedral chapter of Burgos. His loyalty—and property—were for his kin and for those back home.[5]

These examples show, as has already been indicated, the sharp break between donations and protowills written before the 1220s and the testaments for the period afterward. Not only did the language (from Latin to Castilian) and the vocabulary of giving change, but the intent behind these early unrestricted donations was transformed as well. When we look at wills from the early thirteenth century onward, we see a novel and increasing concern with property. Wills after this date included elaborate provisions to ensure that the testator's property remained in the hands of family. In fact, notwithstanding the usual charitable and/or pious donations found in almost all the wills, there are few testaments in which the overriding concern is not the preservation of property for the benefit of family and friends. Moreover, the religious institutions designated as recipients of the donor's largesse would receive, at best, the income or use of the property, but very seldom the *dominium* or title.

Wills, therefore, as legal instruments for transferring property (cash, jewelry, household goods, real estate, books, and other valuable items) to relatives and friends, reflect a shift in attitude toward property itself, in the redaction of transfers of property, in the legal context in which new notions of property were defined, and in the perception of property itself by the middling sorts. The latter group generated the immense majority of these legal instruments. This meant, in a few words, a new conceptualization of what property was—how it could be utilized to promote the individual and the family—and of the language deployed to legitimize such actions. Such development is even more striking when one considers that the largest portion of the extant testaments come from clerics—some of them quite high in the ecclesiastical hierarchy, though almost all of them belonged to prominent bourgeois families—yet, regardless of their ecclesiastical filiation, without a single exception, they reserved the largest share of their property for their own kin (their "lineage"). Even when they donated a portion of their goods to the church, they never did so unrestrictedly. That is, whenever they donated to the church, testators—such as Martín Ibáñez, Gonzalo Pérez, and others—imposed restrictions on access to their legacies and sought to control the distribution of their largesse even beyond death. And, in many cases, they expected very good returns for their investments: innumerable masses, anniversaries, burial in the church or monastery, and other activities that would promote the spiritual well-being of the donor, family, and friends. In the case of Martín Ibáñez, a cloth of gold was to be placed over his body as he was laid to his eternal rest.[6]

Investment Strategies

Property could also be used in other beneficial ways, not just deployed in wills to obtain salvation and the retention of lands and other goods within the family, but also for securing maintenance in old age or in lonely widowhood when there was no family or, at least, not a family one wished to have benefit from one's wealth. I speak here of the sort of transactions, common throughout the medieval West, by which a donor—usually a widow or an old couple—donated their possessions to a monastery or church in return for bed, board, and burial after death. Under the veneer of piety, these agreements reveal practical and shrewd bargaining for the hope of a comfortable old age. It also shows how middling sorts in Castile and elsewhere utilized their property to improve their spiritual *and* physical well-being at the end of their days. Although these types of arrangements, as pointed above, were quite common throughout the medieval West as they are today, they appear in northern Castilian documents in substantial numbers only from the late twelfth century onward, and in clearly spelled-out details only after the transition to the vernacular in the 1220s.

In 1293, Doña María de Sagentes, the widow of Ferrant González de la Población (a member of the lower nobility), donated all her property in Valle de Dios, Villafría, and Sagentes to the monastery of Santa María la Real de Aguilar de Campoo. In return for these donations, the monastery agreed to feed and dress her, to provide a servant woman to tend to her needs throughout the year, and to allow her to dwell in a house near the monastery. Doña María received an *ochavo* of wine (around two liters daily)—of the same quality as the abbot drank. She was also to be given meat on Sundays, Tuesdays, and Thursdays, and one may assume that fish was provided on Fridays, throughout Lent, and on vigil days. This makes for a substantial diet, comparable to that of well-to-do merchants and lower nobility. And she was to receive these provisions for the rest of her life.

In addition, the monastery gave Doña María a cloak and a long robe of *valencina* (imported cloth from Valenciennes or in the style of Valenciennes) every three years, and a cloak and long robe of Flemish cloth (*camelín*) every five years. Shoes and thin furs she was to have whenever necessary. There was nothing devotional or pious in this arrangement, other than Doña María's proximity to the monastery and frequent visits to the church. The monastery, of course, also drove as hard a bargain as it could. Upon receipt of new clothes, shoes, and furs, Dona María had to return the old ones for almsgiving. It was a way to ensure that Doña María did not trade or sell her old clothes, while the monastery was able to recycle its investments into charity for the poor.[7]

In this and similar examples, we see the actual manifestations of new ways of conceiving property, not just as something that must be returned to God—via a donation to a monastery—but as a tangible and physical good that could be employed to advance the success of one's lineage in the world, to secure a comfortable retirement, even to save one's soul.[8] These impulses were not, of course, entirely new nor was love of property invented in Castile in the late twelfth century. The accumulation of wealth, desire for material goods, and other such manifestations of human greed are fairly constant throughout history. Nonetheless, impulsive and overgenerous gift-giving, with little or no restrictions, if we are to trust the extant sources fully, was over. That meant not only hard times for ecclesiastical establishments, but new ways of seeing and experiencing the relationship between self and property.

Legal and Cultural Transformations

The dramatic shift in attitudes toward property in northern Castile was preceded by similar transformations throughout western Europe in the way women and men thought of time, property, and their relation to the sacred.[9] These were accompanied by vigorous scholarly debates and legal transformations in medieval western Europe and Castile proper. The question, of course, always remains as to the causal relationship between ideas and deeds. I, for one, would argue, once again, that ideas emerge from and reflect the context of the material world. To be more specific, legal and philosophical formulations, which legitimized new or recovered perceptions and attitudes toward the material world, resulted from economic and social transformations, from the shift in attitudes toward property, and in the relationship of the individual and community to the physical world. This is what Le Goff has elegantly described as the descent from heaven to earth.

Janet Coleman's excellent summary "Property and Poverty," in *The Cambridge History of Medieval Political Thought, c. 350–c. 1450,* traces not only the changes from feudal tenure to private property throughout the West, but also the rise of "impersonal transactions unaffected by considerations of the status of buyer and seller."[10] The latter is, of course, a reference to the rise of a market for land, a topic that I have already examined in detail elsewhere and that has been much debated by medieval historians.[11] Coleman, following Lester Little, Le Goff, and others, rightly links these new ways of thinking about property to changes in the spiritual climate and a new understanding of poverty. In her article, she goes on to mention briefly the legal, theological, and philosophical elucidations—with no reference whatsoever to the Iberian Peninsula—on the right to own property and the uses of property thereof.[12]

This debate concerned the Church most of all, as it faced the challenge of heretical sects (Cathars, Waldensians, and even radical Franciscans)

TABLE 3.1
Transactions of Land and Real Estate in Burgos, 1200–1350

Purchases made by:	1200–49	1250–99	1300–50	Total
Cathedral chapter	134 (67.7%)	4 (4.3%)	5 (3.2%)	143
Nonnoble knights[1]	0	66 (71.7%)	120 (76.9%)	186
Others	64 (32.3%)	22 (23.9%)	31 (19.9%)	117
Total	198	92	156	446

[1]Includes ecclesiastics who were members of nonnoble families (after 1256) and who purchased property for their own use or for their families.

and their attack on ecclesiastical wealth.[13] The Church also faced the fierce competition of upper segments of mercantile and artisan groups. By the beginning of the twelfth century, these rising patrician elites began to monopolize benefices in cathedral chapters throughout Castile and the rest of the West and to divert Church wealth for their own private benefits. This was certainly the case in Avila, Segovia, Burgos, and other northern Castilian cities where, from 1200 onward, most of the purchases made by canons and other ecclesiastics were no longer made for the benefit of the Church itself, but for the clergymen. They, in turn, as we have seen, willed these properties to their own relatives and friends, with only a small portion of their wealth being returned to the Church (see chapter 5).

It may be useful to show the radical transformation that occurred around 1200 in who purchased property and for what purpose. Table 3.1 contains information on land and real estate transactions in Burgos from 1200 to 1350. Most of the purchases made by the cathedral chapter between 1200 and 1250 took place in the first twenty years. In fact, between 1225 and 1249, the chapter made only seven purchases of property. There are no figures for nonnoble knights (*caballeros villanos*) during this period because it is impossible to identify for sure who had nonnoble knight privileges before 1256. Under the heading of "others," we find rich farmers, well-to-do merchants, city officials, and ecclesiastics who were, in fact, the same families prominent in Burgos in the early thirteenth century, but who cannot be ranked for certain among the nonnoble knights until after the mid–thirteenth century. Nonetheless, they often were part of the city's patrician elite. What is clear is that a dramatic shift occurred with new players appearing in the market for land, but also with members of the great bourgeois families joining the cathedral chapters. Similar developments can be found in Avila, Segovia, and other Castilian towns.[14]

Legal Codes: The Fueros

In northern Castile, concurrent with the shift in language and how wills were written, legal codes exhibited a similar concern with defining property and preserving it within the confines of the family. These shifts in the legal discourse of property resulted, in part, from the recovery and readaptation of Roman legal forms. At the same time, legal codes provided a novel and necessary way, considering the swift social and economic changes of the late twelfth and early thirteenth centuries, of dealing with "impersonal material transactions" (the burgeoning market for land and houses), and the requirements of new urban centers. The *fueros* provide good entry into discussion of urban life and novel preoccupations with property. These urban charters and liberties had been granted by the counts of Castile, and later by its kings, to new or reconquered settlements, and hence exemplify the changes I am attempting to trace here.[15]

Since municipal and rural fueros were imitated but also slightly altered to meet local needs and changing political and geographical conditions, they offer a useful glimpse—though not always a clear one because of the permanent gulf that exists between legal formulations and actual praxis—of changing attitudes toward property. In 950, the count of Castile, García Fernández, granted a fuero to the large village of Melgar de Suso. The short charter established what the inhabitants had to pay in taxes, the dues and exemptions of widows and other citizens of Melgar, penalties for certain crimes, and little else. The fuero's only concerns were jurisdictional and judicial. Essentially, the charter dealt with seignorial rents—what was owed and by whom—and with defining crimes and the penalties to be imposed, which were, together with taxation, a reassertion of rights of lordship and an important source of lordly income.[16]

In the first fuero of Castrojeriz (974), García Fernández, using the same formulaic language as in contemporary pious donations, meaning that the giving of law had the same pious value as the donation of property ("propter remedium anima mee, et animarum parentum meorum, et omnium fidelium defunctorum."), granted privileges to the inhabitants of the town, neatly arranged by social order: knights, clerics, urban and rural workers. The grant consisted mostly of a series of judicial privileges and exemptions from taxes. Similar to the fuero of Melgar, there is no great concern with rights of property, nor with establishing the town's physical limits or jurisdiction.[17] By 1074, the fuero of Palenzuela, while more or less replicating the themes of earlier fueros regarding jurisdictional and judicial norms, exhibits new concern with physical boundaries (see chapter 4), and sought to define the town's territorial jurisdiction in vague spatial terms.[18]

The greatest of these fueros (or to be more precise, family of fueros) was that of Cuenca, a town south of the Central Sierras and thus distant from the Old Castilian heartland. Although the fuero of Cuenca was closely linked with Aragonese urban charters (the fuero of Teruel), fueros in general followed on a long tradition of monastic, seignorial, counts', and, finally, royal privileges to settlers along the southern edge of the advancing frontier.[19]

When we turn to the extensive and sophisticated fuero of Cuenca—which served as a model for other urban fueros or was granted outright to many other towns—many of the preoccupations with judicial (and jurisdictional) matters still comprise a significant portion of the charter (sections on judicial ordeals are extensive and detailed indeed), but they have been now joined by a clear attempt at defining property relationships and rights of property. In the Cuenca fuero, the sections regulating ownership and property transactions leap at us in sharp contrast with the vague references or omissions of earlier charters. Although the fuero's main aim was to order life in a frontier settlement and provide guidelines to contain the violent nature of a town on the vanguard of Christian expansion—and therefore, as pointed out earlier, the numerous entries on ordeals and judicial trials by combat—its treatment of material possessions is significant indeed. Books 1 and 4 of Cuenca's charter dealt almost exclusively with definitions and protection of property, as well as regulating transactions of land and real estate.[20] And these early legal dispositions serve as a fitting prelude to the more sophisticated legislation on these matters found in the great law codes of the thirteenth century.

The fuero of Cuenca's concerns with the material world extended to the safeguarding of one's property: theft, the ploughing of one's field by an outsider, and other such illicit actions denote a growing preoccupation with articulating the limits of one's holdings, as well as providing deterrents to trespassing or illegal appropriations. The world of open fields (not always present in Castilian agriculture) and vague boundaries was coming to an end in Castile. These provisions that legally defined property (mostly land) extended to the "moral" realm as well. Adultery, rape, and other sexual transgressions seen as threatening to women in the kin group, or to the purity of lineage when "tainted" by men of inferior rank, were treated in almost the same manner as appropriation of lands. Crimes against women were handled with equal harshness by a legal system that often made little distinction between a piece of land and a wife or daughter.[21] Testaments also became carefully regulated in the fuero of Cuenca. These entries sought, as wills were beginning to do at the same time, to preserve wealth within the family. Children, to give an example, could not make wills before they married, that is, as long as they remained in the household. Regardless of age, their property was still held by the father (and mother).[22]

The *Fuero juzgo*

Fueros were mostly a Castilian (and Aragonese) invention, aimed at attracting settlers to empty lands or frontier locations. There was, of course, an older legal tradition, strongest in western Iberia (the kingdoms of Asturias and León), among Mozarabs (Christians living under Muslim rule who had adopted Muslim culture) in Toledo, and elsewhere in southern Spain. I refer here to the *Fuero juzgo* or Romance version of the *Lex visigothorum,* the ancient Germanic law code that included a substantial amount of surviving Roman legal tradition. Although the *Fuero juzgo* had some legal play in the areas mentioned above, much of its contents were far beyond the understanding or economic and social context of northern Castile's inhabitants. With changing conditions and the development of new values, however, came legal revisions. It is significant, and certainly no coincidence, that from the first half of the thirteenth century, the Castilian kings revitalized the *Fuero juzgo* and granted it as a municipal charter to many locations in the newly conquered south, but they also did so with many towns in the north. Thus, the *Fuero juzgo* acquired new importance when granted widely throughout the land, and its driving concerns with property fitted perfectly with the kind of mental shifts and transformation of values I describe here.[23]

After defining what constitutes the law, book 2 of the *Fuero juzgo* contains careful descriptions of procedure, including title 5, which describes how wills should be drawn. Although the *Fuero juzgo* does not use the word *will* or *testament* in its Latin or Romance forms, title 5 clearly aims at creating an established legal procedure for monitoring and regulating the last wishes of the deceased.[24] It also sought to transform even oral bequests in front of witnesses into binding legal instruments.[25] Moreover, book 2, title 5 sought to protect heirs' rights and to prevent children, the ill, and the mad from drawing wills.

The code carefully spells out rights of inheritance, establishing clear lines for claims on property—children of the deceased first, grandchildren next—protecting women's right to inherit and advancing other family rights. It forbade excessive donations to the Church that may have impinged on the rights of children and grandchildren (i.e., donations to ecclesiastical institutions were never to exceed more than one-fifth of the total value of the testator's assets). The *Fuero juzgo*, in its original Visigothic version and as reintroduced in the early thirteenth century, forbade clerics to bequeath all their goods to the Church as long as a relative to the seventh degree remained alive (book 5, title 2). The right to inherit and to will, that is, to keep property within the family, was thus guaranteed at the expense of the Church. In this context, it is salutary to remember the changes that took place in the pattern of purchases by the cathedral chapter of Burgos (see table 3.1), and in the nature of the wills from the late twelfth century onward. These changes shifted income and property from the Church to the secular lineages. Here, the law and actual practices marched hand in hand. Similarly, the *Fuero juzgo* dedicates significant portions of its text (books 3, 4, and 5) to questions of marriage, lineage, familial and commercial transactions, all of them deeply intertwined with property. Thus, book 4, "Of Natural Lineage," which discusses rights of succession, wardships, and other familial (and material) concerns, concludes (title 5) with a definition of property by virtue of nature ("de los bienes que pertenecen por natura"), that is, the rights to property within the family as given by kinship and blood ties, "by nature."[26]

Books 7, "Of Theft and Fraud," and 8, "Acts of Violence and Injuries," describe judicial procedures and penalties for dealing with attacks against and damage to one's property. Book 10, "Of Partition, Prescription, and Boundaries," addresses landmarks that defined the spatial limits of property. Seven of the twelve books of the *Fuero juzgo* are directly or indirectly linked to discourses of property, and, although as a legal code the *Fuero juzgo* dated back to Germanic customary law and, in many ways, to a more formidable Roman legal tradition, the new cultural, economic, and social climate of late twelfth- and early thirteenth-century Castile made its adoption widespread. It was a ready-made law for changing notions of the material world.

The *Fuero real*

A few years after Ferdinand III (1217–52) began to grant the *Fuero juzgo* as a municipal code to newly conquered cities and towns in Andalusia in the late 1230s, his son and successor, Alfonso X (1252–84), sought to reform the legal foundations of his realms, primarily Castile, and to create homogeneous legal procedures throughout the land. Although we now know that Alfonso's legislative program had its roots in his father's scriptorium, and that it met with fierce and successful opposition from the nobility and some cities,[27] Alfonso X's legal reforms had two very specific manifestations: the granting of the *Fuero real* in the 1250s as a unifying municipal code, and the writing and enactment of the *Siete partidas* as the normative law of Castile-León. Alfonso X was quite successful in granting (and having cities accept) the *Fuero real* throughout Castile proper, but the towering achievements of the *Siete partidas* had to wait almost a century, until 1348, for adoption and then only as a supplementary code.[28]

The *Fuero real* provided, foremost, administrative and judicial guidelines for city government. It built on the foundations of the *Fuero juzgo* and tried to fill in gaps in the undertaking of judicial procedures. Nonetheless, book 3 addresses in detail questions of wills, donations, and the transfer of property that echo the shift in attitudes toward property and the family occurring throughout most of Castile at that time.

The entire third book of the *Fuero real* focuses on inheritance and material transactions. Title 1 establishes the precedence of lineage, while limiting the family's rights over women in the kin group. If parents, brothers, and other relatives could not arrange a marriage for a kinswoman before she reached twenty-five, she could then marry anyone she pleased without losing her rights of inheritance.[29] Book 3, title 2 provides protection for women's dowries, while title 3 establishes the equal rights of husband and wife to properties obtained jointly. Title 4 explains how inheritances ought to be apportioned among the heirs, and title 5, the most significant for this discussion, outlines how *mandas* (wills) ought to be drawn. Unlike donations in an earlier age, testaments "must be written by the hand of some public scribe or written by someone else, and the testator must put his seal [or mark], as well as that [mark or seal] of someone who is known and who is to be believed (*que sean de creer*) or [was to be verified] by good testimonies (witnesses)."[30]

Thus, the *Fuero real* confirmed new methods of redaction already found in early thirteenth-century Castile. Legal sanction followed praxis. Wills therefore became not only a legal instrument regulated by municipal law after the 1250s but a secular affair as well. The drawing of wills—written now in the same Castilian language in which the *Fuero real* was composed—passed from the hands of monks and canons into that of municipal officials or, in their absence, to the testators themselves. Not coincidentally, most of the public scribes and city officials came from the same social groups as those disposing of their property through wills. Further titles in book 3 include elaborate prescriptions on who was to inherit and what lines of kinship were preferred. They also set the right of legitimate children over illegitimate ones, as well as the claims of collateral branches of the family.[31]

The careful language of the *Fuero real*, which, unlike the *Siete partidas*, was the law of most northern Castilian cities and their respective vast hinterlands, points to a world, both rural and urban, in which rising conflicts (and litigations) about property rights, inheritances, and family claims necessitated sorting out what was legal and what was not. More importantly, these legislative initiatives marked the intrusion of the Crown—of a more vigilant, expansive, and organized royal bureaucracy—into the material concerns of everyday life. After all, what we see in the *Fuero real* and other similar law codes enacted or readopted in the early and mid–thirteenth century—but already foreshadowed in the fuero of Cuenca and other foral legislation of the late twelfth century—are the consequences of an intense market for land and the emergence of new concepts of property. The law codes formalized these material and impersonal transactions, as they formalized and legitimized wills—the transfer of goods within the family—but they also made these exchanges profitable for the Crown by insisting on the exclusive monopoly of royal and municipal scribes in drafting these legal instruments.

The *Siete partidas*

With the *Siete partidas* the great, but failed, legislative achievement of Alfonso X the Wise and his immediate successors, we turn to a discourse of property that was far more explicit and detailed than any previous law code or fuero enacted in Castile.[32] A brief glance at some of the sections of the *Partidas* dealing with property, wills, and impersonal transactions allows us to establish a link between actual material change and legal formulations.

The first partida includes a series of titles and laws that denied the Church the right to the property of parishioners who had died intestate. It also states the reasons under which Church property could be alienated: (1) for debt; (2) to ransom parishioners in the hands of the Moors and who could not afford to buy their freedom; (3) to feed the poor in time of famine; (4) to build the church; (5) to enlarge the cemetery. Other titles define the limits of ecclesiastical property, establish severe penalties for attacks against or alienation of royal property, and set up elaborate procedures to protect the property of those held captive in Muslim lands.[33] Clearly, beyond a preoccupation with rights of property, the first partida also dramatically changed the relationship between secular and spiritual. It granted the Crown significant intrusive and monitoring powers in material and spiritual aspects of ecclesiastical affairs. Title 5, law 18 of the first partida discusses the rights the kings of Spain (by which the *Siete partidas* meant Castile) had in the election of prelates, stating the reasons for these unusual powers. The law begins by appealing to historical tradition: "there was an ancient custom in Spain, which still prevails, that when the bishop of any place died, the deans and the canons communicated the fact to the King . . . and that they asked him to permit them to hold an election without hindrance, and they did *sur-*

render to him the property of the church [my emphasis] . . . the King should grant their request, and send and collect his dues." After the election, the king delivered the property to the person elected (ideally after the king had approved of the election). The *Partidas* argue that the kings of Castile enjoyed these privileges—which harken back to the disputes of the Investiture controversy (1) because they had conquered the land from the Moors and "turned Mosques into churches"; (2) because they founded churches where there were none before; and (3) because they had endowed these churches and favored them with gifts and grants.[34] These claims, based on historical events (the Reconquest) and deeply imbedded in discourses of property, were not idle words. In fact, as we know, thanks to Peter Linehan's work, the Castilian church was very much under royal authority and the victim of harsh royal fiscal demands from the late twelfth century onward. Those were, in many respects, also important aspects of the change in values in northern Castile: the appeal to history over myth, and the changing relationship between spiritual and temporal. The latter, of course, occurred mostly over questions of property and taxation.

Elsewhere in the *Partidas*, legal discussions deal with the integrity of royal property and the realm's castles and other fortifications (partida 2, titles 17 and 18), with captives' (and their heirs') rights to property (partida 2, title 29). The third partida, "On Procedure and Property," concerns mostly judicial procedure, methods of redaction (including a detailed discussion of how wills were to be drawn (title 18), and notaries (title 19), but the concluding titles, from 28, "On Ownership"—which carefully defines property and includes, in its legal discourse, a taxonomy of types of property—to 32, "On Building," articulates a Roman-based legal understanding of property.[35] It did not hurt that the *Partidas*, in these and other matters, so closely paralleled shifts in procedures taking place at the local level. Even if the *Partidas* did not gain formal acceptance, mostly because of resistance from magnates who rightly saw the legislative reforms as a threat to their power, it remained a source known and referred to by lawyers and the court against the fragmented legal standards of Castile.[36]

But wills and legal codes only underpinned a broader transformation in the manner in which Castilians perceived and explained concern about property. Ample additional evidence at the local level testifies to the shift in attitudes toward land and material possessions in late twelfth- and early thirteenth-century Castile. It is to these transformations that we now turn.

CHAPTER FOUR

ITEMIZING THE WORLD:

BOUNDARIES, CONSOLIDATION OF PROPERTY,

AND RIGHTS OF WAY

IN THE LATE TWELFTH and early thirteenth centuries, the northern Castilian landscape began to be radically transformed. These changes followed, in part, from new political realignments in the peninsula and from the new stability and civil order promoted by Alfonso VIII's competent rule in the second half of his reign. Around 1200, Castile, north of the Central Sierras, was firmly in the rearguard of the Reconquest. Threats from Muslim raids were essentially over, and the settlement and organization of rural space was, by then, centuries old. As the twelfth century came to a close, northern Castilians engaged in a vigorous reorganization of the countryside.[1] Those new definitions of property and of rural spaces were signaled by an increased preoccupation with boundaries and landmarks.

Boundaries

In simple terms, one can think of a change in the concept of property as a move from an idea of land or real estate as a form of jurisdiction—in which the connection between legal rights, land rent, and physical space is not fully worked out or defined—to an idea of land grounded on notions of geographical space and location. Here, I am seeking to describe a shift from the concept of seignorial or rural jurisdiction to the concept of physical possession: a material sense that this is my land (either owned or held from someone else) that can be measured and that extends to a recognizable and, often by the thirteenth century, precisely marked boundary. This shift occurred both at the local level and in the wider context of kingdoms throughout the medieval West, where, by the late thirteenth century, custom collection houses and royal outposts established geographical borders, or liminal points between what is ours, as a regional community, and what is theirs.[2] I return to this topic later; my initial concern, however, is with the former, with the emergence of a sense of the physical and measurable character of property at the local level.

From late twelfth to the fourteenth century, the sources in Castile provide us with a veritable mine of information. Throughout northern Castile, village communities, monasteries, and small landholders engaged in costly litigation, sometimes undertook violent action, and appealed repeatedly to the king for inquests to determine not the extent of their jurisdiction, but the actual spatial extent of their property or communal holdings. Even in an earlier age, there had been preoccupation with determining the extent of jurisdiction over specific localities. In 1028, Queen Jimena set the jurisdiction of Vallarta by specifying where its limits lay: "by the fountain of Fonte Vascones, by the valley of Covo ad Sanctum Iustum."[3] At best, however, these definitions of boundaries were vague and lacked the preciseness of later documents.[4] By the late twelfth and early thirteenth centuries, natural features of the landscape, a river, a hill, a road, still determined some boundaries, but the land began to be delimited by artificial markers, the *mojones* or *moiones*. In 1170, a conflict between the municipal council of Oña and the monastery of Santa María de Nájera over their respective jurisdictions in the villages of Trespaderne and Castrillo led to the naming of a group of arbitrators. After an inquest, they proceeded to determine the boundaries between both parties. Although geographical features retained their importance, one of the surveyors, Iohan Adcona, *portarius regis*, placed artificial landmarks (*mojones*) in critical locations.[5]

Shortly after 1170, wills, inquests, land transactions, surveys to determine boundaries, and other sources show renewed concern with measuring property and providing reliable accounts of the physical dimensions of the land, a pattern often missing from earlier sources. In the lands of the monastery of San Zoilo de Carrión (a small town in western Castile and on the road to Compostela), Diego, the *merino* (the main royal official of a *merindad*, a territorial administrative division, similar to a shire) of Saldaña sought to restore the limits or boundaries of lands Alfonso VIII (1158–1214) had donated to the monastery. These lands had been illegally appropriated by the villagers of Gañinas (Gannines) for plowing and pasture. The *merino*'s agents recommended who could graze in which lands and set the boundaries to the monastery's properties. Paths and rivers were still the preferred markers, but there is no doubt, as evident in the language of the document, that the arbitrators were going over the land in person, questioning villagers as to who had rights to it, and, more importantly for our purpose, what was the actual physical extent of the property claimed by the monastery.[6]

This desire to define the boundaries of one's properties extended beyond land to other forms of property: mill rights, use of water, salt wells, and so forth.[7] In Carrión, in 1203, an inquest undertaken by the abbot of Sahagún, Don Pelayo, and ratified by the king of Castile, Alfonso VIII, established how the waters of the Carrión river were to be shared by the monastery of San Zoilo and the villagers of Nogal de las Huertas. This type of inquest always stemmed from some illegal action by one of the parties in litigation. In this particular case, the villagers of Nogal built a dam on the river in the area of Nido del Corcio, which interfered with the dams built by the monastery downriver. Again, the arbitrators, all local men, walked along the banks of the river, questioned villagers, and came to decisions that sought to create a written map—or, as Daniel Smail has argued for Marseilles in a later period, "an imaginary [but also physical] cartography" of the region.[8]

By the early thirteenth century, the trend toward greater clarity in marking boundaries accelerated. This is obvious in a series of charters issued by Ferdinand III in which *quadrilleros*, a team of land surveyors, were commissioned to erect mojones throughout the borders of municipal, ecclesiastical, and lordly lands, to establish, once and for all, the actual physical extent of the property. In the litigation between the municipal councils of Madrid and Segovia over the area of Valdemoro, the royal agents erected forty-two landmarks, some on top of hills, others near roads, some in valleys. The document is quite precise as to where these markers were to be located: "Et xxxv mojón en somo de la Pedriza sobre Valde Ezebreros en las cabeças de don Aparicio" (the xxxvth landmark to be placed on the summit of La Pedriza overlooking Valde Ezebreros).[9] A few years afterward (mid–thirteenth century), in documents then drawn fully in Castilian, measuring and mapping the land became even clearer. When María Gutiérrez and her sister, Doña Mayor, sold all they had in a garden (including a well) to the Hospital del Rey (an important royal foundation in the outskirts of Burgos) for 6 *mrs.*, they sold "all of it, with entry and exit, and with all that belonged to it [to the property] from moion to moion (landmark to landmark)." A year later, María Ibáñez and Ario sold a piece of land to the Hospital in La Requejada for 4 *mrs*. They sold the land "between the rivers, with entry and exit and with all that belonged to it, from moion to moion.[10]

These transactions involved very small pieces of land, bought by the hospital at a very low price, yet both parcels had entry and exit to a public road and were bound by landmarks. The properties lay in areas of intense cultivation—a garden, an area between rivers—surrounded, except for the little path to a public way, by other parcels. In terms of substantial property, in 1262, in the general area of Burgos, the powerful abbots of the monasteries of Covarrubias and San Pedro de Arlanza entered into an elaborate agreement to draw the boundaries between their respectives pasture lands. Mojones were placed throughout the jurisdiction, indicating quite clearly whose livestock was to graze in the area. Alfonso X sanctioned the agreement, legitimizing, once again, a new rural landscape dotted by landmarks. A few years later, another agreement drew the entire population of two Burgalese villages into the setting of landmarks as a way to define the access and utilization of wooded lands (*montes*).[11] Mojones had become the way to identify precisely the extent of one's property, no matter how small or large the holding. But then landmarks already played an important physical and symbolic role in the Castilian landscape.

In the fuero of Cuenca, the fields of battle for judicial trials by combat were bound by landmarks. To step beyond the physical space delimited by these boundaries was to admit defeat.[12] But mojones were not the only way the land was measured. In 1225, once again in the area of Carrión, the property was to be measured with a rope ("ista hereditatem debet esse mensurata cum soga"). The transaction involved an agreement in which an older couple donated their lands to San Zoilo but retained use of the property for their lives and—though not stated—some assurance of support for the rest of their existence. It was at the monastery's insistence that the property was measured with a rope, to ascertain the physical extension of the land.[13] When in 1255 the monks of the monastery of San Pedro in Gumiel de Izán reached a settlement with a contentious rural council nearby, the arbitrators placed twenty mojones to mark the borders of the disputed property, and more than seventeen witnesses, including local petty noblemen (*hijosdalgo*) attested to the newly bounded territory.[14] These are just a few examples of the careful manner in which northern Castilians defined property as tangible and measurable space, a development far more noticeable among the middling sorts and small proprietors than among the well-to-do.[15] Clearly, from the twelfth century onward, slowly and piecemeal, many Castilians became engaged in a broad project of physically mapping out the land and in inscribing these maps made of words into the public record of their localities and kingdom.

Stone mojones erected in this period throughout northern Castile speak to us across time of emerging new concepts of property. The illegal removal of these landmarks by disgruntled villagers, and the bitter controversies and inquests that ensued, tell of the distress brought about by these new ways of defining territorial space. In Gonzalo de Berceo's *Mil-*

agros de Nuestra Señora (c. 1250), miracle 11 tells the story of an avaricious peasant "who loved his land more than his Creator" and who, to increase or gain property (*heredad*) illegally, moved the landmarks bordering his lands.[16] Although in the end, because of his devotion to the Virgin, the peasant's soul is released from hell, the poem denounces the peasant's greed and reveals a new set of standards at work. The world of clear-cut boundaries, marked by artificial means (the mojones), had superseded the ambiguousness of an earlier age, when boundaries were determined by the vagaries of the natural landscape. And in medieval Castile, the artful peasant, who engaged in "all kinds of evil deeds and falsity," including illegally advancing the boundaries of his land, was a reprehensible yet common figure.[17]

In 1288, Doña María, the prioress of the monastery of Santa María in Fresnillo de las Dueñas, protested against the violent actions, land appropriations, and deception of the knights and other men of the village of Montejo. Sancho IV ordered his merino to place mojones between the jurisdiction of the monastery and that of Montejo; nonetheless, two years later, the men of Montejo, armed to the teeth, came into Santa María in the dark of night, removed the landmarks, killed the monastery's cattle, and stole fifteen sheep. Even though the king had ordered an end to the violence and had, through his officials in the area, set the boundaries between the village and the monastery, he now had to commission a new inquest. Once the inquest learned the truth of the monastery's protests, the king sent a royal letter to the region's merino, commanding him to take appropriate action. In his 1290 letter, Sancho IV enjoined the villagers of Montejo and Saint Quirze (another village that seems to have also been connected with the violence) to return the property stolen and to replace the landmarks.[18] In yet another instance, the monastery of San Pedro in Gumiel de Izán entered in litigation against the village council of Fontoria de Val de Aradores over the removal of landmarks in 1301. In a scene that replicated that of the greedy peasant in Berceo's miracle, the peasants of Fontoria had removed or placed the mojones to gain land belonging to the monastery. A team of peasants from the village council of Estudos de Baño placed new landmarks along the boundaries between the monastic lands and those of Fontoria to make clear the limits between the two properties.[19]

One might argue that the thirteenth century was no different from a previous age, and that, were documentation available, earlier litigation over boundaries would also be uncovered for that period. One may also wish to argue that the shift from jurisdiction to spatial property that I am positing here is incorrect. There is, after all, enough evidence from other parts of western medieval Europe that lords understood jurisdiction to be geographically bounded. Many charters, while granting or describing litigation over a specific jurisdiction, also specified the spatial or topographical features of the land. Moreover, by the late eleventh century and afterward, jurisdiction itself had already become part of the monetary economy and could be described, and marketed (bought and sold), as part of the new impersonal (and personal) transactions of the market economy.

This was certainly the case in northern Europe and even, at times, in Castile itself. Nonetheless, the fact is that in most monastic registers in northern Castile, where one finds far more documents extant for the twelfth century than for the thirteenth or fourteenth, what the documents address—donations, transactions of land, and other property exchanges—and how they described these transactions changed substantially. Sources for an earlier period do not provide a clear picture of jurisdiction as already deeply imbedded in the monetary economy or as marketable as the land itself would become in late twelfth- and early thirteenth-century northern Castile.

Of course, one may also wish to voice the same reservations about landmarks. After all, landmarks were already mentioned in earlier medieval sources. In fact, boundary marks date from the beginnings of history, from the beginnings of property. As a common feature in Roman definition of boundaries, roads, and other physical property, mojones could be found throughout Iberia. In his *Histories* (c. 1040) Radulfus Glaber, to cite but one example from north of the Pyrenees, reports some strange occurrences in Burgundy—a rain of stones that fell on someone's house and lands for three years. Among these stones, "many men recognized the boundary stones from their fields."[20] This points to the ubiquitousness of landmarks in Burgundy (and elsewhere) in western Europe. Mojones had a long history in Castile, but references to landmarks, fences, and the shift from jurisdiction to spatially bounded land began to appear more frequently in documentation from the late twelfth century onward.

Landmarks were only one of the new indicators of boundaries. Northern Castilian agriculture differed dramatically from that of northern Europe. Thin soils, the universal use of the Roman plow, and the vagaries of climate precluded the open-field rural landscape found in other parts of the West. Fields were often fenced, certainly before harvest. Vineyards were always protected by hedges, stone fences, and even guards. The Crown determined the exact width of the Mesta routes, the *cañadas*, as they wound their ways from northern Castile to the newly opened grazing lands in Extremadura and Andalusia. When the Mesta went through or close to village lands, the *cañadas* were to be fenced and hedges built to prevent damage to local crops by the transhumant livestock.[21] Wherever Castilians went in the mountains of the north or across their vast plain, they saw physical evidence of bounded property and jurisdiction. It was an indelible presence in their visual and mental landscape.

Did specific pressures on the land prompt such concerns for defining and establishing the limits of one's own lands? Whatever the reason—and there seems to have been growing competition for wooded areas and pasture lands in some regions of northern Castile, despite the general demographic poverty of the realm—new concern with the physical characteristics of the land began to emerge, manifested in two distinct but not always mutually exclusive discourses.

One of these emphasized jurisdiction, or lordship—what we generally, though not always correctly, call "feudal" bonds—and, at a certain level, the formulaic language and social rituals of seignorial power became synonymous with the land or with other types of property.[22] The other discourse, without abandoning the almost ritualized speech of lordly power, expressed a more vivid concern with the concrete realities of the land, with its materiality and physical boundaries. Not surprisingly, the former appears most prominently in the dealing of powerful lords, whether secular or ecclesiastic. Thus, as late as the mid–fourteenth century, as the great *Becerro de behetrías* shows, lordly jurisdiction and rights were expressed in terms of rents (mostly in kind), whereas spatial or geographical preoccupations defined the transactions and litigations of lesser men and rural communities, as they argued among themselves or against their masters.[23] In a sense, the growing presence of small farmers and urban dwellers in the economic life of the realm, and thus in the documentation, contributed directly to these shifts in mentality and values.

I also contend that these changing concerns formed part of a new or alternate discourse of power, grounded in the physicality of the land and articulated in a new language. Not only were the concepts new; the language itself was the vernacular and thus accessible to the people. In wills and in litigations over definitions of boundaries the concern with property thus also functioned as a counterdiscourse, as a language that, asserting the new economic and political power of the middling sorts, succeeded, at times, in resisting noble violence and power. The political counterpart of these new imaginings of land was the growing importance of urban dwellers (the people most active in land transactions) in the life of the realm.

Boundaries Revisited: Consolidating Property

One further aspect of boundaries deserves mention as yet another example of how Castilians conceptualized property in the late twelfth and early thirteenth centuries. By then, many of the extant records of land transactions began to include, in greater number than in the past, elaborate descriptions of surrounding property or geographical accidents that were to serve as boundaries for property being sold. Although most transactions remained rather vague, in certain areas of northern Castile special care was taken to indicate whose lands, roads, commons, or brush served as terminus for one's property.

In Carrión, a series of land transactions, donations, and descriptions of the property (apeos) owned by the cathedral of Palencia and the monastery of San Zoilo de Carrión—written, at least the portions that described boundaries, mostly in the vernacular between the mid–twelfth century and the 1240s—carefully detail the lands, roads, gardens, and other physical features adjacent to the property in the extant sources. Besides offering a clear sense of where the land was situated and to where it extended, many of these sources show how the monastery or cathedral began to build contiguous estates out of dispersed and fragmented holdings.

In 1146, when Palea and his wife, María Andrés, exchanged some properties they owned in Villamuriel for others in the city of Palencia, the bishop gave the couple a store in Palencia, bound by a butcher shop on one side, the episcopal palace on another, the store of Guilelmi Ermegodi on the third, and the main street of Palencia, "callem qui discurrit per mediam uillam," on the fourth.[24] Don Juan Galindo and his wife, María Fernández, donated gardens and houses in Carrión to the monastery in return for a perpetual anniversary and "remedium anima mee et uxoris mee . . . et filiorum et filiarum mearum." One of the houses faced the road to Compostela (a prime location in Carrión); the property was bound on the other three sides by a street leading to the river, a path to the mills de la Puente, and the houses of the donor himself. Another of the houses donated with a garden (*huerto*) had the road on one side, and gardens on the others.[25]

Documents containing detailed description showed up most frequently in well-settled rural areas, as is the case with a long series of transactions undertaken by the monastery of Las Huelgas in a few hamlets in the area of Dueñas between 1229 and 1262 (see table 4.1). During those thirty-three years, the nuns of Las Huelgas made fifty-three purchases (this is the number of extant documents; the actual number of transactions must have been much larger). The elaborate descriptions of boundaries found in this set of documents—and nowhere else, I should point out, with such detail in this period—reflects the monastery's desire to define precisely how much it owned, and where. These transactions, as well as more than a thousand others in northern Castile between 1250 and 1350, reveal a dramatic shift in the way property was acquired and imagined.

TABLE 4.1
Purchases by the Monastery of Las Huelgas of Burgos in Frausillas (Dueñas), 1229–62

Total number of transactions (Land exclusively)	53
Sellers	
Total number of peasants mentioned as seller	108
Males	65
Females	43
Families/Groups	14
Couples	20
Males	19
Females	4
Range of Prices	
0–5 *mrs.*	43
5–10 *mrs.*	10
Highest amount paid for land:	9 *mrs.*
Lowest amount paid for land:	4 *ss.*
Average price per transaction:	3 *mrs.*
Peasants selling plots twice	4
Peasants selling land three times	1
Number of times the descriptive Don or Doña is used	
Don	30
Doña	34
Boundaries of the Property Sold to Las Huelgas	
Land owned by other peasants	71
Of this amount, land owned by John Adrian	9
Monte (wooded, uncultivated rough)	100
Carrera (roads, byways)	22
Land owned by Las Huelgas	13
Land owned by another ecclesiastical institution	5
Vineyard	1

Source: *FMCL*, vols. 30–31; Ruiz, *Crisis and Continuity*, 155.

Elsewhere, I have already examined how throughout northern Castile, municipal councils, monasteries, and a few members of the urban elites carried out an aggressive policy of land acquisition in the Castilian countryside.[26] Village lands close to important towns (Burgos, Segovia, Avila, Dueñas, Soria, and others) became monopolized by a few rich men (urban oligarchs) and institutions and turned into contiguous estates. Although I have previously studied this evidence as an example of urban intrusion into the market for land, and reexamine it in the next chapter as the material counterpart to the construction of lineages, this tendency to consolidate land—to purchase land adjoining one's existing property—shows that the perception of property as fragmented rights, rents, and holdings changed to one of property as ownership of an undivided physical space. There was, of course, also an increased awareness that working contiguous lands (often with hired agricultural labor rather than with dependent farmers) was far more profitable, but this awareness was in itself part of the change of values under discussion.

The broad movement to consolidate property can be traced back to the critical period between the late twelfth century and the mid-thirteenth, even though isolated examples can be found earlier.[27] It coincided with the transformation of the economic structure of the realm and the rise of northern towns as centers for long-distance trade. The rise of a monetary economy, the shift from trade with al-Andalus to trade with northern Europe, and the commercialization of agriculture paralleled and led to new understandings of property.

My book *Crisis and Continuity* provides overwhelming evidence for the trend toward the consolidation of landholdings and the construction of single, undivided estates, or what later would become entailments. This occurred not only among the well-to-do but even among small landholders; that is, the phenomenon was replicated at the village level. A few examples will suffice. Almost twenty years ago, as I sought to provide prosopographical information for two important nonnoble knightly families of Burgos, the Sarracín and the Bonifaz, I traced their patterns of acquisitions in the Burgalese hinterland for more than a century. In the next chapter, I examine the Sarracín's role in the market for land from a different perspective, but it may be useful to point out here that from the late twelfth century, members of the Sarracín family engaged in a conscious policy of purchasing lands in a number of locations in and around Burgos. The first member of the family documents reveal was active in the land market was Pedro Sarracín I; who held the position of *alcalde* (a judicial and executive office of the municipal council) in Burgos at least in 1187, 1193, 1200, 1202, 1207–8, and 1210–12 but probably more often. He was obviously an important man, as was his brother, Gonzalo, canon and sacristan of the cathedral of Burgos. Pedro not only held an important political office, but together with his brother undertook extensive purchases of land in the villages of Villatoro, Prado, and Valdecardeña, as well as buying shares in Atga, the city's main water mill. His children and grandchildren continued to hold important positions in Burgos's civic and ecclesiastical bodies. One of his sons, Juan Pérez I, became alcalde of Burgos; another, Pedro Sarracín II, became dean of the cathedral. The latter acquired extensive properties in Burgos's hinterland, but all concentrated in the aforementioned villages. Villatoro, above all, was clearly on the way to becoming an entailment (see chapter 5). The Sarracín and the Bonifaz in Burgos, Blasco Blázquez of Avila, who made forty purchases over a few years—most of them in and around the village of Serranos de Avianos in Avila's hinterland—and Miguel Pérez, who bought land in the Segovian hinterland toward the mid–fourteenth century, tended to concentrate their property in one locality. This pattern of acquisitions, as I have argued before, reflects a new understanding of the land itself and of the profit to be made from it.[28]

In one sense, this shift in understanding what property was and how it could be held rang the death toll, the slow demise, of the village community; in another sense, however, the consolidation of property, very much as the demise of the village community, was subverted, slowed down, and, often, reversed by partible inheritance among the peasantry and by ancestral village customs. What we witness in Castile from 1200 onward, therefore, is a complex conflict, and, at times, parallel process, between the nobles' and urban oligarchs' construction of large and entailed estates through purchases and royal donations on one hand, and the continous fragmentation of mostly rural property among the peasantry on the other. Although Castile did not suffer the development of large latifundia that Andalusia did, it too witnessed the emergence of substantial consolidated holdings. These stood in contrast, and opposition, to the strong communal claims of the village and the peasants' tendency (and desire) to partition their holdings among their children. This conflict between privatization and communal traditions, between consolidation and fragmentation is the crux of Castile's rural history, as it is for most other regions of western Europe. It remains a continuous presence of the past even into the present.[29]

Rights of Way

Further supporting evidence for a shift in how northern Castilians understood and defined property comes from the many purchases or exchanges of land for rights of way that can be found in the extant documentation of the late twelfth and early thirteenth centuries. From the earliest date, land transactions or donations sometimes included such formulaic language as "illa hereditate in loco que dicitur Villota et Villateca, et Sancti Stephani, cum sus hereditates et divisa, in montes, in fontes, in pratis, cum exitus et introitus."[30] Exchanges of land, in fact, continued to use the expression in Castilian—*con entrada y con salida*—into the late thirteenth century.

Rights of way, the prerogative to enter and exit one's own lands, have

Fig. 7 Partial view of Gallejones de Zamanzas
Sixteenth-century houses in Gallejones de Zamanzas, the author's ancestral village in northern Castile. Dating probably from the ninth century, the village still retains a sharp distinction between communal (unfenced) lands and private property marked by stone fences and landmarks. (Photo by Scarlett Freund)

been part of the Castilian mental landscape since the emergence of the county as a political reality in the ninth century. The changes of the late twelfth and early thirteenth centuries were, as with boundaries and the consolidation of property, of degree and intention. Our best evidence for these changes comes from the diocese of Burgos. Luis Martínez García's pioneer study, "La concentración de la propiedad urbana burgalesa mediante la concesión de 'pasadas de tierra,' 1150–1250," examines 291 exchanges and purchases of land with rights of entry and exit. These types of transactions, which are peculiar to Burgos (the largest diocese in northern Castile, and, in some respects, synonymous with Old Castile)—no similar transactions can be found to the same extent elsewhere in northern Castile—reveal an intense preoccupation with rights of way. Martínez García uses the transactions to illustrate how the urban oligarchy of Burgos consolidated their property, but, as he points out, they were essentially concessions of a right of way or of an easement to a public road from someone else's lands through one's own property.[31] For example, in August 1202, Guillermo Gascón, his wife, Estefanía, and their son, Ordonio, exchanged property they owned in Quintanilla Muniocisla for "unam passatam terre, in longo et in amplo, cum introitu et exitu, ante domun uestram qua habetis in Quintanilla, et desuper XI morabetinos alfonsi."[32]

The extant documentation is essentially urban in nature—although the previous example concerns a small village in the Burgalese countryside—and deals mostly with exchanges of rural property and money, or mill rights and money, for "una passatam terre, cum intrada et exida" within the city. This was the case in a transaction of July 1212, in which passage was sought through the property (*in casa de*) of Don Martín, the alcalde of Burgos. Doña Perdona and her husband, Juan de Pamplona, gave Domingo Escriba part of a garden, a quarter of a house, and 110 *mrs* for "unam passatam terre, cum intrada et exida in casa de Don Martin, el alcalde."[33] What we witness then, at least in Burgos, is a large number of transactions aimed at providing a right of way through someone's else property and legal access to a public way. Beyond the attempts to deal with a chaotic urban development in the late twelfth and early thirteenth centuries, these land and monetary exchanges for rights of way institutionalized a new spatial understanding of property.

Although easements and rights of way remain a feature of life to this very day—the eternal conflict between ancient and communal rights of way and private interests—the numerous transactions for *pasadas de tierra* in late twelfth- and early thirteenth-century Castile represent a defining moment in time, a paradigm shift. These exchanges indicate a growing awareness of the link between rights of way, spatial boundaries, freedom of movement, and power. I argue that the disappearance of such transactions after the 1220s marks the transition to a period in which an urban property or a farm *without* access to a public road or street was inconceivable, and that property—all property—was useless without the right to "enter and exit." The influential fuero of Cuenca spells out these new shifts:

> Every *eredad* (property owned outright) which would not have entry or exit, whether it is fields (land) or vineyards, the sworn *alcaldes* [would] go to that *eredad* and for that part [of the property] in which they will see that they will cause the least damage, they will give entry [provide access], and let it be stable (permanent), and whosoever would alter, close, or destroy the path that the *alcaldes* made, pay 10 *mrs.* [in penalty], so that the *carreras* (road, paths) and the *exidos* (pastures) that the *alcaldes* set will be firm and permanent forever.[34]

Between the original Latin and the Romance translation, important mental changes had occurred, reflected in the greater emphasis on rights of entry in the vernacular. Lands without entry and exit were nothing but potential sources of conflict in Cuenca and elsewhere, and the situation had to be remedied either by purchases or exchanges of land for the right to an easement, or, in the case of Cuenca, by legislation. But the Castilian version implies that there must have been some resistance to these redrawings of the land. Not unlike the fictional peasant who removed the mojones to extend his property, villagers in Cuenca and elsewhere must have also plowed and fenced rights of way. This was also true of the Mesta. The sheepherders' guild often fenced its *cañadas* or transhumance roads as they went through or near village lands, only to have them overthrown and their paths plowed by enterprising peasants.[35]

By the late fourteenth century, although the formulaic "I sell you such and such lands with [the rights of] entry and exit" continued to appear in most documents, some transactions no longer included such language. By then, it was a given that land could not be sold or bought without access to a public road or street. Most records of transactions began to include a more careful description of property and its boundaries, and these boundaries already implied easement to a public way.[36] There is another way to read these newly found concerns with boundaries, rights of way, and consolidation of property. They also reflected new political realities: the emergence of oligarchical elites in Castilian towns, the growing economic and social gap between rich farmers and impoverished peasants within village communities. Shifts in how property was defined and measured articulated new ways of wielding power in northern Castile, from the royal court down to the most remote hamlet. The power of patrician elites, of noble lineages, of well-to-do farmers became inscribed, therefore, in novel discourses of property.

Inventories

Inventories, a type of document quite common throughout the medieval West, further confirm changing attitudes toward property and the rise of a transformed system of values in northern Castile. I refer, of course, to the proliferation of inventories of land and other forms of property found in late twelfth- and early thirteenth-century Castilian documents. In many respects, the wills and exchanges of property in return for guaranteed support examined above were inventories. These types of legal instruments included itemized lists of lands, houses, households, and other material goods bequeathed to family, friends, and ecclesiastical institutions. Similarly, exchanges of property for monastic support and life-long maintenance listed property given and, as has been seen, itemizations of what the monasteries were to provide in return. One must note, once again, that donations before 1100 always mentioned property in a general manner—lands, vineyards, and other material possessions—but without ever specifying number, boundaries, or other characteristics. How many houses? How many pieces of land? How many villages? The monastery and the donor probably knew, but nothing in the documents allows us to know.

Wills and exchanges of property in return for an annuity, however, were only part of a broader movement in the late twelfth century toward itemizing material possessions and the physical world. As such, inventories are very much part of the same processes that led to elaborate descriptions of the actual size of the land, to mentions of bordering properties, and to attempts to define legally rights of way. From the 1180s onward, monasteries, cathedral chapters—from which most of the extant documentation comes—municipal councils, and even a few individuals from the middling sorts engaged in a rather active process of counting and inventorying property. Of course, nothing of this was really new. As with the other developments I have been presenting as evidence for shifts in values, inventories existed long before the twelfth century. The great ninth-century polyptychs of the Abbey of Saint Germain des Prés or the Domesday Book in eleventh-century England are only the best examples of such inventories. In the kingdoms of Asturias-León and in Castile itself, there are, however, few examples of such early activities, and some of the inventories found among the extant documentation barely qualify as such.[37] An exception can be found in Liébana, where an inventory itemizing all the property held by the church of Sant Fagunt de Tanarrio was imbedded in a will dated in 941; another appears in a 1048 donation to the monastery of San Martín de Turieno.[38] Though quite detailed, these two inventories were not meant to be an actual record of property owned, but a of what was donated or willed to specific monasteries. New in the late twelfth century was the frequency with which inventories were recorded and the careful manner in which they detailed what was owned and by whom.

The monks of the monastery of San Zoilo de Carrión undertook two significant inventories in February 1213. The first itemized all the valuable objects and religious ornaments held by the church of San Zoilo. Altogether sixty-seven categories of objects were listed, ranging from silver chalices to a gold reliquary holding a piece of the True Cross, to ivory objects, to silk liturgical vestments, silver crosses, and a motley collection of other treasures and liturgical objects. Altogether San Zoilo's holdings comprised more than 150 individual items; the objects were inventoried by number as well as by type.[39]

Around the same time, the monks of San Zoilo inventoried all the property held by, rights owed to, and vassals (peasants) of the monastery. The apeo listed all the localities in which the monastery held property and what was due to San Zoilo. Altogether thirty-eight places are named, ranging from distant locations, such as Ciudad Rodrigo, to holdings in nearby cities and substantial towns, such as Salamanca, Aguilar de Campoo, and Toro, and, finally, to small villages. The monastery also had *collaçios*, that is, peasants who owed work service to the monastery, and *heredad para duos iuga boum*, the spatial extent of land that could be plowed by two teams of oxen in a day, in the village of Badielo. In Villaoueco, the monastery of San Zoilo owned lands (one team of oxen) and peasants who paid for *infurción* (an annual territorial tax) six loaves of bread, two pieces of bacon, two hens, two measures of wine, and one *emina* of barley. But San Zoilo's inventory did more than just list properties and dues. It also itemized the income assigned to the sacristy, to almsgiving, to the kitchen, to the wardrobe, and to the infirmary.[40] In describing these inventories, the word used is the Castilian *remembrança*, that is, remembrance, a written memory of what rents, properties, and other goods the monastery had at a specific time.

San Zoilo's and Santo Toribio's inventories belong to a genre quite common in northern Castile from the end of the twelfth century onward. It was followed in the next century and a half by some of the most extensive and detailed inventories in Castilian history—themselves among the most valuable sources for understanding the social and economic structures of the realm. The timing of these extensive inventories and accounting books is not coincidental. After the early thirteenth century, they were composed exclusively in the vernacular and became the main instrument of the Crown, monasteries, cathedral chapters, municipal councils, and the well-to-do in order to map possessions, dues, and jurisdiction. The great *Repartimientos* of Seville, Jerez de la Frontera, Cádiz, Murcia, and elsewhere carefully recorded what had been granted to settlers in the newly conquered lands of southern Spain. They were also elaborate inventories of property, now measured spatially.[41] Around the same time, the cathedral of Burgos began its long series of *Cuadernos de contabilidad* (account books), which every year or so, for the next two centuries, itemized all the property owned by the chapter, the rent collected from them, and, often, the name and occupation of the tenant. Not yet fully explored, these account books are one of the most formidable sources for the social and economic history of the region, but they also reveal a distinctive new way of thinking about property and how to itemize it.[42] For example, in the *Cuadernos* for 1279 and 1280, the mills owned by the cathedral chapter of Burgos are listed. The inventory notes the name of the mill, the tenant, when and how much rent was collected. In 1279, the mill of Villa Ayuda was rented by García de Tremello, paying 103 *mrs.* and 4 *dineros* (*ds.*) by the feast of St. John. The following year, the renter was Martín Sedano, and the rent amounted to only 60 *mrs.* We can follow the fluctuation of rents for more than a century, as well as the changing cast of tenants. For the canons of the cathedral chapter, the *Cuadernos de contabilidad* produced a clear map, an itemizing, of their material resouces.[43]

Similar developments can be found in the inventories of the cathedral chapter of Avila in the early fourteenth century, or in the lands of the monastery of Santa María de Aguilar de Campoo around the same time.[44] The movement to greater precision in keeping track of one's property culminated in the extensive *Becerro de behetrías*, which, unlike other inventories, itemized feudal dues—a seignorial discourse quite distinct from the one I have examined here.

These great inventories, repartimientos, apeos, and account books are just the tip of the iceberg. The extant sources for the thirteenth and fourteenth centuries reveal an explosion of such documents. They were, in fact, taxonomies of material possessions, rents, and rights. And as complementary cultural artifacts to landmarks, boundaries, rights of way, they were an essential part of the process by which Castile was mapped and spatial property and material goods obtained a legal and discursive reality. This new reality differed radically, in its intensity and intent, from the vague formulations of an earlier age.

From Local Community to the Late Medieval Monarchy in Castile

I wish to conclude this chapter with some reflections on a point raised earlier: the link between local boundaries and the construction of the territorial monarchy in Castile at the end of the Middle Ages.[45] Without the perception of local boundaries and limits, the new concepts of territorial space, tied as they were with nascent ideas about sovereignty, could never have been formulated. Peasants, merchants, lords, and kings had to start thinking about local borders and measurable local space before they could even imagine larger territorial units.

In the accounts of the travels of Leon of Rosmithal, a Polish nobleman who visited Spain and Portugal with a large retinue in 1465–67, several passages describe crossing boundaries from one region or country into another. Signaled by a river crossing, the fiscal demands of a toll station or customhouse, or a vigilant castle the liminal points that separated one land and jurisdiction from another never failed to be noted by late medieval and early modern travelers. Upon crossing one of these transitional points on the road, Rosmithal's account alerts the readers that this was "where Biscay ended and Spain"—by which the author meant Castile—"began."[46] Crossing the Duero river, "the frontier between Portugal and Castile," the traveler described a castle on the Portuguese side of the border, which carefully monitored incursions by Castilians into Portuguese territory.[47]

Late medieval and early modern travel accounts include many such moments of transition or encounters with physical (a customhouse, a toll station, a castle) or geographical (a river, a mountain) barriers between two different kingdoms or regions. Although political jurisdiction, the rule of one king over a particular territory, is always implicit in these descriptions, the travel accounts emphasize the spatial transitions and geographic and physical markers that determine that this land, in this case Castile, has ended and another, in this case Portugal, has begun.[48]

Such a development, certainly in Castile but most probably elsewhere as well, emerged from the lower classes. Medieval men and women could not have thought of territorial frontiers and, therefore, of sovereignty without having previously begun to imagine their own local communities, lands, and other types of property spatially and boundaries as physical signs that defined one's own property from that of others. Essentially, a theoretical formulation of sovereignty cannot be articulated without a grounding of this idea in an imagining or perception of the kingdom as a territorial entity with recognizable limits or boundaries. This is what Benedict Anderson describes in his *Imagined Communities* as the transition from a "dynastic realm organized around a center to the modern concept of state sovereignty signaled by a legally demarcated territory."[49] I am not arguing, however, that the territorial monarchy in Castile emerged exclusively from a new awareness of the measurableness of the land. The genesis of the idea of sovereignty also resulted from a complex set of circumstances and the slow theoretical elaboration and transformation of the concept of sovereignty itself. Beginning in the twelfth century, a succession of civil and canon lawyers, political philosophers, and other scholars began to enunciate political principles that would, by the sixteenth century, come to be identified with the indivisible power of kings and/or people.[50]

Borrowing from the practical aspects of nation building from the thirteenth century onward—embryonic as these efforts may have been—and underpinned by the reception and reformulation of Roman law in the twelfth, Augustinus Triumphus, Marsilio de Padua, Bartolus of Sasseferrato, and others began to explore new ways of conceiving the realm and the links between rulers, power, land, and subjects.[51] Although based, as they were, on Roman legal tradition, these early definitions of sovereignty (even if the term was not employed yet) had also to take into account—notwithstanding its Italian roots and praxis[52]—the growing sense of territoriality and of territorial boundaries emerging at the regional level throughout most parts of the medieval West. In many respects, to restate the case once again, early notions of sovereignty in late medieval society were imbedded in a new sense of borders, of the spatial and geographical character of the kingdom, on territorial frontiers now dotted with customhouses, fortresses, and other physical signs that marked territorial liminality. In other words, the evolution of the idea of the kingdom as the community of people, believers, language, and those bound by ties of fidelity to a broader concept of the realm had to include all or some of the above within specified spatial limits. There are, of course, other ways of looking at the emergence of frontiers and the relationship between local boundaries and the construction of broader regional political communities. In many respects, as Joan Cadden suggested while commenting on an earlier version of this chapter, the boundaries of emerging realms could also be seen as the boundaries of towns writ large. Walls and tax collection houses at the gates of the cities or of urban markets (charging taxes on incoming and outgoing trade) also provided a powerful example for the construction of a sharply defined royal territory.

The development of frontiers and recognizable boundaries occurred at different times throughout the West, and was not fully accomplished until after the French Revolution. In France, a system of customhouses, which jealously kept track of goods brought in or taken out of the kingdom, was in place by the late thirteenth century. It is unnecessary to point out the financial benefits of such toll stations. They became, in time, an important source of income for the nascent centralized monarchies, a training ground and source of jobs for the expanding royal bureaucracies, and a sign of the power of kings and their territorial claims. This was certainly the case in Castile, where the collection stations in the ports of the Bay of Biscay, Laredo, Castro-Urdiales, San Vicente de la Barquera, Santander, San Sebastián, Fuenterrabía, and others generated considerable income for the Crown. Moreover, many of the royal officials listed in the accounts of 1293–94 (another example of inventories), the only extant fiscal record of these ports, show many of the men who had worked in the toll stations holding other important positions in the royal bureaucracy.[53] Furthermore, customhouses were not limited to maritime boundaries, mountain passes, or river crossings but were extended, in Castile, to other points throughout its frontier in the next two centuries. Henry III's

(1390–1406) charter, confirmed by John II (1406–54) in 1446, established customhouses to control traffic and collect export and import dues on merchandise coming from Aragon and Navarre. *Puertos secos*, that is, land entry points with their respective customhouses, were established in Vitoria, Calahorra, Logroño, Agreda, Soria, and Molina in 1435, when John II determined that all the merchandise coming from or going to Aragon and Navarre had to pass through these border towns and pay the appropriate dues.[54]

As María Asenjo González has argued, the *territorio de la frontera* (the frontier land) in the late fifteenth century was defined by customhouses, royal toll takers, and a military presence. Although in this early period the frontier allowed for "fluid and frequent social and economic ties between local communities on both sides of the border, it also delimited distinct sovereignties on either side." Moreover, following Asenjo González and others, the frontier had its own peculiar political and institutional reality, one that demanded military defense and fiscal vigilance.[55]

These aspects of the material construction of territorial boundaries had their counterpart in the ideological formulation of *patria* as land, that is, the conflation by Castilian chroniclers and political writers of the concept of *patria*, inherited from Roman sources, with the larger idea of the *tierra*, that is, of the land. This, in turn, was paralleled by the transformation, taking place at the local level, of the way property was imagined from the twelfth century onward. Ariel Guiance has shown how by the late twelfth century, Castilian chronicles and historical treatises began to identify and justify the war against the Moors in terms of defense of the land—meaning that at least in the twelfth and thirteenth centuries and most probably in the next two centuries, the modern concept of *patria* had not yet been formulated fully in Castile. As Guiance argues, "the idea of *patria* as part of a larger concept, that of land (both terms are not yet synonymous) is closer to Castilian reality than any other claims for the emergence of the concept of motherland in its modern meaning."[56] In the end, the land—the *tierra*, as it was beginning to be defined in late twelfth-century Castile at the local level—served as the foundation for the construction of a broader territorial community.

CHAPTER FIVE

FAMILY AND PROPERTY: LINEAGES AND PRIMOGENITURE

"IT IS A TRUTH universally acknowledged, that a single man in possession of a good fortune, must be in want of a wife," wrote Jane Austen in her extraordinary *Pride and Prejudice*. Writing at the beginning of the nineteenth century, the incomparable Austen reiterated a well-known commonplace: the inextricable link between property and the family. We have already seen how new ways of thinking about property translated into novel forms of disposing of one's earthly goods, of consolidating land estates, and of transmitting them to one's heirs. In this chapter, I reexamine the links between family and property from a different perspective. Although here I look briefly at the northern Castilian family and its social organization, my main concerns lie elsewhere. Rather than study the family per se, this chapter focuses on how certain families deployed new strategies not only to secure the preservation and transmission of their property but, far more importantly, to advance their individual and collective political and social power.

Although this is indeed a difficult and complex topic, itself worthy of a monograph, this chapter concentrates solely on three specific but related themes: (1) the formation of bourgeois lineages and familial clans; (2) the emergence of great noble lineages; (3) the development of primogeniture (royal as well as noble) and the establishment of undivided and unalienable inheritances. The shift in values I have sought to portray in previous chapters was paralleled by concomitant social transformations, although these latter changes were never clear-cut or complete. In the period under consideration, the new links between family and property were still uncertain and contested. In many respects, that contestation—with social pressures in the form of partible inheritance and internal competition between branches of the family that thwarted or reversed the formation of lineages or the emergence of primogeniture—also constitutes an important part of this story.

The Structure of the Family in Northern Castile

In the last few decades, historians have paid a great deal of attention to the family, its composition, size, internal structures, and the organization of households.[1] From the innovative work on urban families carried out by Christiane Klapisch-Zuber, David Herlihy, and others, to the examination of rural households, these works have provided a clear portrait of the history of the family in trans-Pyrenean medieval Europe and methodological models for this particular area of historical research.[2] Unfortunately, such a plethora of works does not exist for medieval Castile.

I begin this chapter examining the family in northern Castile in part to signal the remarkable shift that occurred from the central Middle Ages onward in family organization, but also to emphasize the social forces at work within the family and the enduring presence of patterns of property distribution that significantly deterred new concepts of property, lineage, and primogeniture. Above all, partible inheritance—traditional and well-established models of equal property distribution among heirs (male and female alike)—worked as a powerful instrument in slowing down the powerful and the middling sorts' growing desire to consolidate land into contiguous and undivided estates, later called *mayorazgos* or entailments. Partible inheritance and dowries (*arras*), which were kept by the wife at the end of her husband's life and which added to the wide circulation of property, were part and parcel of noble and peasant customary practices and remain a vital force in the organization and reorganization of property into the present.[3] But what about the family, that unit of material and emotional production so deeply intertwined with property?

In this brief summary of family structures, "at once, the most central and elusive institution of social organization,"[4] I make, for the sake of clarity, an artificial distinction between urban and rural families. Although differences between bourgeois and peasant families in northern medieval Castile rested mostly on social filiation rather than on place of habitation (most urban oligarchs in Castile spent half of the year in the countryside anyway), I deal with them as separate categories. Indeed, the size of a particular village or city had a great deal to do with the nature and size of kin/clan networks. The basic household, however, was, with rare exception, organized around a nuclear family, and that nuclear family was, on the average, quite small.

Although our own present family structure has been radically transformed in the last several decades, the typical family unit in Castile from the twelfth century onward included parents, children, and, occasionally, an elderly grandparent. Once children came of age, they were expected to establish separate households and start a family of their own. The nuclear family therefore undermined, to a certain extent, the formation of lineages. In Castile and elsewhere, such developments, then and now, depended on the family's financial viability and on individual members' ambitions, determination, and allegiance to the family's wider goals. Size of dowries, access to wealthy brides and to land, and other such factors determined the ebb and tide of the marriage market and, thus, of family fortune and organization. Extended households and those consisting of a single individual—usually a widow or widower—could be found in medieval northern Castile, but large family units occupying one household were restricted to the Basque region and the northern mountains, where distinct models of family organization and kindred households, arranged around a central courtyard, survive until the present.[5] The pattern of children coming of age, marrying, and settling elsewhere was more common. Yet, settling elsewhere could mean living on the same street, or in the same neighborhood, thereby promoting the social and economic advantages of kin networks.

The Family in the City

In Burgos, a city for which we have far more extant sources from before 1350 than for any other urban center in northern Castile, the membership lists of two confraternities or brotherhoods (the first of merchants, the second of nonnoble knights) give the place of residence of large familial clans. These lists illuminate a later period than the one I have focused on until now. Nonetheless, the references we have from the late twelfth and early thirteenth centuries for the city's leading families show that these patterns of inhabitation—members of the same clan living close to each other but in separate households—had a long history.

The 1338 membership list of the Real Hermandad of the Santísimo y Santiago includes an impressive collection of individual portraits. Through these lists and the iconographic representations therein, one is able to establish family connections, recognize the different generations within a specific family, and learn family members' different addresses. Young members of important oligarchical families set up independent households close to their parents' abodes. John Mathe, one of the sixteen citizens of Burgos named by Alfonso XI to the *regimiento* (the Crown-controlled ruling body of the city) in 1345 and a member of one of the most powerful familial clans in Burgos, lived on the *cal* (street) of Sanct Llorent, the most prestigious Burgalese address in the thirteenth and fourteenth centuries. Four of his sons, already adults and members of the

Fig. 8 Illustrations from the rules and membership lists of the Real Hermandad of the Santísimo y Santiago, 1338. (Photo by the author)

Real Hermandad as well, lived within a block or two of their father's residence: one on Sanct Llorent itself, another on the street of Armas, and two on that of Sanct Esteban.[6] Similar information can be gleaned for the Bonifaz clan, with three brothers holding office in the regimiento, and eight of their respective children (named in the confraternity list) living within four blocks of each other. This accounts for at least eleven different Bonifaz households (there were, in fact, other, female Bonifaz households in the neighborhood as well) all of them within the orbit of the head of the family and subordinating, as we know from their political lives, their own personal ambitions to the collective needs of the senior branch.

One should inject a note of caution into these pronouncements. Comparable patterns of familial relations and inhabitation can be found among lower social groups. The cathedral of Burgos's *Cuadernos de contabilidad*, a formidable inventory of property discussed in chapter 4 as an example of the itemizing of the material world, show that artisan and laboring groups in the city—those who rented their abodes from the chapter—followed along the same lines as their social betters. That is, coming of age and marrying meant, with almost no exceptions, creating an independent household, albeit within short walking distance of the family home. Yet this did not entail forming lineages or accumulating property for the greater benefit of the family. There were, of course, other types of households; for instance, women, presumably either widowed or unattached; living by themselves. In Burgos and in Avila, where the extant documents allow for partial reconstruction of patterns of urban inhabitation, the number of women (usually renters) living on their own is quite significant. In the census of property owned by the cathedral chapter of Avila in 1303 numerous houses were rented or owned (those noted in boundary descriptions) by women alone. Interestingly, several of these women belonged to religious minorities, providing additional evidence of the parallels among Christian, Jewish, and Muslim families.

Indeed, these social patterns of settling independent households crossed social and religious boundaries. Some cases are not easy to explain, as they defied the logic of kinship and economic rationality. In 1332, the cathedral of Burgos's *Cuadernos de contabilidad* showed a certain María Pérez, a *curandera* (healer), renting a house from the chapter for 15 *mrs.* per annum. Nearby, her daughter, Marina, rented another house for 14 *mrs.* Fifteen years later, María Pérez, presumably dead, no longer appeared among those renting from the chapter, but Marina, still a tenant in the same cathedral chapter house as in the 1332 document, was now listed as a healer.[8] Here, in an urban setting, two women related by the closest blood link possible, sharing the same trade, lived close to each other but not in the same home. Why did they incur the double expenses of maintaining two households? What personal animosities or social forces led them to these separate yet proximate lives? Such fragmentation of the family and the renting or owning of a house by what we may suppose was a single individual (often a woman) or a couple was not uncommon in the countryside either.

The Family in the Countryside

Among the peasants paying *infurción* (a seignourial due) in the small village of Piedraportún (Per Apertum), one of the monastery of Santa María la Real de Aguilar de Campoo's rural holdings, most of the villagers formed part of an extensive kin network. Twenty-seven different units of production were listed in a late thirteenth-century census.[9] Of these, as far as one can gather from the documents, seven plots were in the hands of individual members of one family, the Miguéllez; three were in those of another, the Martínez. Two women, Illana and Illana Peláez, held lands from the monastery, while their respective sons, Miguel and Domingo Peláez, held lands elsewhere in the village. María Miguéllez, whose infurción payments to the monastery amounted to 1 *modius* of rye and 17 *dineros* (*ds.*)—one of the largest payments in Piedraportún, thus denoting a large holding—had at least two sons: Iuan (Juan) and Domingo Martínez, both of them paying 1 *modius* of grain (a combination of rye, wheat, and barley), plus 18 *ds.* each.[10] The Miguéllez and the Martínez were closely related, and one must assume that in this particular village almost all the inhabitants were part of a large kin group, as found in small villages in northern Castile today. The point to be drawn here is that grown-up children, either because of existing social structures or because the monastic and lay fiscal units of production were often fragmented and resistant to consolidation, set up independent households not unlike those we find in towns. Although holding and working different plots of land does not always assure the existence of a nuclear family structure, the internal evidence of the *apeo* (census) of Santa María's rural holdings, in which peasants are identified as being the son of such and such person, points quite strongly to this type of family unit.[11] Thus both in the countryside and in cities, large kin groups existed.

Lineages and Familial Clans

If the social structure of the family worked against tightly knit kin networks and tended, through the nuclear family, patterns of inhabitation, and partible inheritance, to lessen the collective importance of specific family groups, other forces sought to reverse these trends. Property and power, that is, the preservation and increase of property and the enhanced exercise of power, whether in a village, a town, or the wider context of the realm, led to the strengthening of the ties that bound disparate family members into some form of cohesive unit. Through wills, career decisions, and marriage, lineages were constructed, bourgeois and noble alike, in the context of new visions of the material world. These processes continue to operate in modern society and pit individual ambitions against the collective needs of the family, an endless swaying back and forth in the unfolding of family histories.

I have been using the words *lineage* (*linaje*), *familial clans*, and *kin networks* as if they were synonymous. This is, of course, untrue, and the terms themselves, especially *lineage*, provide a clue as to the link between linguistic production, family structure, and values. For early thirteenth-century Castile, lineage meant direct descent through one specific bloodline, or, to be more precise, semen line. That is, one descends from the *simiente* (semen) of someone. As such, the term began to be deployed in legal texts and literary works. In Corominas's *Diccionario de autoridades*, the word *linaje* is traced back to line (*linea* or *liña*), a word that, not coincidentally, is also used to describe spatial boundaries. Corominas traces some of the variants of the word *lineage* to Catalonia, arguing that it first appeared in Castilian in 1209. This is precisely around the time new links between family and property were being created.

Whether in Berceo's work or in Alfonso X's legislative compilations, lineage carried two different and contradictory meanings. On one hand, all humans are of the lineage of Adam. This usage could be reduced metaphorically, and for ideological purposes, to one religious group. This is certainly the case of the example given by Corominas: Muslims "descended from Muhammad's semen." Jews would also be described as forming one lineage or group.[12] Yet, lineage also functioned as a powerful and developing discourse on blood and property. This was most evident among the royal family and the great magnates, but it was articulated by patrician elites as well.

This meaning of lineage as a classificatory and exclusionary discourse operated at several levels. At that of individual families or a particular family line, it translated into a growing concern with genealogy, the creation of a mythical ancestor and family history. This meant keeping records, mostly property transactions and wills, as permanent testimonies of the family acquisitions and wealth. After all, wills and even exchanges of properties functioned as genealogical markers. They provided verifiable evidence for family descent. At the level of particular groups, it made all Christians "brothers." It constructed all Castilians as the children of a newly conceived territorial entity: the kingdom, the land. In that sense, the emphasis on Visigothic blood and Visgothic descent found in thirteenth-century chronicles was part of the broad discourse of blood and lineage. One must therefore not lose touch with this linkage between property, an emerging sense of collective identity, and the family. At the same time, one must also note the connection between a new discourse of blood and lineage—grounded on the family and on property—and the rising legal and literary pejorative representations of Muslims and Jews. This was an extended racialized and blood-based discourse that located religious minorities outside the common family of Christians.

Familial clans, whether noble or bourgeois, were different from lineages in late medieval Castile. In this period, as shall be seen below, a branch of a specific family, usually the oldest or richest, might leap into the undisputed leadership or prominence within a more extended kin network. In theory, specific lineages stood at the center of familial clans. But this already presupposed growing awareness among bourgeois families of the benefits of primogeniture and entailment. Among great noble families, the leadership of one branch was maintained by backing their blood claims with the building of large estates—a late twelfth- and early thirteenth-century phenomenon. This is yet another example of the close relationship between property and the family's new social and economic functions.

In northern Castile the term *linaje* came, in time, to stand for the broader familial clan. For lesser branches of the family, it was always advantageous to claim solidarity with the main family stem. Among urban elites, social, political, and economic ties were so profitable as to bring together several family groups into overlapping networks. Marriage and business partnerships were the conduits for these developments.

Bourgeois Lineages

I have long been interested in the formation of large urban kin groups and their monopoly of political, social, and economic power in Castilian cities. More than twenty-five years ago, I undertook a detailed prosopographical study of two Burgalese patrician families, the Sarracín and the Bonifaz, and, more recently in *Crisis and Continuity*, of Avila's leading family, the Blázquez.[13] My focus, then, centered around the emergence of urban oligarchical elites and their relations with the Crown. Here, I revisit some of these families but focusing now on the patterns of inheritance, property transactions, and their political manifestations. Familial clans have long been well studied in the social and economic history of the medieval West.[14] Although northern Castile lacks the extensive monographic literature available for other parts of Europe, studies of specific cities in the last twenty years have gone a long way toward elucidating the origins of bourgeois (or patrician) lineages, their power, and their role in urban politics and kingdomwide affairs.[15]

Property alone did not make for power over the long term. The extant sources are filled with information about individuals or multiple members of a family actively engaged in purchasing lands or houses for a short period of time. And, then, they vanish from the documentation either because the records are missing or because the individual or the family itself faced adverse conditions that prevented them from continuing to accumulate property. Success, the establishment of enduring lineages, depended on different factors, but, clearly, the conjunction of the accumulation of property and the long-term holding of secular and ecclesiastical offices became the key for some families' rise to social prominence and power within Castilian cities and their hinterland. Despite the linkage of these two elements—acquiring property while holding lay or ecclesiastical office had long been a practice among the nobility, even if not always systematically in pre-twelfth-century Castile—the middling sorts do not appear to have consciously decided to follow this course of action until the late twelfth and early thirteenth centuries. Once they began along this road, the secret was to maintain such practices and privileges over several generations. A few families or, in some cases, specific lines within a family were able to do this, and their reward was substantial influence and status within their respective localities and even within the realm as a whole. This also meant eventual entry into the nobility, through marriage, royal grant, or outright purchase of a noble title in the fourteenth century.

The Sarracín family is a very good example of both the development of an influential line and the creation of a strong lineage over four generations. Gonzalo, a canon of the cathedral of Burgos, and his brother, Pedro Sarracín I, appear in the Burgalese records for the first time in 1179. That year, the two exchanged land in Villatoro (a small village near the city of Burgos) for land (most probably a *pasada de tierra*) in the neighborhood of Santa Coloma in Burgos.[16] This particular purchase marks the beginning (though there is a great possibility that the family had long been engaged in purchasing property and that the records of those transactions are no longer extant) of the two brothers' and Pedro Sarracín's direct descendants' long-term investments in Villatoro and the surrounding area. By 1180, the family had clearly obtained some distinction. Gonzalo was already a canon in Burgos, one of the richest sees in Castile. That year, he paid four gold *maravedíes* and a piece of land (another *pasada*) for another parcel of land in Villatoro. Although on the surface the amount paid does not seem very high, gold *maravedíes* were markers of fairly high economic standing. It is also clear that in 1180, Pedro Sarracín was not yet a player in city affairs, and, as far as the extant documents reveal, he had not yet been called to witness documents in Burgos proper. The latter was often a sign of one's holding either an office in the city administration or a prominent economic position. Most probably, the family had originally come from Burgos's hinterland, that is, from a village under the jurisdiction of Burgos, most probably Villatoro itself. Education—although Gonzalo is not described as a master, he must have had some schooling—and an ecclesiastical benefice provided a good entryway into Burgalese affairs. Of course, some kind of position and financial well-being was required to enter the cathedral chapter, but, once there, Gonzalo and Pedro Sarracín used their position to the family's advantage. Two other transactions (one in Villatoro) in 1181 and 1186 showed the brothers still buying in unison and active in the market for land.[17]

By the mid-1180s, Pedro Sarracín must have been settled within the city, but he did not hold yet a position in Burgos's municipal government. In 1187, he witnessed a document drawn at the monastery of Las Huelgas, an important Cistercian monastery, founded by Alfonso VIII and his English wife, Eleanor, in the outskirts of Burgos just a few years before. All the other witnesses were important royal and municipal officials or prominent Burgalese citizens.[18] While their acquisitions continued apace, both Gonzalo and Pedro rose within their respective spheres. Gonzalo, continuing to serve as canon (with its substantial flow of income), also became sacristán of the cathedral of Burgos. The latter position probably meant an additional source of income. By the mid-1190s, Gonzalo appeared second in the list of ranking witnesses for important ecclesiastical and secular transactions; Pedro also figured prominently among the list of witnesses in several property exchanges.[19]

By 1195, Pedro Sarracín was already one of the city alcaldes; and he owned a substantial house or houses in the Burgalese neighborhood of Santiago.[20] He also seems to have had special links to the monastery of Las Huelgas. He witnessed a good number of their transactions—important and not so important ones—and from 1195 onward, he did so as a municipal official as well. This connection with Las Huelgas, difficult to describe in any detail, opened up possibilities for royal patronage and connections with the court. Alfonso VIII and Eleanor spent a great deal of time at Las Huelgas. Moreover, as one of the city alcaldes, Pedro Sarracín represented to the king the affairs and interests of perhaps the realm's most important urban center in the late twelfth century. Pedro Sarracín was not directly involved in either long-distance or local trade, nor were any of his direct descendants ever mentioned as active in the city's commercial life. Since social promotion in Burgos was often related to mercantile activity, this made the Sarracín quite unique among the city's influential families. They were a family, and eventually a lineage, built around the accumulation of land property and without direct connection to long-distance trade.

Pedro Sarracín occupied the important administrative and judicial position of an alcalde for what appears to be an almost uninterrupted tenure until 1211.[21] With their fingers already in the political and ecclesiastical life of Burgos, Pedro, together with his wife, Estefanía, and his brother, Gonzalo, continued a systematic policy of purchasing lands in Villatoro, Prado, and Valdecardeña, all near the city. Their purchases were part of the process of consolidating property in a few locations and building contiguous estates. This represented a departure from earlier purchase patterns and confirmed the dramatic transformation in the way property was understood in late twelfth-century Castile.[22]

By 1211, Pedro Sarracín had either died or withdrawn from public life. His wife, Estefanía, is mentioned in a land transaction as a house owner

Fig. 9 The monastery of Las Huelgas
One of the earliest Gothic buildings in northern Castile, the monastery of Las Huelgas of Burgos (late twelfth century) became a royal pantheon under the patronage of Alfonso VIII and his wife, Eleanor. Located in the outskirts of Burgos, and one of the stops along the pilgrimage road, Las Huelgas played an important role in the economics and political life of Burgos. The Sarracín family was associated with the monastery; Pedro Sarracín I often served as witness for important monastic transactions. (Photo by Scarlett Freund)

in 1212; the text implies that she was Pedro's widow.[23] Marriage alliances were, of course, an important part of lineage formation. Estefanía may have been a member of the Bonifaz family, a rising lineage of foreign merchants, settled in Burgos in either the late twelfth or early thirteenth century. Estefanía's and Pedro Sarracín's names surfaced again, probably after Estefanía's death, when the six surviving children divided their parents' property according to the terms of a will no longer extant.[24] Although I have detailed the fortunes of every member of the Sarracín family elsewhere,[25] here I am mostly concerned with the careers of three of them, probably the three oldest male children. From the 1225 partition of property, we know that one of Pedro and Estefanía's sons was Gonzalo Pérez, probably named after his uncle Gonzalo, canon and sacristan of Burgos. Gonzalo Pérez followed in the footsteps of his uncle. He became archdeacon of Valpuesta, an important ecclesiastical benefit, and abbot of Salas, a midrange monastery in Burgos's hinterland.[26] Another son, Juan Pérez, continued his father's political career. For at least the entire decade of the 1220s, Juan Pérez is listed as one of the alcaldes of Burgos. He also appears prominently in the documentation of Las Huelgas, witnessing important transactions involving the monastery. Juan Pérez, his wife, Doña Alda, and some of their children continued to purchase property in and around Burgos. Juan Pérez and Doña Alda's offspring came to occupy an important place in mid-thirteenth-century Burgos as ecclesiastics, municipal and royal officials.[27] None, however, attained the success of their first surviving son, Pedro Sarracín II.

A university-trained *maestre* (master), Pedro Sarracín II rose through the ranks of the church at a meteoric rate. Between 1256 and 1262, he moved from one profitable archdeaconry to the next (including that once held by his uncle Gonzalo Pérez) and, between 1274 and 1276, he became dean of the cathedral of Burgos and a serious contender for the episcopal chair. His ecclesiastical career, his philanthropic and patronage activities (as head of the family-founded Hospital of San Lucas), and his strong family connections to Burgos's lay officials was paralleled by his long life of investment in the land market. Building on almost fifty years of continuous purchases of land and consolidation of property by his ancestors, Pedro Sarracín II proved to be the most active buyer in more than two hundred years of city history. Altogether we have thirty-three extant transactions, accounting for an investment of more than 30,000 *mrs.*, with the bulk of the monetary outlay coming after his election as dean. These purchases were strictly personal, and almost all his property passed into the family's hands at the dean's death in 1290 or 1291.[28] In his life, we see illustrated some of the patterns of property accumulation, social mobility, and recirculation of goods within the family (through wills) discussed earlier. A good number of interfamily transactions, among nieces and nephews following Pedro Sarracín II's death, show the redistribution of property within the family, as exchanges and purchases resettled what must have been the fairly even distribution of the dean's holdings among his relatives by a no-longer extant will.[29]

Pedro Sarracín III, the son of Rodrigo Ibáñez (Juan Pérez's son and the dean's nephew), followed in the footsteps of his namesake. He entered the church, became a canon of the cathedral of Burgos, warden of the family's endowed Hospital of San Lucas, and an active buyer of lands in the Sarracín-dominated localities of Villatoro, Temiño, Castro Val, and in the city itself.[30] Thus, for four generations and extending more than a century, the main branch of the family, together with some collateral lines, played a prominent role in the city's political and ecclesiastical life.

Many other family members held important positions in the church, the municipal council, and the royal administration. Through marriage alliances, they linked with other great familial clans, monopolizing Burgos's political, financial, and religious life. And they bought property, again and again, in targeted locations, building contiguous estates in Burgos's hinterland between the 1180s and the early fourteenth century.

Their trajectory was not unique. It was paralleled in northern Castile, in the rest of Iberia, and in western Europe by similar familial groups—the Bonifaz, also in Burgos, the Blázquez in Avila, the Dávilas in Segovia—who, by combining municipal and ecclesiastical office holding with property acquisitions, promoted themselves into unchallenged prominence. That we find certain names, Sarracín, Bonifaz, which were not yet fixed as family names, repeated over several generations bespeaks of a sense of continuity and of the firm construction of family identities built on the solid foundation of property. Their individual and collective history was, however, short-lived in terms of the *longue durée*. Success within the city and the ownership of estates in the countryside led them away from and bourgeois aspirations. These led them, as with the Sarracín and the Blázquez, into the nobility.[31]

Noble Lineages

As lofty as the Sarracín, Blázquez, Bonifaz, and other urban familial clans were, their fortunes and prestige did not compare to the power of the great Castilian noble lineages. Unlike the history of bourgeois lineages, which has only recently begun to be reconstructed, the history of the Castilian nobility has long attracted a great deal of attention. From strictly genealogical reconstructions, that is, finding out as much as possible about one great noble family or group of families, to more recent concerns with the social aspects of noble lineages, our knowledge of these matters is quite extensive. This has become even more so in the last few years. The works of Marie-Claude Gerbet, Isabel Beceiro, Simon Barton, Margarita Torres Sevilla, Simon Doubleday, and others point to the transformation of noble life toward the end of the twelfth century and the conflation, once again, of family, property, and the holding of office (in the case of the nobility, at the royal court or at the highest ecclesiastical rank) in the construction of lineages.[32]

Although the broad outline of these transformations has been well depicted, we do not have a clear connection of change in the structure of noble families to other forms of social change or shifts in value systems. The complex and uneasy development from "aristocracy to nobility," as described by Gerbet, implied a vast remapping of the nobility's mental landscape and of the high aristocracy's relations to the Crown, to the land, and to its own concept of family. In Castile and León, the great magnates came into being out of opportunities generated by warfare against the Muslims. Their rise to positions of power was underpinned by the fabulous booty and tribute garnered in the south. Yet, in the late eleventh and early twelfth centuries, there was not yet a full understanding of the family's, as opposed to the individual's role in the wielding of political, social, and economic power, or in the relation between property, family, and power. Partible inheritance, the heavy weight of the Visigothic legal tradition, thwarted the emergence of an individual or a family line recognized as head of the family group and as spokesman for the family's collective will and ambitions. As was the case with the royal family, a capable aristocrat could accumulate lands and offices and rise in his own lifetime to dazzling heights within the royal court and the realm. But, though the firstborn male tended to inherit some of the offices and the choicest lands, the prestige and power acquired through years of service and warfare were often undone by the demands of partible inheritance (which included women), cognatic kinship, or the lack of a male heir.[33]

Moreover, in the twelfth century the foundation of magnate power in Castile-León rested, to a large extent, on royal largesse. Unlike the aristocracy elsewhere, which, although also the beneficiary of royal grants and gifts, had begun to build its own territorial base, often quite independent from royal control, in Castile-León a fairly powerful king prevented the formation of autonomous political entities.[34] Not only was the king the ultimate source of offices, land grants, and income; he was also the undisputed leader of the Reconquest, organizer, and military commander of raids against al-Andalus. As such, the kings of both Castile and León could command service from the nobility on grounds quite different, and far more appealing (because of the access to large tribute money, the *parias*), than the unstable feudal obligations north of the Pyrenees. Of course, these aristocratic groups could and did rebel, joined princes of royal blood angling for the throne, even joined Muslims against their lords, but the thought of establishing a quasi-autonomous fiefdom à la Normandy, Flanders, Brittany, Languedoc, or many of the German principalities was out of the question. One could say, however, that the history of Castile is essentially that of the nobility's resistance to royal power. The many conflicts and rebellions, especially in periods of royal minority, from the twelfth century until the reign of the Catholic Monarchs attest to the historical contradictions between a fairly centralized royal authority (by the standards of the age) and a perennially rebellious nobility.[35]

Partible inheritance, a strong royal power, and gifts and offices accumulated as part of regal favor led to another reality. Aristocratic holdings, mostly in land, did not play an important role, as Doubleday has pointed out in his study of the Laras, in the family's transition from important aristocrats to one of the leading noble lineages in the late twelfth century.[36] Their power base still rested in royal gifts, and their actual landholdings were not yet significant or were dispersed over the realm, negating the advantage of continuous estates. The fragmentation of property may have provided convenient resting stops for a peripatetic nobility, but it made their lands difficult to manage and less profitable.

By the late twelfth century in Castile and elsewhere in the peninsula, the rise of a monetary economy (already explored in some detail in chapter 1) and the growing expense of maintaining a noble establishment led to a dramatic shift in values and attitudes toward property and lineages.[37] During the political crises following the minorities of Alfonso VIII and Henry I, the great noble houses, the Castro and the Lara, sought to gain control of the regency, but also to build an economic base independent from uncertain royal largesse.[38] It is to this crucial period, the late twelfth and early thirteenth centuries, that we can trace the acceleration in the formation of large noble contiguous estates (though this should not be exaggerated) and the nobles' effort to rationalize their holdings and concentrate them in specific locations. These regions would become, in time, identified with the power of certain nobles, even though the families might hold other lands throughout the realm. The Haro family, which owned large estates in northern Castile, the Rioja, and the Basque region in the thirteenth and fourteenth centuries, is just one example of the growing link between the accumulation of lands in one area and the heightened power of a family lineage. Ahead, and beyond the chronological terminus of this book, loomed the great entailments of the mid- and late fourteenth century and the rise of great territorial lordships: the Haros in the north, the Medina Sidonia in the south, and other great families throughout Iberia.[39]

This transformation involved a concomitant change in lifestyle, excessive and costly displays. By the mid-thirteenth century, this was already so evident that the Crown, through a series of sumptuary edicts, sought to curb the nobility's growing appetite for material goods and their conspicuous consumption. If these laws tell us anything at all—and they were also aimed at the great bourgeois lineages—it is that the high nobility had been transformed into a social group capable of rivaling the king in terms of social display (eating, dressing, lifestyle) and that their great estates, though always under the threat of royal confiscation for treacherous behavior, had made them economically independent from the Crown.[40]

This broad and sketchy outline does not reflect the complexities of this process, nor the ebb and tide in the shift in values. By the late twelfth century, the great noble houses in northern Castile began to image property in ways altogether different from the fragmented rights and rents that kings had granted them in the past. Many great noble families began to concentrate their estates in locations associated with the family's history or ancestry. Awareness of a family history (even when it had been fictionalized or was part of genealogical mythification) was itself part of the shifts in values that occurred in this period, and bore fruits in the late Middle Ages with noble emphasis on a mythical Gothic descent and blood.[41]

Estates became economic units, lordships (*señoríos*) independent, to a certain extent, from royal jurisdiction and interference. But one could not build such estates without a parallel and emerging notion of lineage and, far more importantly, of lines of authority within the lineage itself.[42] This seems, of course, far too neat. Reality was otherwise. The noble discourse of property operated at different levels at the same time. As late as the mid–fourteenth century, the *Becerro de behetrías*, the formidable census of noble rights in northern Castile, indicates that what the great noble houses accomplished by consolidating their property was not true for all noble families. The lower and middling nobility still suffered from extremely fragmented holdings and often maintained a view of their possessions as forms of income and rights rather than as physical and measurable property. These diverse notions of property and lineage were all bound in questions of inheritance and in the slow acceptance of primogeniture among the powerful.

Primogeniture and Lineage

There could be no lineages without primogeniture.[43] In parts of western Europe kings from at least the eleventh century or even earlier passed their power undivided to their firstborn son or to the next male within a specific bloodline. In England and in France, working out primogeniture or descent through a specific family line did not always go according to plan, and the principle of primogeniture itself, which solidified royal authority, was challenged repeatedly by an ambitious and powerful aristocracy. The French practice of coadopting the first child as king, a practice that remained in place until the first half of the thirteenth century, is a vivid reminder of the fragile position kings occupied in this period. But neither William the Conqueror's descendants in the English and Norman lands, their Angevin successors, nor the Capetians slowly expanding their domain outward from the Ile-de-France would have thought of dividing their fledgling possessions among their male children.[44]

The success of primogeniture in securing a dynastic line and in strengthening the English and French monarchies was not lost at all among their rivals—the great noble houses. These aristocratic clans, often led by princes of the blood royal, also embraced primogeniture and undivided or at least preferential lines of descent and claims to the family's property. This placed certain family lines or lineages in a privileged position, basing their enhanced status on the conjunction (as seen above) of defined territorial power and the identification of a geographical location with a family. In time, for both the royal family and the great noble lineages, property and thus the family's rights and privileges became inalienable.

In the Iberian Peninsula these developments were checkered at best. At the level of the individual realms, specific political developments (examined below in some detail) deterred the early appearance of primogeniture. At the level of individuals and specific families, partible inheritance, women's right to property, and the whims or dislikes of the testator dictated myriad types of legacy. These particular arrangements subverted the desire of lineages to establish patrilineal inheritance and primogeniture. A simple example illustrates the vagaries of inheritance in Castile and the manner in which the legal system remained fluid enough to call into question the sort of arrangements that became normative in northern kingdoms.

In 1337, Sancha Alfonso, a citizen of Frías, a small town north of Burgos, wrote her testament. Her husband, John Pérez, was still alive and entered a monastery in 1341 or earlier. There is a very good chance he took the habit while his wife was still alive, and this action may have prompted this peculiar will. Sancha requested burial in the grounds of the Hospital of Santa María de Frías, a male monastery (though not the one where her husband had taken or would eventually take his vows). She also donated vineyards and the rents of her cereal lands to several different monasteries and churches, asking in return for anniversaries and masses: sixty masses for her mother's and sister's souls and one hundred for her own salvation. A considerable amount of money (in rents garnered from her lands) was assigned for lamps to burn perpetually in different churches, candles, and other pious bequests. No masses were offered for the souls of her father, husband, or any other male relative. No alms were assigned to her husband's monastery, even though her largesse was spread far and wide in the area of Frías. To her husband, she gave 60 *mrs.*, a sum so small compared to her other legacies as to be an insult. Moreover, after twelve years all her lands and rents were to go to her immediate relatives and kin on her mother's side. Nothing was left to those related to Sancha through her father's side or to her husband's (or ex-husband's) relatives. We do not know what hatreds were played out in this will, but it is also obvious that a well-to-do woman in mid-fourteenth-century Castile could feel, and articulate in her will, that her real family were those in a matrilineal line. Furthermore, she could get away with it. In the conclusion to her testament, Sancha Alfonso defiantly stated that "if any of her relatives contested her will, they should inherit nothing."[45]

In northeastern Iberia the compromise between ancient political forms and the new demands of family and property created a unique and odd (by medieval standards) political union. The Crown of Aragon emphasized the continuity of individual kingship and inheritance while maintaining the division of kingdoms (or regions) and preserving their individual institutional, linguistic, political, and cultural autonomy.[46] When the ruler of Catalonia, Ramón Berenguer IV (1131–62), married Petronila, the sole heir of the kingdom of Aragon, the two kingdoms were joined under one ruler and one ruling house (Valencia was added to the Crown of Aragon as an independent kingdom in 1238). Although these kingdoms remained, as indicated, quite distinct from each other in every sense, primogeniture, or next male kin succession was firmly established. Yet, the rulers of the Crown of Aragon could not fully escape their Iberian inheritance. Whether dealing with the Balearic Islands, Naples, or Montpellier, the kings of the Crown of Aragon were not unwilling to create new kingdoms for younger sons or bastard children. These were not appanages in the French fashion or great lordships as among the Angevins, but full-fledged kingdoms undermining the supposed advantage of undivided inheritances. A further, and much later, example can be found in the sixteenth century, when Charles V, on his resignation, divided his possessions between his son Philip II and his brother Ferdinand.

This is, however, a circuitous way to get to late medieval Castile and its history of royal succession. I do not wish to imply here that one form of political organization was superior to the other, that is, that the French and English successions, with their early adoption of primogeniture, were the norm from which Castile and the Crown of Aragon deviated (a lot in the case of the former, less so in the latter). To postulate one as paradigmatic and the other as exceptional privileges northern realms to the detriment of Iberian ones.[47] Specific circumstances took Castile down a different road to primogeniture than other western medieval realms. To begin with, the kingdoms that eventually comprised greater Castile had their own peculiar history. Galicia, Asturias, León, and Castile proper all had long and separate histories as independent political entities. Although these different kingdoms were often ruled by the same king or dominated politically and culturally by a neighboring realm, there were strong historical precedents for their autonomy in the tenth and eleventh centuries.[48]

Moreover, the strong Visigothic tradition, recaptured or reinvented in early tenth-century Asturias, and the partiality of Visigothic law (the *Lex visigothorum* or its vernacular version, the *Fuero juzgo*), for partible inheritance encouraged those who had united these diverse realms by great labor and military campaigns to divide them again at the moment of their death. Similarly, the Muslim influence, with its unstable political system and uncertain succession rules, served as an important model for Christian rulers. After all, Christian kings had, for almost three centuries, lived under the shadow (and threat) of Andalusi political practices.[49]

To complicate matters further, each of these Christian realms in northwestern and central Iberia (Galicia, Asturias, León, Castile, and, to a lesser extent, Navarre) developed along distinct social, institutional, and economic lines. Galicia had become or was becoming by the late twelfth century a backwater, located in the rearguard of the Reconquest. Although Galicia could count on Santiago de Compostela as a great shrine, the terminus of one of the greatest medieval pilgrimages and with claims to ecclesiastical primacy in the peninsula, the conquest of Toledo (1085) meant the emergence of a powerful rival for spiritual leadership in Iberia. Galicia did not have the economic resources to play a major role after the early eleventh century, and though it remained, in theory, an independent realm—listed in the litany of titles of the rulers of Castile and later Spain—its possibilities for true independence were, in fact, over by the early twelfth century. That was not the case with Asturias-León. The kingdom of León, as it came to be known in the twelfth century, had a long history. Unlike Galicia, it had a frontier with Islam and the possibility of expansion southward into the rich grazing lands of Extremadura. With a rich tradition of independence and great historical cities (León, Sahagún, Oviedo), León was a viable political entity—which made the final integration of the kingdom under one ruler in the early thirteenth century all the more remarkable.[50]

The political developments of the late twelfth and first half of the thirteenth century deserve brief retelling. The adoption of primogeniture at such a late date could not be explained without some dramatic shift in how Castilian and Leonese kings perceived their rule and, far more important, their relationship to the land. In the end, the process was not without difficulties nor without compromise. As we have already seen, Alfonso VII, despite his imperial ambitions, divided his kingdom among his two eldest sons. Sancho III (1157–58) received Castile, the lion's share of the inheritance and of Muslim tribute. Ferdinand II (1157–88) inherited León, Asturias, and Galicia. Sancho's sudden death left a minor child, Alfonso VIII (1158–1214), as heir. Although Ferdinand interfered in Castilian affairs, hoping perhaps to follow an ancient precedent of division of the realms by partible inheritance and their reconstitution as an undivided holding by military intervention, Castile, though plagued by conflicting noble lineages in-fighting, was able to retain its independence. In the late twelfth century, the two realms appeared to be diverging. Antagonisms and frontier conflicts were far more frequent than cooperation and amity. Expansion into the south was a perennial source of strife, and the Leonese were reluctant to join in Alfonso VIII's campaigns against al-Andalus. When Alfonso IX succeeded his father to the Leonese throne in 1188, it seemed as if the two kingdoms were set on independent courses. Attempts at reconciliation between the two cousins through the arranged marriage of Alfonso VIII's daughter, Berenguela, to Alfonso IX of León ended in failure when the marriage was annulled because of the close blood ties between bride and groom. The ill feeling between the two rulers was most evident in Alfonso IX's refusal (or reluctance) to join Alfonso VIII in the great enterprise of Las Navas de Tolosa (1212), and, thus, missing out in the signal victory against the Almohads and the subsequent territorial expansion into western Andalusia. Eventually, the offspring of the brief marriage between Alfonso and Berenguela, Ferdinand, through a series of fortuitous events, came to inherit both kingdoms.[51]

As yet, the events that led Ferdinand to become king first of Castile and then of León had little to do with the establishment of primogeniture or of a clear line of descent in Castile. Ferdinand's younger uncle, Henry I (1214–17), died at an early age. The throne passed to Berenguela, the eldest daughter of Alfonso VIII of Castile, who immediately relinquished the throne to her son in 1217. When Alfonso IX, king of León, died without a male heir from his second marriage in 1230, the energetic Ferdinand bribed, threatened, or convinced his two half-sisters to surrender their legitimate rights to the throne to him.

By 1230, Ferdinand III ruled over both kingdoms with a strong and sure hand. His expansionist polices were to be vindicated when he led his armies to great victories in the south and to the dramatic conquests of Córdoba in 1236 and Seville in 1248. Nonetheless, his rule rested on very shaky grounds. He was the issue of an uncanonical marriage, and his claims to both crowns were surrounded with illegalities and unlawful use of force.[52]

That Ferdinand united the kingdoms of Castile and León is unremarkable. That he willed them undivided to his oldest son, Alfonso, in 1252 is. In doing so, Ferdinand broke away from almost four centuries of well-established tradition of dividing the realms among male children, instead embracing primogeniture as the guiding criterion for royal succession.

This change in how the king thought of his possessions was deeply imbedded in a new awareness of his rule as extending over a territory, that is, over a defined and bounded expanse of land. This was most obvious in Ferdinand's last injunctions to his son, when he equated good rule with territorial expansion and indicated royal success was to be measured by the ability to hold on to recently acquired territory:

> Son, you are rich in lands and in many good vassals—more so than any other king in Christendom. Strive to do good and be good, for you assuredly have the means to do so. And he also said to him: "Sir, I leave you all the lands on this side of the sea which the Moors won from King Roderick of Spain. All this now lies within your power, one part of it conquered and the other laid under tribute. If you should manage to hold it all in the way in which I leave it to you, then you are as good a king as I; and if you should enlarge it, you are better than I; and if you should lose any of it, you are not as good as I."[53]

Before Alfonso VIII's and Ferdinand III's reigns, Castilian and Leonese kings thought of conquest, but they also thought of booty and tribute as the most profitable reward for their military campaigns. The victory at Las Navas de Tolosa in 1212 underscored the vulnerability of al-Andalus and opened the way to the south, but there was also a shift in how the kings viewed the land. In Ferdinand III's admonitions to his son, partition of the inheritance was clearly no longer acceptable. It was not yet a matter of recently conquered territory. The traditional realms themselves could no longer be partitioned or new kingdoms created out of conquest. In many ways, this paralleled similar developments in northern Europe that led to the inalienability of Crown lands, to undivided succession, and to the development of primogeniture.[54]

Other factors also influenced these developments. The Castilian royal family had become intertwined with other royal houses in western Europe from the late twelfth century onward. The example and influence of royal brides played a role in leading Castilian kings to new awareness of the relationship between the land and royal succession. The same development could be observed among the high nobility, the *ricos hombres*. These magnates began to acquire, as pointed out earlier, permanent and fairly contiguous estates in the late twelfth century, which led to the emergence of lineages and primogeniture. The appellation itself, *ricos hombres* (rich men), which only began to be employed regularly in thirteenth-century texts, serves as testimony to how contemporaries understood the link between property and power.

Tradition, however, always dies hard. Alfonso X's succession in 1252 was not an easy one. Ferdinand III's younger sons also wanted to be kings, and now there were many more kingdoms to be had. The secondborn, Henry, rose up in arms and caused enough complications in Alfonso X's early years as a ruler to delay the implementation of the new king's ambitious programs.[55] Henry's rebellion set the tone for a series of revolts by members of the royal family, either struggling over contested regencies or even, as occurred with Henry II in the second half of the fourteenth century and with Isabella in the late fifteenth, overthrowing the rightful heir for their own benefit. Not surprisingly, Alfonso X promoted legal reforms—the *Siete partidas* is the centerpiece—that emphasized primogeniture and an indivisible line of succession from eldest son to eldest son.[56] In this, he failed. When Alfonso X's heir, Ferdinand de la Cerda, died in 1275, leaving a small child of five (Alfonso de la Cerda), Alfonso X's second son, Sancho IV, wrested the crown from his minor nephew (though Sancho himself was only seventeen).[57] In fact, Sancho also wrested the crown from his father's head and the last years of Alfonso X's rule were consumed by the open hostility between father and son. This became so extreme that in a second will Alfonso disinherited Sancho and cursed him as a traitor.[58] The troubles this usurpation brought about were not quelled until the first half of the next century, when the Infantes de la Cerda reached a compromise with Alfonso XI, Sancho IV's grandson, by which they gave up their claims to the throne in return for a substantial bribe.

These stories, Henry's failed rebellion, Sancho's successful coup d'état, are grim reminders that the road toward primogeniture and the "rational" integration of land, rulership, and family were never smooth. In fact, all these shifts in values, above all those in political culture, were always contested territories, as the dynasty change in 1365 and Isabella's ascent in 1474 were to prove. Nonetheless, from the late twelfth century onward, lineages and primogeniture became the dominant means of preserving and transmitting property and asserting political and social power among the royal family and a handful of magnates. By the fourteenth century, entailments (*mayorazgos*) guaranteed the inalienability of most important noble property and served as a powerful factor in the construction of a high aristocratic caste: the magnates (*ricos hombres*) or, in the early modern period, the grandees.

Royal acceptance of primogeniture also eroded the peculiarities of individual kingdoms, ruled until then by the peripatetic energy of Castilian kings. In many respects, though, primogeniture and the end of the dividing of royal titles reflected not only shifts in values but Castile's rise to a hegemonic and undisputed position in western Iberia. The Castilian heartland's dominance over peripheral kingdoms could be fully articulated only through the establishment of a single line of descent. In the end, it was about changes in family structure and the links of the family to property, but it was also about the exercise of naked power.

CHAPTER SIX

HEAVENLY CONCERNS: CHARITY AND SALVATION

IN THE PRECEDING chapters of this book, I have sought to describe a shift in northern Castile's values system and the impact of these transformations on the material world, on language, and on the religious culture of Castilians. In this and the next chapter, I turn to very different concerns: charity, salvation, and political culture. These inquiries continue the trajectory of providing evidence for a shift in values in late twelfth- and early thirteenth-century Castile while moving away somewhat from earthbound issues into more religiously bound or heavenly concerns.

I have focused on hard-nosed problems of the here and now and of material life, whereas this and the next chapter address the construction of certain types of mental categories from the late twelfth century onward. This does not mean these topics are separate from those discussed earlier. Shifts in attitudes toward property, new concepts of primogeniture and of the family underpinned novel negotiations for salvation, changes in attitude toward the poor, as well as the manner in which Castilians imagined new ways of exercising power. All these transformations were intimately linked, and each has to be seen and understood in the context of the whole.

Revisiting the Wills

In chapter 2 I examined the way donations and wills changed in the late twelfth and early thirteenth centuries and sought to explain how and why these changes signaled new attitudes toward salvation—or, rather, to be more precise, how wills began to be utilized to negotiate for salvation.[1] Prior unrestricted donations were, of course, also meant as a form of bargaining for heaven, but in them, as shown earlier, how the donation was to be deployed was left entirely to ecclesiastical intermediaries. The latter assigned the property or income donated as best suited the needs and obligations of specific churches or monasteries. Again, as has been seen, from the late twelfth century onward, wills and even donations reflected the donors' greater concerns with controlling what they gave, and even their legacies—that is, the nature of what they gave—changed.

In revisiting wills in this chapter, I am mostly concerned with a series of extant testaments—not as many as one would expect but sufficient to give us insights into attitudes toward the indigent and toward charity— that made specific provisions for feeding and clothing the poor. These wills, beginning in the early thirteenth century and continuing into the early modern period, followed a distinct pattern in their negotiations for salvation.[2] What I am suggesting here is that in the years after 1200, how one gained salvation and thought of the afterlife often became intertwined with legacies to feed and clothe the poor. The latter became one more instrument in a complex strategy of salvation and of taxonomies of pious legacies (candles, masses, chaplaincies, pilgrimages, rescue of prisoners, and the like). Together with legal shifts throughout the realm and in municipal legal practices ordering how and to whom to give (see chapter 3), the wills' changing language and content also signal a significant change in attitudes toward those in need, toward charity itself, and toward what was understood as salvation.

Three important shifts took place. The first is obvious. From the early thirteenth century until the onset of the early modern era, wills came to include elaborate provisions to help the poor. This was markedly different from an earlier period in which such provisions are rarely found in either donations or the few extant wills (see table 2.1), but post-1200 legacies to feed and clothe the poor may also reflect a transformation in the institutions that generated our sources (from rural monasteries to urban municipal scribes). Changes in the method of redaction and in who dictated and wrote the extant wills in this period may reveal social and economic changes, but not necessarily a sweeping shift in how charity was articulated and practiced. In many respects, what one may observe after 1200 is a more active and direct attention—perhaps as the result of vigorous Mendicant preaching and new forms of religious observance sweeping the medieval West after the Fourth Lateran Council—to the Gospels' injunction to feed and clothe the poor. In that single sense, the wills demonstrate not a move from heaven to earth but a complex relationship that moved back and forth between acute concerns for the here and now, longings for the hereafter, and new forms of spirituality.

But—and this is an important qualification and the second shift I wish to signal in these introductory remarks—these stipulations to help the poor, as shall be seen below in detail, were imbedded in careful calculations and forms of investing in salvation that somewhat belied their altruistic intent. Furthermore, gifts to the poor may also be seen as purposeful gestures to assert one's social standing. We know that gifts, whether in the context of religious devotions, kin relations, or material exchanges, always carried with them a complex set of obligations and expectations.[3] Castilian wills belong in this category of giving as well. What, then, really did change? Clearly, as I have been arguing, the transformations were many and closely related. There were changes in methods of redaction, from ecclesiastical scribes to secular ones; changes in the very nature and language of the sources, from Latin to Castilian, from rural to urban; and a sharp increase in the number of wills drawn after 1200, and in the number of merchants, ecclesiastics (from bourgeois families), and other middling sorts writing wills. All these changes led to new ways of thinking about this world and the next, including the poor and the relationship between charity and salvation. This does not mean that the relationship did not exist before, or that in pre-twelfth-century Castile charity had been selfless. Nor does it mean that with a new mercantile mentality emerging, charity turned selfish, a matter purely of self-interest. It is apparent from many of the wills that those donating property or assigning income to feed and clothe the poor felt deeply that this was indeed the right and Christian thing to do.

A third and significant shift is the partial move, from the mid–thirteenth century onward, from private charity to municipal and royal assistance. Charitable donations in wills remained, as did ecclesiastical assistance, part of the fabric of life in medieval Castile, but, in the overall attempts to help the needy, these earlier forms became secondary to secular efforts. The latter, the actions of municipalities and the Crown to relieve poverty, turned the indigent into a social question. Though still couched in a highly idealized Christian discourse of charity, these secular attempts to help the poor obeyed other political imperatives (social control, order) and can be seen as a move from charity to welfare.

As sincere as many of the testators may have been in their legacies to the poor, the way they organized the distribution of their wealth and sought to make arrangements for the afterlife reveals new ways of thinking about their own relation to the sacred and the connection, to reiterate, between property and salvation. As noted above, the setting had changed. Donors and testators were now mostly urban dwellers, unlike the pre-1200 donors of rural provenance. The number of poor had increased dramatically, as social and economic conditions deteriorated in thirteenth-century Castile. The way of thinking about God and religion, under the impetus of Mendicant preaching and new spiritual concerns, had also changed. The coming together of these different social, cultural, and economic strands had a profound impact on the values and mentality of northern Castilians, and thus, as detailed below, on how they thought about the poor and their own salvation.

The Debate on Poverty

Charity cannot be isolated from poverty and the poor. Changes in ideas about what charity meant or who was deserving were linked to actual social changes in the nature of poverty in Castile, to the increase in the number of poor, and, far more significantly, to new ways of perceiving the poor, and of constructing new categories of poverty.[4] These issues, naturally, bring us back full circle to the issue of property and to what, I have argued, were new ways of thinking about and imagining the material world.

The debate in the twelfth and subsequent centuries over who was poor and how the poor were to be treated did not reach the virulence of the early modern period. In sixteenth-century Spain scholars and ecclesiastics, such as Domingo de Soto, Cristóbal Pérez de Herrera, and others, engaged in a passionate defense of the poor and a social critique of the harsh (and becoming harsher) treatment they received in early modern Europe. In their works, these writers sought to answer the attacks that other Catholic scholars, such as Juan Luis Vives, and Protestants, such as Martin Luther, had directed against begging and against the concept of almsgiving itself. Quoting from St. Paul's 1 Corinthians—one of the fundamental texts in the idealized definition of Christian charity—Pérez de Herrera stressed that to love one's neighbor, meaning specifically the poor, was, to a large degree, the foundation of individual salvation. Similarly, earlier in the sixteenth century, Domingo de Soto in his *Deliberación en la causa de los pobres* argued that almsgiving was indeed the duty of all Christians and that to deny charity to one's neighbor was a mortal sin.[5]

Implicitly and, at times, explicitly these early modern debates reflected the notion of a transformation in the way de Soto and Pérez de Herrera's contemporaries dealt with the poor as compared with what was thought to have been a more sympathetic treatment in an earlier time. This change was evident, in other parts of early modern Europe and in Spain itself, in the repressive early modern legislation against beggars and their freedom of movement, as well as in the attacks on indiscriminate almsgiving. In recent scholarship the debate on poverty and charity undertaken in sixteenth-century Spain has been viewed as an anomaly when compared to developments elsewhere in Europe. Because of Spain's supposed economic backwardness and/or its military and aristocratic ideology, historians such as Gutton, Lis, and Soly have argued that harsh condemnations of the idle and of begging, which could be found in the rest of precapitalist Europe, were either absent from the Iberian Peninsula or softened by the survival of indiscriminate charity. Linda Martz has already dealt aptly with these contentions, and there is no need here to rehearse her arguments.[6] The question remains, however, whether Spain's—and, in our own particular inquiry, Castile's—assumed tolerance toward the poor and benign views of charity in the early modern period were grounded on medieval precedents.

Michel Cavillac, for example, in his thorough and valuable introduction to Cristóbal Pérez de Herrera's *Amparo de pobres*, places special emphasis on the evangelical dignity of the poor in medieval Castile and on the survival of traditional Christian concepts of charity into the early modern period. Yet, as in France and England—where already in the Middle Ages the sanctity of poverty began to be rejected—in Castile we also find repressive measures against the poor after the disasters of the mid–fourteenth century, specifically the Plague. But in Castile, argues Cavillac, "the apostolic dignity of the poor had far deeper roots since it was supported by aristocratic disdain for manual work."[7] Besides stereotyping Spain, however, early modern apologists and recent scholars have been mistaken in this. The most perfunctory glance at the extant documentation for the period before 1350 shows that medieval Castile was not a place where the poor were invested with "apostolic dignity" or any kind of dignity for that matter. In many ways, both medieval Castile and early modern Spain were "different" from England and France—but not in the Castilians' treatment of the poor, which was far more complex than the black-and-white dichotomies presented in early modern polemical works.

If, as I argue, charity was imbedded in new strategies of salvation, and these, in turn, were deeply imbricated in new perceptions of the material world, then a shift in the Castilians' attitudes toward the poor and toward charity—which appears in the documentation in the late twelfth and early thirteenth centuries—gives us a window onto the development of a new system of values. One might examine those instances in which the sources show private charity—here understood to be mostly the feeding and clothing of the poor. Obviously as Christians medieval Castilians could not cast aside the mental baggage of centuries of Church teachings and the lessons taught almost daily by the Gospels, the Epistles, Church Fathers, and Mendicant preachers. As petty-noblemen, merchants, and landholders, they were also part of a world in the midst of important social, economic, and cultural changes. I contend that although Castilians, and men and women elsewhere in the medieval West, understood charity according to evangelical prescriptions, the way they practiced it, as revealed in their wills, showed important variations and a special emphasis on the social meaning and uses of charity. In Castile, at the moment of death—when charity must have been most poignantly urgent—those executing their wills most often left nothing to the poor, or did so in a limited, almost formalized fashion. I wish, therefore, to examine how and why private and even ecclesiastic feeding and clothing of the poor often turned into highly ceremonial and public displays, how charity was often deployed to promote social visibility and employed as another tool in the negotiations for heaven. In doing so, we can see how this ritualized giving reaffirmed the existing social distance between rich and poor, reminding those receiving charity of their place in a well-defined hierarchy of eating and dressing.

We must keep in mind other types of private charity that cannot be documented by historians. I refer here to the impromptu giving of alms and food to beggars in the street, on the steps outside the church, or at the door of the house, when the poor would ask for donations "for the love of God." Before 1350 there is little or no documentary evidence for this type of charity though one must assume it existed. Later, in early modern Spain, this direct charity would reach impressive and well-documented levels. In fifteenth-century Valladolid, members of the urban patriciate kept careful accounts of their daily almsgiving to the poor—which is, in itself, revealing as to new attitudes toward charity and in line with the move to itemize the material world. The count-duke of Olivares, as a child, was expected to devote 10 percent of his monthly expenditure to charity; and Ruth Behar has shown how, until recently, private charity was "institutionalized" in Leonese villages. Such activities, however, whether documented or not, only represent the other side of more ritualized forms of charity.[8]

Poverty and the Poor in Northern Castile before 1350

In the late Middle Ages, the kingdom of Castile had to face serious economic, social, and political problems. Endemic political and noble violence, troubled minorities, civil wars, and demographic dislocations beset the realm from the mid–thirteenth to the late fifteenth century.[9] But even before the great Christian conquests of western Andalusia in the 1230s, 1240s, and 1250s, which reoriented Castile toward al-Andalus and which, as I have argued elsewhere, triggered significant economic transformations,[10] the emergence of a mercantile culture in late twelfth-century Castile (see chapter 1) and the shift in how property was defined dramatically redefined the relationship between different social groups. In this specific instance, it altered the social and pious negotiations between middling sorts and the poor.

These transformations, economic and mental, influenced the number and status of the poor and forced Castilians to take notice of the needy in their midst and eventually make halfhearted attempts to help as well as control the poor. In thirteenth- and fourteenth-century Castile, it is next to impossible to define exactly what the sources meant by the "poor," or indeed to calculate their precise number. Although poor people certainly existed in the centuries before the twelfth, documentary references to the poor, even in monastic sources, and individual legacies to help feed and clothe the poor are rare before the 1220s. This, of course, does not mean that beggars were not found in the streets of Castilian cities, nor does it mean that almsgiving—whether impromptu giving in the street, or regulated monastic charity—did not exist. Rather, what I am seeking to pinpoint here is the process by which the poor came to signify something different for the rest of the population—not just as poor people per se, but as part of a complex strategy of salvation and social promotion.

Historians have already dealt with specific aspects of poverty, such as attitudes toward the poor and social assistance in medieval Castile, but to my knowledge no one has yet examined private charitable efforts as a whole nor has anyone studied charity in this period as part of broad social and cultural changes.[11] What is clear, however, is that the sources for the thirteenth and the first half of the fourteenth centuries seem to indicate that the number of poor was on the rise and their plight evident for anyone to see. This poverty was made more visible now by its concentration in urban centers.

With the growing number of poor people and their greater visibility came a transformation in social attitudes toward poverty. As occurred elsewhere in the West, hostile views of poverty and of the poor surfaced in the legal and literary sources of the period.[12] Even the Christian command of almsgiving was redefined, establishing gradations and categories that ran counter to the teachings of the Gospel. Alfonso X's *Siete partidas* recommended the following guidelines for those unable to give to all the needy: (1) help Christians before non-Christians; (2) help poor men captive in Moorish lands first; (3) help those in prison because of debt next; (4) choose the appropriate time to give alms; (5) do not give excessively or to just one person; rather divide alms among many; (6) be charitable to poor relatives before helping strangers; (7) give to the aged before the young; (8) help the handicapped or sick before the healthy; (9) give to noblemen or to those who were rich and have fallen in hard times (the *envergoñados*) before giving to those who have always been poor. Some of these recommendations sought a more rational utilization of almsgiving (help the aged, the poor, and the ill first), but others reflected the martial (help captives) and aristocratic character of Castilian society, as well as the social hierarchical distinctions in existence then.[13]

Moreover, Castilian legal codes from the late twelfth century onward, as seen in earlier chapters, sought to protect the family's right of inheritance, principally the rights of children and grandchildren, against excessive donations to the Church, often limiting donations to just one-fifth of the estate. Yet, in the typical ambivalence of the period, the *Partidas* allowed the testator to name the poor as his or her heirs, but establishing, once again, a clear order as to how the estate was to be divided: first, to those sick in hospitals and unable to beg; second, to the handicapped and orphan children; third, to the very old. Although still emphasizing the spiritual nature of charity, that is, that alms without love are no aid to salvation, the *Partidas* also commanded "that alms should not be given to those who were healthy and refused to work the land." Even if the *Partidas* may not have had the force of law until 1348, they represent the normative legal vision of that age. As such, Castilian law around the mid-thirteenth century reflected traditional concerns with the poor but also growing intolerance with the idle and with beggars. The harshness of such legal commands is also evident in the legislation of the cortes. Beginning as early as 1268 and continuing throughout the next century and a half, the edicts of the Castilian and Leonese cortes encouraged royal and municipal officials to arrest peasants who were idle but able-bodied and to force them to work.[14]

At the same time as these coercive measures were being introduced to force the idle to work and to define the deserving poor as just the aged, the sick, the very young, and the widowed, begging itself came under attack. In the fourteenth century even religious orders had to obtain royal licenses to beg, and in 1338, when Alfonso XI granted such a permit to the monks of Silos, he did so because "many men go around the land (begging) with lies and tricks, and the simple men of the land receive much harm." Moreover, late medieval Castile witnessed the emergence of a new category of poor, the *envergoñados*, poor men or women who, until recently, had had enough means to live. Not surprisingly, most of the relief allocations in the 1338 accounts of Santo Domingo de Silos, one of the most important Benedictine houses in northern Castile, were destined for the *envergoñados*.[15]

The construction of taxonomies of the poor—the deserving and the undeserving, the weak and the able-bodied, those who had money once and lost it (thus deserving a return to their former status) and those who never had anything (and were, therefore, to go to the bottom of the list)—reveals an intense preoccupation with the social and economic meaning of poverty and, far more important, with how certain forms of charity became more valuable in the social and moral economy of salvation. One could now quantify and itemize poverty and the poor. This sharply contrasted with the ideals of Christian charity still espoused in ecclesiastical and devotional texts and sermons.

In thirteenth- and early fourteenth-century Castile, poverty began to be justified "because of man's necessity to give alms as a way to cleanse his sins," but more often, as in the *Poema de Alfonso XI*, in the writings of López de Ayala, and in the *Libro de miseria de omne* (all written toward the middle or second half of the fourteenth century), poverty was the outcome of royal and noble violence and excessive fiscal demands.[16] In Juan Ruiz's *Libro de buen amor* (first half of the fourteenth century), where to be rich was certainly more desirable than to be poor, and to eat well far better than to lead an ascetic life, one also finds that giving to the poor is simply not enough. The giver must, in the true spirit of charity, share in the pain of the needy. This must be done with love; the gift must be both spiritual and material. And, yet, Juan Ruiz cannot help but emphasize, with a touch of irony, the reciprocity of all giving. As the poor scholar begs for money, he promises to his credulous listeners that "for every ration that you give, God will return a hundred," and in the bargain will even cure your cough.[17] Here, it is worth emphasizing Juan Ruiz's praise for what one may call—using modern terms—a solid investment strategy. Charity was indeed, in the new moral economy of salvation, a worthy investment. It brought spiritual returns far beyond the amount of money assigned to the poor.

Nonetheless, true charity must be, following the example of St. Martin of Tours, at least sharing fully what one has. In the *Libro de Apolonio* (mid–thirteenth century), a destitute fisherman finds king Apolonio on the shore reduced to abject poverty. After hearing his plight the fisherman presents Apolonio with half of his only garment and half of his meager dinner. In Gonzalo de Berceo's *Milagros de Nuestra Señora*, also dated to the mid–thirteenth century, a beggar for the love of God and the Virgin shared half of the alms he received with other beggars. At his death the Mother of God herself came to take him to heaven, where he was fed "as the angels are" with *candeal* (white wheat) bread.[18] This last reference is intriguing. One one hand, Berceo, one of the most representative authors of the period, provides examples of charitable acts he had borrowed from a well-known hagiographical tradition. On the other hand, the rewards of charity are not only heavenly but material as well. The poor beggar eats the bread, the pure white bread, consumed by the powerful (and by angels as well). Social hierarchy, so evident in eating and dressing, once again plays an important role in Berceo's representation of charity. In any case, for all the worthy descriptions of charity present in literary sources, I have yet to find a similar real example in the documents of thirteenth- and fourteenth-century northern Castile.

The diverse discourses of charity found in literary works and legal codes, tilting between idealized Christian charity and new ways of imagining help for the poor, was also inscribed in the language of these works. Castilian, deployed after the early 1200s in wills and donations, provided new meanings for such words as *charity* (*caridad*) and *alms* (*limosna*), which embraced the material aspects of giving to the poor as a means to salvation. In thirteenth- and fourteenth-century literary works, *limosna* denoted, as it does today, something material. This could be money, clothes, food, or drink. Such is the meaning in the *Libro de Apolonio*, in Berceo's *Milagros de Nuestra Señora*, in the *Vida de Santo Domingo de Silos*, in Don Juan Manuel's *Conde Lucanor* (a work from the first half of the fourteenth century), and in the *Libro de buen amor*. In the latter, alms are identified with the giving of material things, but one line makes distinction between *limosna* (alms) and *ración* (the giving of food).[19]

Charity (*caridad* or *caridat*) has a much wider semantic spread. As indicated before, charity was a thing of the spirit, love of one's fellow man, but in thirteenth-century Castilian it could have other meanings. The word appears in a series of literary works: the *Poema de mío Cid*, Berceo's *Milagros* and *Vida de San Millán*, and Ruiz's *Libro de buen amor*. Although the meaning is at times ambiguous, charity is still the Christian love for the poor, as seen in the examples above. Nonetheless, in Berceo's *Vida de San Millán*, the monks take some mourners to their refectory to eat and drink, that is, "fueron al refitorio, la caridad tomar"—they (the mourners, the poor) went to the refectory to take charity in the tangible form of food.[20]

Feeding and Clothing the Poor

My focus here is on settlements to feed and clothe the poor, but this narrow understanding of charity does not always correspond to how medieval men and women perceived almsgiving. Castilians in the Middle Ages may have thought they fulfilled their duties to Christ and the poor by giving to churches and monasteries.[21] That they thought about these matters somewhat differently after 1200 is yet another sign of a shift in values.

On 6 May 1107, the count Gómez González and his wife, Urraca, "pro remedio animarum nostrarum," donated land, a vineyard, and the parochial church of San Miguel to Michaeli Didaz, abbot of the monastery of San Miguel de Busto. The opening paragraph of the donation, obviously a formulaic device since it is often repeated verbatim elsewhere in Castile, expressed, in corrupted Latin, the general equating of pious and charitable gifts: "Evangelius preceptis ammonitus, in quibus dicitur: 'date elimosinam et omnia munda erunt vobis,' ceterisque in quibus subinfertur: 'abscondite elimosinam in sinu pauperis et ipsa orabit pro uobis ad Dominum, qui sicut aqua extinguit ignem ita elimosina extinguit peccatum,' ob peccatorum meorum diminitionem et infernalis ignis feci hanc scedulam."[22]

The theme of *elimosina* extinguishing sins as water does fire is common before the 1220s, but for all the references to the poor, donations were to the monastery, not directly to the secular poor. It can be argued, of course, that these types of indiscriminate giving did eventually make their way to the stomachs of the needy through monastic charity. After all, monastic property was in theory the patrimony of the poor. But this specific donation as well as many others in northern Castile show clearly that their purpose was not to feed or clothe beggars but to assure salvation and to fend off those menacing infernal fires.[23]

Churches, monasteries, and hospitals did care for the poor, but in the late Middle Ages, as shall be seen below, they did so in the same limited and ritual manner as their secular counterparts. In any case, in their charitable programs, here understood as feeding and clothing the poor, the Church could only make a small dent in the growing problem of poverty. Society's greater involvement was needed. After the 1250s, one begins to witness the first steps toward a partial transferring of ecclesiastical responsibility for the destitute to secular bodies. The Crown and municipal corporations took greater steps to provide legal services for the poor, set up hospitals, and create a royal almonry.[24] To a certain extent, however, this also marked a growing realization of the social benefits of controlling the poor through confinement in hospitals and through welfare, a transition from charity to control that paralleled the ceremonialization of private charity and pointed to similar developments in the early modern period.

Charity after 1200

A statistical sampling of donations and wills conveys a general idea of trends in pious and charitable giving and shows the minor role that feeding, clothing, and other such provisions to help the poor played in such bequests (see chapter 2). We must take, however, a closer look at the few wills that did include provisions for the poor. In them we can often see delineated the terms of such aid, as well as attitudes toward the poor.

Most of the wills included in table 2.1, as well as those examined below, were generated by northern Castile's urban middling sorts, clerics, merchants, or petty-nobles, but in most respects these testaments did not differ a great deal from those of kings and high nobility in how property was deployed in exchange for the hope of salvation.[25]

In the appendix, I provide a typology of legacies and a monetary breakdown—as far as the sources permit—of three wills in the regions of Logroño and Burgos. It may be useful to revisit these testaments and to focus, this time, on the specific aspects of donations to the poor. Before doing so, however, one must remember that such legacies played a secondary role to far more complex strategies of salvation. In fact, and this is worth reiterating, legacies to feed and clothe the poor, or other such provisions that directed part of one's income to benefit those who were neither relatives, friends, or ecclesiastical establishments, appeared, especially after the 1250s, in most wills, but as an afterthought, included among other more significant legacies. In most cases, bequests to the poor represented a small monetary investment in the wills' overall financial settlement.

Nonetheless, such deployment of the testator's income in the economy of salvation provides insights into the changing attitudes toward salvation and charity, toward the increasing tendency to fragment legacies, and toward the need to satisfy very distinct constituencies. Although the early thirteenth century has to be seen as a turning point in new testamentary concerns with the poor, the late thirteenth and fourteenth centuries witnessed a marked increase in these types of legacies until new forms of spirituality—devotion to the Eucharist, pious lectures, and the like—dictated new strategies.[26]

Sebastián, a cleric of the church of Santa María la Redonda in the Rioja region, dictated his will (written in Latin) in 1230. This was, as pointed out earlier, a very modest testament. For convenience, I have created categories of donations and measured them in terms of the money deployed to satisfy each of these categories. He bequeathed an annual income of 113 *sueldos* (*ss.*) for masses and anniversaries for his soul and the souls of his relatives. He also gave a one-time donation of 4 *mrs.*, a silver chalice to Santa María la Redonda, and a barrel of wine to Santa María de Roncesvalles. The latter donation clearly associated Sebastián with the devotional practices of the road to Compostela. Logroño was, after all, on the pilgrimage route, and, thus, linked commercially and culturally to the shrines along the road that meandered through most of France and northern Spain.

Bread, wine, meat, or fish—"all that is necessary"—was to be made available for funeral feasts on the very day of his burial, and on the second and seventh days after his death. The will does not specify who was to partake of this meal, though one must suppose it was restricted to fellow clerics and intimate relations. In what we may describe as pious social legacies, Sebastián gave annual amounts (3 *mrs.*, 24 *ds.*) to confraternities in Logroño. His donations to feed and clothe the poor were even smaller. For feeding the infirm at the hospital of Santa María de Rocamadour, Sebastián assigned 2 *ss.* annually. Similar amounts for the same purpose were given to the hospital of St. John "*ultra Iberum*" and to the hospital of St. Egidius respectively. He also made a one-time donation of 12 *ds.* to the lepers in the hospital of St. Lazarus, 6 *ss.* to give bread to the poor over his tomb, and 100 *cannas de cordat* (100 measures of very inexpensive cloth) to dress them.

These are very small amounts indeed, and those legacies that were given in perpetuity went mostly to institutions north of the Pyrenees and associated with the hospitable and caring activities of the pilgrimage road to Compostela. Most significant here is the amount allocated to give bread to the poor over Sebastián's tomb. Below, I examine in some detail what I describe as the symbolic gestures of an economy of salvation. For now, it is sufficient to imagine the scene: a small cemetery in northern Castile, a fresh tomb, the clerical administrators of Sebastián's will standing around his grave and ritualistically handing loaves of bread to a predetermined number of poor men and women. Giving charity beyond death, Sebastián linked his dead body into a system of religious and social gestures. Through them, he continued to bargain for salvation and reiterated his social distance from those who received his charity.

To his relatives and friends, he gave all his movable property and real estate outright (lands, vineyards, houses, clothing, wine barrels, bed and bed linen, pigeon coops, cupboards, all his books, and all his remaining cash). His family received the bulk of Sebastián's property, and legacies to churches and to the poor represented less than 10 percent of his entire estate.

Pedro García's will (1331) shows similar patterns in the distribution of legacies in the Rioja region. Pedro was a prebendary of the church of San Martín de Albelda (a small town near Logroño). Most of his property went to his nephews and nieces; small annual rents were directed to pay for anniversaries and masses for his soul and the soul of his son, oil for lamps to burn in churches, and other such pious bequests. As is the case in many ecclesiastical wills, there is ample evidence that the testators had children and even, in some instances, concubines. Such was the case of a Burgalese cleric, Pedro Ibáñez, who left a legacy to "the woman who lives with me."[27] In Pedro García's will, there is no evidence of a concubine (*barragana*), but he gave a crossbow—what was a prebendary doing with a crossbow?—to the friars of the monastery of the Trinity.

Pedro García gave a one-time legacy (the amount is not stated) to dress ten poor men and women with burlap (the least expensive cloth available in Castile) and to feed another ten with wine, bread, and meat until they were satisfied. This he did for his soul. His charity was not aimed at addressing the growing number of poor in northern Castile—the region faced enormous economic problems and civil unrest in the 1330s and 1340s—but, rather, including them, in a very limited fashion, in a complex negotiation for salvation.[28]

This was even more obvious in the case of Martín Ortiz de Agonçiello, a merchant and citizen of Logroño. In his will (see chapter 2), entered on 2 September 1347—a testament that, as has already been seen, was most likely composed in a moment of great illness and close to his death— Martín engaged in a series of gestures aimed at placating the impending fires of hell. Beyond the usual large number of masses, anniversaries, candles, and the like, Martín sent pilgrims, for his sake and that of his brother's soul, to Compostela, to the Church of San Salvador in Oviedo, to Santa María de Rocamadour, and to Santa María de Cameno, reflecting the enduring hold the pilgrimage to St. James's tomb had on the spiritual life of those who lived alongside the Milky Way.

Martín also apportioned 2 *mrs.* for rescuing captives and gave small amounts to other monasteries along the road to Compostela. His legacies to the poor were, however, quite restrictive. On the day of his death, thirty deserving poor men and women (*envergoñados*) were to be fed meat, wine, and bread. These were people he knew and with whom he may have, at one time, shared a similar social status. The *envergoñados* were still citizens of Logroño; thus, people who still held some property or rights within the town and who were, perhaps, too proud to beg in the streets. Martín also gave 100 *varas* (a *vara* was close to a yard) of sackcloth to dress a preselected number of poor men and women in his neighborhood. Again, these were people he knew and met often in his own neighborhood in Logroño. To his family and friends, as indicated previously, he gave the lion's share of his substantial estate.[29]

A good number of similar wills can be found for the period after 1250.[30] One could gloss them for several pages, but this may prove a rather tedious exercise. Some of these testaments included laconic entries on charity, as if the poor had been added as just another entry in a long list of activities aimed at securing forgiveness. In an instance or two, they appear as a last thought, as something one remembers at the very last minute and included just in case it may help the donor escape hell or purgatory. On 20 July 1315, Iohana Peres, a woman of some property (but not rich at all) entered her testament in Barcelona, even though she was from the area of Santander. This will provides an extreme example of fragmentation of donations to churches and monasteries. She distributed her income among thirty-one different institutions, her bequests ranging from 1 to 40 *mrs.*, but mostly between 3 and 5 *mrs.* Altogether 247 *mrs.* and two pounds of wax were dispersed among ecclesiastical institutions; other legacies went to friends and servants—including a teasing 10 *mrs.* to a certain García Amor "for he knows the sin he has from me." In the last entry of her will, Iohana Peres ordered that "whatever they find [left over] in the chest [that the executors use] to dress a poor man or woman as well as they could."[31]

Iohana Peres's example does not necessarily reflect the entire range of giving found in northern Castile. Severe wills, although still reserving the bulk of the property for relatives and friends, took careful steps to provide a larger and more regulated share of their largesse to the poor. A few examples will suffice to show how concerns with the afterlife became articulated through material concerns and with itemizing help to the poor.

Elaborate Legacies to Feed and Clothe the Poor

On 15 April 1289, Doña Elvira Alfonso donated most of her property in Varenciella de Río Pisuerga to the monastery of Santa María la Real de Aguilar de Campoo. She offered this gift "for her soul and the soul of her children and husband." The abbot of Santa María promised, in return, a perpetual chaplaincy for her soul in the altar of St. John. Moreover, on the day of Our Lady (15 August) fifty-four of the poor were to be fed every year. To this end Doña Elvira allocated one *fanega* and a half of wheat, two *cántaras* of wine, and a piece of mutton for every two poor men or women (sixteen pieces to the animal).[32] Doña Elvira's will allows us to reconstruct more or less the typical fare of the poor at these ritual feedings, and thus to contrast it with the diet of other social groups. This testament also permits a rough estimate of the actual cost of such giving, providing a way of assessing what percentage of the total cost of pious, charitable, and personal donations the feeding and clothing of the poor represented.

In her testament Doña Elvira requested wheat bread, which was not common fare for the destitute. Rye bread and a mix of grains (wheat, barley) was the bread of the poor: Doña Elvira's feast was one of those rare occasions on which the poor ate the bread of the rich. We do not know exactly how much grain made up the *fanega* at the standard measure of Aguilar de Campoo, but it probably averaged out to between half and three-quarters of a kilogram of bread per person. This is a good amount for a seating but short of the kilogram of bread (mostly wheat) assigned to monks daily (between twelve and fourteen *fanegas* a year) in 1338. Two *cántaras* of wine at sixteen or sixteen and a half liters per *cántara* gives us around 0.61 liters per person. Although an account of travelers from 1352 shows a daily consumption close to two liters per person, the poor sitting at Doña Elvira's anniversary table certainly had enough. As to meat, scholars have speculated that in the late sixteenth century a ram may have yielded around twelve kilograms per unit. Adhering to this calculation, we can assume around 375 grams of meat per person, or a bit more than a third of a kilogram. Since the meat was probably accompanied by greens or served in a stew, those poor people benefiting from Doña Elvira's largesse should have left the table, at least once a year, with full stomachs. These are, of course, very rough estimates and do not take into account waste or pilfering by ecclesiastical cooks or executors. And yet the price of such a meal was quite low. Even including expenses for preparation, vegetables, and other incidentals, the total budget for the meal should not have exceeded 30 *mrs*.[33]

If we accept this tentative estimate of the cost of charity, then the gulf between the diet of the well-to-do and the poor was indeed extreme. The comparison can be drawn simply in monetary terms. Thirty *mrs*. was a paltry sum in 1289 and contrasts vividly with the 2,000 *mrs*. granted to each magnate and his retinue for daily expenses when at the court of Ferdinand IV in the early fourteenth century, or the daily allowance for food of 150 *mrs*. each to which Alfonso X and his wife promised to adhere as a measure of austerity in 1258. At this level the differences between the rich and the poor, already evident in terms of clothing and housing, becomes more poignant in terms of income assigned for food.

Equally revealing are the two extant wills of Ferrant Pérez, a scribe in Frías, a small town north of Burgos. The first will dates from 1334, and it was drawn jointly with his wife, Catalina Ruiz. By then, Ferrant was already a prosperous municipal official with properties in and around Frías. We also know that some of his income derived from moneylending, for two months before drawing up his first will he had lent 900 *mrs*. to Ferrant Sánchez de Velasco, a powerful local nobleman. In their first testament, Ferrant and Catalina made important donations to the Augustinian monks of the hospital of Frías. In return, they requested burial at the hospital, a chaplain to "sing masses" for their souls forevermore, and anniversaries to be kept on the feast of Our Lady for Ferrant and on that of St. Catherine for Catalina. Moreover, they settled 20 *mrs*. annually on the hospital for the upkeep of a lamp, and 300 *mrs*. for repairs of the church. Finally, they made provisions for the clothing of fifteen poor men and women with cloth, half *sayal* (sackcloth), half *estopazo* (burlap).[34]

By 1344, when the second will was drawn, Catalina was already dead, and Ferrant's fortune had increased dramatically. The long list of debtors mentioned in the testament, his own debts, and the many references to transactions with Jewish moneylenders lead to the conclusion that Ferrant was an important usurer and perhaps an intermediary between Jewish bankers and Christian borrowers. By 1344, care for the poor had also become an important concern, a development that may have been closely linked to his usurious economic activities.

The new will opened with a bequest of up to 1,000 *mrs.* to build a hospital of stone with ten beds to house and feed the poor. Separate settlements were made to support spiritual services at the hospital chapel, wax for candles, oil for lamps, purchase of a chalice. To the monastery of San Vicente Ferrant gave 300 *mrs.*, and an equal amount to pay for five hundred masses because "he was a sinner and for those debts he owed and did not remember." There were other pious donations, including money to send men to Compostela, to Santa María de Roncesvalles, to Santa María de Rocamadour, and to Jerusalem. In addition, a modest contribution of 5 *mrs.* was made to the Crusade. These gestures, similar to those in some of the wills examined above, can be interpreted as a compromise between direct help for the poor and legacies to churches, that is, actions and donations outside the direct control of ecclesiastical administrators or that would benefit the needy directly.

In another entry, Ferrant ordered that his executors dress three hundred of the poor of Frías (half wool, half burlap), and that on the day they received their vestments they also be fed. The amount to be spent on clothing and feeding the poor is not spelled out, but a later entry in the will assigned 70 *mrs.* to dress ten poor people. If these figures hold for the other three hundred, then 2,100 *mrs.* were required to clothe them, plus additional income for food.[35]

I have found only one other will in northern Castile before 1350 in which wool is requested as a fabric to clothe the poor—other such donations explicitly asked for burlap or sackcloth. Coincidentally, the testament also dates from the 1340s, a period of great need in northern Castile. In 1349, in a will discussed earlier, Don Gonzalo Pérez, canon of the cathedral of Burgos, bequeathed funds for the foundation of a ten-bed hospital for the poor. He also left instructions for two hundred of the poor to be clothed, one hundred with wool and the other hundred with linen. This is the sole will, as far as I know, in which the poor are described as hungry. Gonzalo supplied his hospital with "good blankets, firewood to keep the poor warm, and enough food for the *pobres flacos*," literally, the thin poor but here meaning the hungry poor. He did this "for the honor of God, (so) that He would wish to forgive my sins." Elsewhere in the will, besides a multitude of masses, anniversaries, oil for church lamps, money for the Crusade, and more, Gonzalo provided funds to feed one hundred poor men. As with most wills in this period, however, settlements on relatives and friends took most of the estate. Moreover, Gonzalo, as we saw earlier, insisted that the chaplaincies he had endowed were to be reserved for his kin as long as there were living relatives, and, in their default, were to be held by citizens of Aguilar de Campoo, his hometown.[36]

The Ritualization of Charity: The Gestures of Salvation

Examples from wills do not bring us any closer to better understanding what medieval men and women intended to do in their testaments or why. Nor does the use of such an expression as the ceremonialization or ritualization of charity convey the complexities and pitfalls inherent in dealing with this topic. For one, ritualized giving implies perhaps an orderly transition from an ideal form of Christian charity and care—represented by the normative lives and examples of Christian saints—to the operative instrumentality of a later age, as manifested by a few surviving wills. In earlier sections of this chapter, I rejected positing such a transition. Nonetheless, there was a change in how wills and other pious donations articulated legacies or gifts to the poor. This transformation was, of course, neither simple nor orderly. After all, regardless how small a portion of the estate was bequeathed to the poor or for what reasons, the examples we have seen above are still manifestations of Christian charity. As such, they were far more vocal, in their careful assignment of gifts for the poor, than donations before 1200.

Part of the problem lies in the use of such words as *charity*—here meaning love—*ritual*, and *ceremonialization*. All three terms can be understood and misunderstood at diverse levels. Nor can we ignore the different cultural contexts to which we apply these terms. When defining *caritas* as Christian love, we refer to a peculiar kind of love, involving a triangular relation between the giver, the poor, and Christ. What happened to that triangular relationship in Castile after the 1220s is one of the topics of this book.

In Castile, long before 1350, the poor began to lose their charismatic value and often turned into a mere social and religious symbol. In this remaking of the triangle into a dual relationship between the donor (whether a private individual, a municipal corporation, or the Crown) and the needy, we have the basis for modern attitudes toward social assistance. And here it is worth noting the growing distinction between voluntary poverty, often assumed from positions of power and wealth, and the lot of the involuntary poor, a condition more often than not associated with weakness.

When speaking of rituals or ceremonialization of giving, we must consider actions that resulted from things other than beliefs. Clearly, there were and are today rituals that depend exclusively on the faithful repetition of certain words or the faithful performance of specific gestures. Examples are magical incantations, the mass, or the sacrament of baptism, all of which are ineffectual if words or gestures are missing. Most of the examples I have given above do not belong to this category of rituals, and if they do, only partially. Instead, the ceremonial feeding and clothing of the poor was often meant to convey a message to other human beings through a vocabulary of gestures and actions. This difference is crucial, for formalized charity allowed for insincerity. One gives, but not too much, and in such giving the donor reinforces the existence of social boundaries. Indeed, that in itself is part of the message. And this makes the range of possible actions wide and fluid, adaptable to differences of personality, circumstances, and messages.[37]

As we have already seen, to those near death or settling their affairs in anticipation of death in the period before the mid–fourteenth century, feeding and clothing the poor, though more frequent than in the centuries before 1200, was often only a secondary concern or no concern at all. In fact, it may have appeared merely as a function of that fragmentation of "good deeds" we see in wills drawn after the 1200s. Such dispositions almost invariably constituted a ritualized form of giving, ritualized in the sense indicated above.

Feeding and clothing a preselected and symbolic small number of the poor on the day of the donor's burial, on the anniversary of his or her death, or even over his or her tomb was in one sense a reciprocal arrangement: food for prayers, food and clothing for remembrance. The donors, however, may not have made these gifts because they loved or cared for the poor, but because the poor symbolized Christ. This notion was, of course, hardly peculiar to Castile or to the late Middle Ages and echoes the command of the tenth-century English *Regularis concordia*, which admonished the monks to administer the maundy "with the greatest care to the poor, in whom Christ shall be adored." At yet another level, these practices harked back to ancient and pre-Christian traditions that survive to this day throughout the world in the form of the wake or the offering of food at funerals.[38]

Furthermore, the gathering of canons, priests, and a number of the poor for a ceremonial feast on the day of the donor's burial spoke of the deceased's standing in the community. It showed others, beyond the grip of death, the extent of his or her wealth and piety. But the food the poor ate was different from the food eaten by the rich. The quality of the wine, often the quality of the bread, and the types of meat consumed by the poor at these ritual feasts were inferior to those served to the ecclesiastical administrators of private charity, inferior to what the donor himself had eaten before departing this world, and far inferior to what kings and magnates ate in late medieval Castile.

Their clothes were inferior as well. Dressed in burlap and sackcloth, ten, twelve, three hundred of the poor, symbolic representatives of Christ, came in ceremonial pilgrimage to partake of the funeral meal and to offer witness, to give confirmation by their clothes and by what they ate, to the rigid social hierarchy, the social boundaries that existed in Castile and elsewhere in the West at the dusk of the Middle Ages. The information on the eating habits and clothing of the northern Castilian bourgeoisie, the high nobility, and the royal court points to a pattern of conspicuous consumption, a pattern reflected in sumptuary legislation, travel and monastic accounts, and literary works from the mid–thirteenth century onward.[39]

The ordinances of the cortes dealing with these matters sought, often unsuccessfully, to restrain the eating, feasting, and clothing excesses of the high nobility and the ostentatious displays of the rising urban oligarchies. Yet, sumptuary edicts did not represent draconian measures; rather they were mild attempts at providing a ceiling to what appear to have been exaggerated and wasteful expenses.[40]

These nonnoble knights and merchants, who dressed in gold, silk, and scarlet cloths,[41] insisted, in those wills that included legacies to clothe the poor, on burlap and sackcloth, confirming the widening gulf between those above and those below. Thus, while donations to the poor here and there added to each person's heavenly account of good deeds, they also reinforced and sharpened, whether consciously or unconsciously, social distinctions in northern Castile, as they did elsewhere.

Of course, the poor did not depend exclusively on this so-called charity. Otherwise, they would have faced impossible conditions. Feeding and clothing the poor was largely the work of the Church but, increasingly after 1300, municipal corporations stepped in. And yet, in the twilight centuries between charity and welfare, between the scattered-shot approach to giving and the early attempts to rationalize assistance to the poor that marked the coming of the early modern period, monastic efforts showed the same tendencies toward ritualization observed above.

In monastic institutions, in this particular case Benedictine monasteries in northern Castile, the amounts dedicated to charity in 1338 were quite small when compared to other expenses. Moreover, the cost of administering monastic welfare was quite high, eating further into the monies or grain reserved for the needy. At the monastery of San Salvador de Oña, of 635 *fanegas* allotted to the office of the almonry only 429 were left for the poor after expenses. Of the total expenses of 5,290 *mrs.* assigned for alms annually, only 2,745 *mrs.* were left for charity while the other 2,545 *mrs.* went either to fatten the purses of those in charge or to cover general expenses. Of this money, the 200 *mrs.* reserved for clothing the almoner seems at first glance an obvious abuse, and a confirmation of the popular dictum that charity begins at home. Altogether, at Oña the total amount spent on charity represented 5.45 percent of the monastery's budget, and of that only 2.8 percent really went to the poor. Obviously, the monastery exercised its Christian duties in other ways: hospital care, teaching, burial of the poor, though some of these expenses were already included in the figures mentioned above.[42]

We must compare these expenses with what these same monks ate in 1338. As García González has shown, allocations for food and wine for the monks was one of the most important items in monastic budgets. Departing from strict adherence to St. Benedict's rule, meat was served around 160 days a year; in places such as San Pedro de Cardeña, near Burgos, the monks ate fish every day in addition to meat. Eggs were part of the menu three days a week at Santo Domingo de Silos, and vegetables, fruits, bread (one kilogram daily), and large quantities of wine (more than two liters per day) completed the rather splendid collation of monks. Altogether between 250 and 295 *mrs.* a year were necessary for feeding each monk, almost 100 *mrs.* more than was required to feed one poor person for a year according to the terms of Doña Elvira's will.[43]

The amounts that monasteries reserved for the poor allowed only a fraction of them to be fed. I have calculated the number of those fed at Oña to between fifty-two and fifty-five daily, but no provisions were made to accommodate emergencies, bad crops, or periods of extreme need. Likewise, the cathedral chapter of Segovia, which had forty canons, fed forty poor men and women daily, one for each canon, regardless of actual necessity, in a ceremonial act of charity.[44]

Hospitals, both ecclesiastical and secular, offered assistance as well, but here again many of these institutions did not yet have a clear concept of their functions. The case of Burgos is instructive in this respect. Although there were many hospitals in the late medieval period, some Burgalese hospitals took in the poor only when there were not enough pilgrims to fill their beds. In contrast, other institutions founded toward the mid–fourteenth century, such as the hospital endowed by Ferrant Pérez de Frías, were reserved exclusively for the needy. In Burgos proper, the Hospital del Rey, the largest in Castile, had as many as eighty-seven beds and two infirmaries in the late fifteenth century, but this was exceptional.

Most of the hospitals in Burgos and elsewhere in Castile in the late Middle Ages limited their number of beds to ten, twelve, or thirteen, symbolic numbers in remembrance of Christ and the apostles.[45]

In the early thirteenth century, with changes in the nature of poverty and a marked increase in the numbers of urban poor, municipal authorities began to take a more active role in social assistance. Often, however, this did not come about as a result of a well-planned program but was the outcome of pressing need or even direct requests by the poor. In 1312 the poor blind of Burgos petitioned the city council to build a hospital for them in the neighborhood of San Gil. We know the hospital was built, for in 1338 Alfonso XI ordered the municipal authorities to forbid those who were not blind from living there. By 1366 the hospital housed not only the blind but also the lame and deformed of the city, yet the unfortunate inmates were often robbed and subjected to other acts of violence.[46]

Conclusion

Contrary to recent views on the idealized nature of Castilian private charity and of the apostolic dignity of the poor in the period before 1350, evidence shows private donations for feeding and clothing the poor were meager and often ceremonialized forms of giving. Ecclesiastical and public efforts to deal with the poor suffered from the same defects. If, as Gregory of Nazianzus insisted, to feed and clothe the poor was to feed and clothe Christ, then in terms of the charitable dispositions at the end of one's life, poor Jesus would have had a difficult time in northern Castile—or throughout most of western Europe, for that matter.

From the earliest examples of wills and donations to those in the mid-thirteenth century we observe a fairly uniform pattern. Before 1200, pious donations and testaments followed a preset formula; gifts to ecclesiastical institutions were on the whole unrestricted. In them, expectations of prayers or masses for the souls of donors and their families were only implied. Seldom in this extensive documentation do we find direct settlement on the poor. By the first half of the thirteenth century, donations decreased in number, reflecting perhaps worsening economic conditions and new secular concerns. At the same time, testaments became very specific.

As indicated earlier, unrestricted giving was replaced by very explicit demands for masses, anniversaries, and other pious and charitable ends. In return, the donor settled a fixed amount of income or property on the Church. In those cases in which property was donated, however, a relative or executor kept some financial control. Moreover, most donors sought to spread their bequests among as many institutions as possible. Unlike the wills of an earlier period, the donor's family, friends, and business obligations—that is, his or her secular concerns—began to command the greatest attention.

Two important developments began to take shape in the cultural and social mental landscape of northern Castilians by the late twelfth and early thirteenth centuries. The first marked a shift in the perception of how one secured salvation or reduced one's time in purgatory. New strategies were conceived and implemented in obtaining those ends. The fragmentation of donations, and taking direct charge of one's heavenly concerns, away from ecclesiastical control, point to a new sense of individual responsibility and more hard-nosed and complex attitudes toward the here and now and the world to come. Although donors kept a very close rein on their property and sought to manage their material wealth beyond their deaths and for the overwhelming benefit of family and friends, their wills expressed new spiritual concerns and a more direct relationship to the actual work of salvation. This meant a new and profoundly distinct attitude toward the material world; it also meant new forms of individual piety and spirituality.

This perilous balancing act between heaven and earth in many cases, turned the poor into one more instrument in the increasingly frantic bargaining for salvation. As the poor grew in number threatening the social fabric and economic order, charity—often a limited, restricted, and ceremonialized charity—became one more tool in a larger strategy of salvation. But these new forms of charity, institutionalized now through wills and donations written in the vernacular by secular scribes, also mapped the boundaries of social difference and reiterated the social prominence of the testators in stunning and dramatic ways.

CHAPTER SEVEN

TOWARD A NEW CONCEPT OF POWER:

UNSACRED MONARCHY

CONCERNS WITH salvation and charity had their counterpart in the world of politics. Deeply intertwined with shifting notions of property, territorial boundaries, negotiations for salvation, and changing attitudes toward the poor, the kings of Castile, from the second half of the twelfth century onward, also began to restructure how regal power was exercised and represented. At the same time, Castilian chroniclers and intellectuals, most of them in the Crown's service, began or, in some cases, continued to construct an idealized image of Castile and its people. New concepts of royal authority—most of them secular in nature—were imbedded in economic and social transformations that occurred in Castile in the late twelfth and early thirteenth centuries (see chapter 1). This also formed part of a complex process through which Castilians began to forge a larger regional identity. Self-representation, both individual and collective, of king and people, required drawing new mental boundaries between one group and another. In many respects, these constructions of psychological and social borders paralleled, and not just as a chronological coincidence, the emergence of physical boundaries in the Castilian countryside.

Unlike the movement to define property spatially and to bargain for salvation that originated with the middling sorts, the transformations of political culture and communal self-representation came from the top down. One cannot fail, however, to notice the connections between the two. The former seems to precede and trigger the latter. In other words, when the kings of Castile began to conceive of their power as one requiring the discarding of rituals and ceremonies traditionally associated with their station, it may have been because in the late twelfth century the political climate, the very foundations of their power, had shifted as well. In this chapter, I wish to focus on two specific topics. First, I illustrate how, beginning in the mid–twelfth century, the kings of Castile-León abandoned the sacral trappings of ritual monarchy and instead embraced ceremonials and rites of power of a distinctive secular nature. I have examined these topics in detail elsewhere, but now I consider this transformation in the wider context of social and cultural change throughout the realm. Second, I focus on the practical and political counterparts to the ideological development of a martial and unsacred kingship—Castile's growing bureaucratization and laicization of its governmental structure. Were the two linked? What was the connection between the new ways of exercising royal authority and the day-to-day governance of the realm?

The Making of Unsacred Monarchy

The history of how the French kings became identified with ceremonies of anointing with holy oil and crowning has been documented elsewhere; this particular model of French kingship and, to a lesser extent, its English counterpart have long been held as worthy examples of sacral monarchy.[1] In these kingdoms, an unambiguous Christological and ecclesiastical symbology sought to place kings above their subjects, to command their loyalty and devotion, and to lay the foundations for the nation-state.[2] But French and English solutions to the question of regal power did not always apply to the historical realities of other medieval realms. In the southern lands of the greatest of the Hohenstaufen, Frederick II, as well as in the kingdoms of Castile-León and Portugal, ceremonies such as the anointing and crowning of kings by high church officials did not play the same significant role in the festive ceremonials marking heirs' ascent to royal title and power.

In an article published in *Annales E.S.C.* in 1984 I described how the kings of late medieval Castile, either consciously or unconsciously, refused to submit to the practices of anointing and crowning. Instead, with a few exceptions, these rulers chose other ways of heralding their assumption of power. Although there were ample historical precedents for sacral kingship in Castile, dating back to the Visigothic and Asturian monarchies, from the mid–twelfth century onward Castilian kings sought different means of legitimizing their authority.[3]

The kings of Castile-León rose to the throne by right of descent, by popular acclamation, or by force. There were no dauphins, waiting patiently for Reims to be liberated so that, by the charismatic mediation of sacred unction, they could be turned into kings. From Castile's inception in the eleventh century as a kingdom to the present king, few monarchs were either crowned or anointed. Pointedly, King Juan Carlos, the current king of Spain, was neither consecrated nor crowned. The few who were either had spurious claims to kingship or chose to do so for peculiar and personal reasons. Moreover, and this is worth emphasizing, in those exceptional instances in which crowning or anointing took place, neither the timing nor the nature of the ceremonies resembled the experiences in trans-Pyrenean realms. The crowning and anointing occurred long after the heir's assumption of power as king, in some cases by more than a decade. These ceremonies, therefore, were not intrinsic to the making of a king, but, as with Sancho IV (1284–95) and the first Trastámaras, they sought to legitimize usurpation of power and the setting aside or murder of the rightful heir or king.[4] Moreover, the mise-en-scène of the Castilian kings' crowning and anointing, whenever this took place, subverted the expected nature of the ceremonial. This was most evident in Alfonso XI's anointing and self-crowning in 1332, twenty years after his becoming king. Instead of being crowned by any of the high ecclesiastics present, Alfonso XI crowned himself; he also discarded the ordo that had been commissioned specifically for the ceremony, replacing it with a ritual that lessened clerical participation.

To put it bluntly, the kings of Castile did not depend on anointment and coronation, not even those few rulers who engineered such displays for their own political ends, to exercise their rule. Their power was not mediated by the Church or its representatives. Their passage to the title and authority of kingship was marked by symbols, rituals, and ceremonials of distinctive secular and martial flavor. I have described these symbols and ceremonies elsewhere; for the sake of brevity, I simply outline them here.

Throughout the Middle Ages, Castilian chroniclers and writers—and those engaged in producing iconographical representations of Castile's kings—emphasized the kings' martial role and successes against the Moors. New kings were often raised on a shield or a chair, a ceremony harkening back to Germanic war bands and the election of kings in the battlefield. They traced the source of their authority to "popular" election or acclamation. This included an exchange of oaths between the new king and representatives of the nobility, the clergy, and the towns gathered at special meetings of the cortes, as well as a public acclamation in an open square, accompanied by the raising of the standard of Castile to the traditional cry: "Castilla, Castilla, por el rey." Moreover, the kings of Castile insisted that no one else could knight them. After a vigil over their arms at the tomb of the Apostle St. James in Compostela, they girded their swords themselves. Later in the fourteenth century, they were knighted by the mechanical arm of an image of St. James.

My description and interpretations of the nature of late medieval kingship in Castile have not gone unchallenged. Although non-Spanish historians have more or less agreed with my conclusions, this has not been the case with some of their Spanish counterparts, above all, the talented and prolific scholar José Manuel Nieto Soria. While attempting to respond to his reservations—though Peter Linehan has already done so far more cogently and comprehensively than I can—I wish to focus on Castile's political transformation and expansion from roughly the late eleventh to the mid–thirteenth century.[5] I also place the shift from royal ceremonials, sacral trappings, crowning, and anointing to the demise (partial demise in some instances) of these rituals within the context of broader changes in Castile's system of values. There is a dramatic link between the emergence of royal primogeniture, undivided royal inheritance, and the construction of unsacred kingship—as well as the subsequent development of Castilian and Spanish history.

Nieto Soria's arguments in favor of a sacral monarchy are found in a short article, "La monarquía bajomedieval castellana: Una realeza sagrada?" and elaborated further in his book *Fundamentos ideológicos del poder real en Castilla, siglos XIII–XVI*. Through an exhaustive gleaning of the extant literary, legal, and documentary sources, Nieto Soria has sought to show how the kings of Castile utilized religious images to promote and define the nature of their power. These images he classifies into four separate groups: theocentric, sacralizing, moralizing, and organicist. Moreover, literary sources, from the thirteenth century on, describe the king in language pregnant with religious and Christological references. From the king "by the grace of God" to the monarch as the vicar of Christ, Nieto Soria mines late medieval sources to expose the close relation between the sovereign's image and religious ideology. And if the kings of Castile were not anointed or crowned, it was, Nieto Soria argues from the advantage of fifteenth-century sources, because God had done so directly and secretly without the need for public or ecclesiastical participation.[6]

I have several responses to these contentions. First, we cannot expect medieval rulers or their agents to abstain from a language rich in religious symbolism and metaphors. Sacral formulas and expressions, associations of the ruler with the divinity and with the Church's work, were an intrinsic part of the medieval cultural landscape. Just as we operate within the constraints and boundaries of our own culture, so did medieval men and women. This is simply common sense. While it is indeed peculiar that in most instances the Castilian monarchs refrained from actual public ceremonies of crowning and anointing, it is inconceivable that they would have sought to define and legitimize their power in a language other than that available. When Franco claimed to be caudillo of Spain "by the grace of God," the appeal to divine support sounded not only preposterous but anachronistic to most Western ears (though perhaps not so to all Spaniards then). Current cultural constructs and our own secular view of the nature and origin of political power could no longer accommodate such ideology in the West.

Second, although I firmly believe in the usefulness of literary texts as windows onto the mentality or, to use a better term, the values of a particular period, Nieto Soria's selective use of evidence to support his own point of view often neglects the political context in which these views were expressed. Most of his references come from the mid– to late fifteenth century, almost three centuries after the Castilian kings had successfully resisted clerical interference with the ceremonies marking their ascent to power. The writings of such figures as Diego de Varela, Fernando del Pulgar, Andrés Bernáldez, and others reflect a period of civil wars and noble violence. They expressed, above all, the yearning for order and for sources of authority capable of granting Castile a stability anchored in religion and law, not in force. Furthermore, a good number of Nieto Soria's examples reflect the apocalyptic agitation of late fifteenth-century Castile and the identification of the Catholic Monarchs—tamers of the nobility, restorers of the public order—with long-held messianic expectations that often had little to do with sacral monarchy.[7] Moreover, with some exceptions, these tractates or literary works came from the pens of ecclesiastics, people whose place in Castilian society had been progressively weakened and who, in Alvarus Pelagius's damning words, were "vile Spanish prelates, accustomed to kissing the king's hand."[8] To say that some in Castile entertained and sought to promote a different model of kingship is not the same as accepting that such a model existed, not even in petto, as the supposed divine and secret anointing of kings. To go from a quote dealing with ecclesiastical and divine unction of kings, taken from an ordo of coronation prepared for Alfonso XI and later discarded in toto by the king for the actual ceremonies, and then to claim, as Nieto Soria does, that this makes "comprehensible the attitude of Castilians toward [divine anointment] in the late Middle Ages" requires the kind of historical contortions for which great faith or gullibility is needed.[9]

Third, while Nieto Soria ignores the documentary evidence that contravenes his own point of view, he also sidesteps important iconographic references. While referring to my own work on royal seals, he neglects to point out that the kings of Castile chose thoroughly secular images: an equestrian design, a king on horseback with a naked sword and the symbols of castles and/or lions in the reverse. This stands in direct contrast to the majestic seals of other medieval kingdoms with rich sacral symbology.[10] And seals were among the most visible and readily accessible vehicles for royal propaganda, one over which the kings had, within the boundaries set by tradition and culture, direct control. If, as Nieto Soria claims, the rulers of Castile saw their power as having a religious basis, why did they so carefully avoid any ecclesiastical or sacral motifs, except the formulaic *rex Dei Gratiae*, and emphasize military and secular themes instead?

Finally, there is a clear distinction between a gleaning of legal and literary views supportive of sacral kingship and historical reality. Political events often stand in sharp contrast with literary ideals and legal formulations. What Nieto Soria argues were the "ideological foundations of royal power" belong, in part, to the realm of the ideal, with little reference to the way kings ruled and acted, above all, in the crucial period before 1250, before the full flowering of Alfonso X's *scriptorium*. But there is little purpose in continuing this old and tired debate. This digression has taken me away from the focus of this book, that is, to explore a shift in value systems.[11] For all Nieto Soria's objections, the question remains: Why were most kings of Castile neither anointed nor crowned?

The Origins of Nonsacral Monarchy

In weaving a narrative of historical events with close scrutiny of extant sources, one must seek to understand the motivations of contemporary chroniclers in their reconstruction of the past. These chroniclers provide us with insights into Castilian political reality but also into their own mind set and that of the social order from which they came. Even when they altered the historical evidence to serve their own purposes, they provide a vista into both the real and the idealized basis of kingly power. The chroniclers, who were eyewitnesses or close to the crucial period of the making of a nonsacral royal tradition in Castile, do not provide support for Nieto Soria's contentions at all. With some exceptions, their emphasis rests on the martial nature of the Castilian monarchy, not on its religious character. These contemporary accounts are closely linked, following each other's narratives almost to the letter, but with some politically important variations. In chronological order of composition they are Lucas de Tuy's *Chronicon mundi*, Rodrigo Ximénez de Rada's, *Historia de rebus Hispanie sive historia gothica*, and the *Primera crónica general*.[12] The first two were the works of high church dignitaries, the bishop of Tuy and the archbishop of Toledo respectively, and they were, as expected, written in Latin. The *Primera crónica general*, written in Castilian, was the "official" history, a version of Castile's past written by royal agents and financed by the Crown. In spite of its close links to the monarchy, the *Primera crónica general* contains sections that may also have served a particular ecclesiastical agenda, sometimes in opposition to royal interests. One must, therefore, tread carefully when dealing with these sources. Peter Linehan has already shown the extent to which Lucas de Tuy sought to promote León as a liturgical center. In the same vein, Rodrigo Ximénez de Rada made the interests of Toledo and its place as primate church of Spain central in his work. Some of the accounts found in the *Primera crónica general*, specifically the description of Alfonso VII's coronation and presumed anointing in 1135, may have aimed at legitimizing Sancho IV's illegal usurpation of the throne in 1284.[13] With these caveats, it may be useful to review the period between 1060 and 1252 for clues as to the origins of unsacred monarchy.

Sancho the Great's (1000–35) conquest of most of northwestern Iberia brought a new dynasty to the incipient kingdom of Castile and the ancient throne of León. These Navarrese rulers came with historical and legal traditions that differed from the Visigothic or Neo-Gothic claims of the last kings of León.[14] Popular acclamation of kings, the raising of a newly selected monarch on a shield or chair, and the "tendency . . . to partition [at the king's death] royal lands among the surviving children" were among the new features added to the political life of Christian Spain.[15] The Navarrese royal house also shunned any elaborate genealogies or idealization of its ancestry. In fact, in their myth of origins Yennego, an obscure knight nicknamed Ariesta, migrated from Bigorra into "Espanna." "In the plains of Navarre he won many skirmishes against the Moors so that the people of that land gathered together and made him king, because he was such a good warrior and could defend them well." Later Yennego's son, García, married Doña Urraca, a woman of royal lineage.[16] The simplicity and lack of pretense of this account is indeed disarming. But this short tale also shows unequivocally that heroic feats of arms, especially against the Moors, merited kingship, and that a warrior, or in this case the son of a warrior, was worthy of a princely marriage. Moreover, Yennego was elected by the people, without any references to sacral ceremonials or ecclesiastical intervention. Power ascended from below, sanctified by martial deeds.[17]

These early Navarrese kings of Castile-León bring to mind the late Merovingian rulers: their realms were divided among male heirs only to be reunited again by violence. Brother fought or betrayed brother, seeking to consolidate political rule. The sons of Fernando I (1035–65) provide a good example of these types of fratricidal wars. In the end, Alfonso VI (1065–1109), originally ruler of León, defeated or outlived his brothers, Sancho II of Castile (1065–72) and García, king of Galicia (1065–72). After some early reverses and exile in Muslim Toledo, Alfonso became the sole ruler of Castile, León, and Galicia in 1072.[18] The chroniclers emphasize the contractual nature of Alfonso VI's ascent to power. His claiming the throne of Castile after Sancho's assassination at the siege of Zamora could take place only after a frightful oath had been exacted. In a dramatic ceremony, captured for us in the chronicles and legends, the Cid pressed Alfonso VI to swear his innocence regarding Sancho II's death. Again, there is no reference to ecclesiastical presence—except that the oath was taken at the church of Santa Gadea of Burgos. Rather, the great lords, the warriors of Reconquest Castile, led by the Cid served as background to Alfonso VI's swearing.

After such a shaky beginning, Alfonso proved to be a competent and active ruler. Victories within the realm were soon followed by a dramatic advance of the frontier and by the taking of Toledo in 1085. With the conquest, the Castilian king appropriated anew the rich legacy of the Visigoths and their ancient claim to suzerainty over the entire peninsula. The Visigothic imperial tradition was also enjoined by the influx of newfangled ideas about the relations between the spiritual and the temporal in Christendom. These new concepts, intrinsic components of medieval culture in the late eleventh century and part of the broader debate within Christendom over Church reform and lay investiture, flowed into Spain with the Cluniacs and French pilgrims on their way to Santiago de Compostela.[19] But Alfonso VI resisted both tendencies, the Visigothic and the Frankish. The king refused to reinstate Toledo to its ancient place of prominence. As Peter Linehan has pointed out, the demands of the Reconquest prevailed and the king was not willing to make Toledo the capital of his newly enlarged realm.[20] Moreover, Alfonso's acclamation as emperor had nothing to do with sacral notions of kingship, nor was it invested with any special symbolic ceremonies. The laconic references in the chronicles are a bit misleading, for they seem to imply a link between the conquest of Toledo and the assumption of the imperial title. In fact, although such acclamation might be connected with former Visigothic claims, Bernard Reilly has shown that the title of emperor appears in Alfonso VI's charters as early as 1079, six years before the actual conquest of Toledo. Furthermore, Reilly argues, correctly I believe, that "Alfonso VI began . . . to make a formal claim to suzerainty over the entire peninsula, 'imperator totius hispaniae,' as a countermeasure to the papal pretensions and its accompanying strategy of dealing severally with the 'regibus, comitibus, ceterisque principibus Hyspaniae.'"[21] This is yet another instance of what was to become a constant theme for the Castilian Crown: its fierce resistance to any Church attempt to control or interfere in its affairs. In the case of Alfonso VI, this found an echo not only in the language of the chancery but in the king's public behavior as well. The *Primera crónica general*, embellishing the account of Rodrigo Ximénez de Rada, tells the story of the adoption of the Roman liturgy in Castile and the demise of the cherished Mozarabic ritual. Ordeals by test of arms and fire showed the people in attendance God's approval of the Mozarabic liturgy and his rejection of the foreign one. Yet, the king twice refused to accept the verdict of the ordeal and imposed the French (Roman or Cluniac) ritual on a reluctant realm because "quo volunt reges vadunt leges." In this case, the king's will superseded that of the Church and even God's judgments.[22] The exertion of royal will at the expense of the Church—most evident in their financial exactions—has vivid counterparts in later centuries. There are numerous examples of the slavish subservience of the Church to the will of the Castilian kings in the thirteenth and fourteenth centuries; such evidence is also available for the fifteenth and the early modern period.[23]

The question for us here is what Alfonso VI claimed as the source of his authority. The rule over Galicia, León, and Castile was his by inheritance, by conquest, and by approval of the magnates and knights assembled at Santa Gadea of Burgos. It had been confirmed and sanctified by the Toledan conquest. There was, therefore, no need for religious mediation or those ceremonies that elsewhere marked the making of a king. But the conquest of Toledo also changed Castile's relations with other political entities in Iberia—Aragon, Navarre, and al-Andalus—and thus the assumption of the imperial title without any of the concomitant sacral ceremonies and ecclesiastical investiture that defined imperial power in the West.

It did not matter that within a year of Toledo's conquest, the coming of the Almoravids checked any further expansion. Toledo remained Christian, and the political relations between Christians and Muslims, already tilting in favor of the former after the demise of the caliphate in the early 1030s, followed the course, with the unavoidable reverses and delays, that led to Las Navas de Tolosa in 1212 and the final confirmation of Christian hegemony in the peninsula. Toledo also signaled Castile's ascendancy within the peninsula, a primacy reflected in the acclamations of Alfonso VI and his grandson, Alfonso VII, as emperors.

In this context, the making of unsacred monarchy was closely related to the course of the Reconquest and Christian settlement in Muslim lands.[24] Perhaps the constant appeal to the Reconquest seems too convenient an explanation for our queries, but we ignore its long-term impact on Castilian society at our own peril. The dynamics of victory, territorial conquest, and the long and inexorable movement of the Christians south provided a setting unlike any other in the medieval West. The triumphalist vision that began shortly after the taking of Toledo and culminated with the conquest of Granada in 1492 made victory in the battlefield and the expansion of the realm's boundaries the ultimate test of a king and his most important source of legitimacy. Thus, the *Primera crónica general* ends with Fernando III's admonitions to his son (already cited in an earlier chapter but worth repeating here for a different purpose):

> Sir, I leave you all the lands on this side of the sea which the Moors won from King Roderick of Spain. All this now lies within your power, one part of it conquered and the other laid under tribute. If you should manage to hold it all in the way in which I leave it to you, then you are as good a king as I; and if you should enlarge it, you are better than I if you should lose any of it, you are not as good as I.[25]

Regardless of the pious pronouncements in literary and legal works, neither sanctity nor goodness nor defense of the faith were the marks of a true king. Rather, more practical considerations applied: What had been conquered lately? By how much had the income of the Crown increased? How well could the Moors be met on the battlefield? When the infante de la Cerda died, the magnates of Castile requested that Alfonso X ignore the rightful claims of the infante's young son and name the Infante Sancho as heir because "he defended the land and defeated the Moors."[26] These were precisely the standards worthy of kingship.

The chronicle of Alfonso X, a hostile account written long after the king's death, opens with a denunciation of the king, blaming him for the decline in tribute from the Moors. Alfonso X's unwise pretensions to the imperial throne and his appeals for papal support in this venture were roundly condemned as detracting from Castile's vital mission in its southern frontier.[27] More significantly, the march against al-Andalus in search of land and booty, whether actual or fictional, was also the raison d'être for the crown's merciless exploitation of the Church. I do not need to detail here the peculiar subservience of the Castilian church to the wills of Castilian kings; this has already been illustrated elsewhere.[28] Nor do I need to describe the command of financial and military resources that the rulers of Castile enjoyed long before the kings of England and France could count on such support for the "defense of the realm."[29]

In Castile the call was not for the defense of the realm but for the *ida contra los moros*, the offensive against the Moors. In periods during which the Reconquest was, for all practical purposes, paralyzed by internal difficulties, the *ida contra los moros* remained a call few, if any, could ignore or resist. We find impoverished monasteries and churches selling parts of their domain to meet the royal call for support of expeditions against the Moors. In the same vein, the charges against Henry IV of Castile, two hundred years later, emphasize his failure as a warrior and the lull in the war against Granada.

The dynamics of a military society and a military kingship also worked powerfully against the foundation of a capital, a sacral center, and a royal pantheon. The kingdom did not lack candidates for the honor of being the center of the realm, and individual kings sometimes sought, and failed, to identify their power and the fortunes of their dynasty with a particular city, church, or monastery.[30] Alfonso VI, Alfonso VIII, and Sancho IV attempted to establish royal pantheons, albeit without success, since kings were measured by their conquests. In most cases, monarchs chose to be buried, regardless of ecclesiastical plotting, where they had achieved some signal victory. Thus, Ferdinand III lies in Seville; Alfonso X requested that part of his body rest in Murcia, a place he had conquered as an Infante; and the Catholic Kings were buried in Granada.[31]

The military needs of the Reconquest prevented the establishment of a fixed capital, and the social and economic structures of the realm did not foster the creation of a permanent administrative center. Peripatetic kings, the rulers of Castile-León moved restlessly from the frontier with Islam to those regions of the kingdom where, far too frequently, rebellious magnates challenged the power of the Crown. Without a formalized feudal structure to provide the links that gradually tied vassals to the service of the Crown north of the Pyrenees, the Castilian kings found resting at one place dangerous indeed. How remarkable then that when a capital was finally chosen in the late sixteenth century, Philip II's willful selection of Madrid represented a city without any ancient religious or historical tradition: a new city. In present-day Spain, many medieval historians bend backward to emphasize the similarities between Castile and the trans-Pyrenean realms. It is inconceivable to think of French history without Paris, Saint-Denis, and Reims, of English history without London, Westminster, and Canterbury. Yet there were no such places in Castile. But let's return to our narrative of twelfth-century history and its impact in the making of unsacred monarchy and on shifts in the system of values.

Alfonso VII's coronation as emperor in 1135 did not, despite the fabrication of the *Primera crónica general*, involve anointment. Ximénez de Rada's description is of a self-coronation and nothing else.[32] This was, however, little more than an empty gesture. Within a few years, the new political realities of the peninsula showed that Castilian imperial ambitions could bear no fruit. By the mid–twelfth century, before Alfonso VII's death in 1157, Iberia was divided into five stable and enduring political units. With some variations and realignments, this political division remained fairly unaltered until the late fifteenth century.[33]

After Alfonso VII's death, Sancho III's (1157–58) untimely demise after a promising but short rule led to a period of anarchy and civil war during the minority of his son, Alfonso VIII (1158–1214). Sancho III's ascent to the throne was not marked by crowning or anointing, nor were those of his brother, Ferdinand II, when he wrested León from his infant nephew, or of Alfonso VIII. In these three instances, the throne was claimed by right of inheritance, and in the case of Ferdinand II, by a combination of illegal force and appeal to a tradition of division of the realms. The chronicles barely mention these crucial periods of transition from heir to king, nor is there any reference to the imperial title.[34]

Let's look briefly at the second half of the twelfth century. León, under Ferdinand II (1157–88) and Alfonso IX (1188–1230), made modest gains in the frontier. No spectacular victories were achieved; no great city was conquered, but the Leonese expansion opened Extremadura to Christian occupation and to their transhumant livestock. The Almoravids, after their early success, had fallen victim to the internal strife that characterized Andalusi politics; the Almohads were already on the move. Aragon and Catalonia waxed mightily on the eve of their Mediterranean expansion. Castile, meanwhile, lived through a long night of civil war and foreign interference. The task of restoring order and securing the realm fell to Alfonso VIII. Once he came of age, he was able to check the Leonese and Aragonese advances and to impose his will on the Castilian nobility.[35] More importantly, Alfonso VIII promoted Christian unity and a joint effort against the new threat of the Almohads.

In 1212, at Las Navas de Tolosa the Christian armies—the most important contingent being that of Castile—delivered a crushing blow to Muslim hopes. The course of the Reconquest was set once and for all to the advantage of the Christians, particularly Castile. Despite his victory, his connections with the English royal house (with its tradition of sacral kingship) through his wife, and the opening of Castile to the intellectual currents of the twelfth-century Renaissance, Alfonso VIII did not seek any ecclesiastical confirmation of his rule and role in the peninsula through anointing or crowning. Indeed he ruled by the grace of God and sought to establish a royal pantheon in his newly founded abbey of Las Huelgas in Burgos, but any attempt at linking his rule with the sacred ended there. For what else was needed to sanctify his rule than Las Navas de Tolosa? The large booty found in the tents of the fleeing Almohads, the green banners captured in battle and carried to decorate the royal pantheon at Las Huelgas—those were the proofs of the king's right to power. Similarly, Alfonso's grandson, Ferdinand III, rose to the throne of Castile in 1217 and to that of León in 1230 amid ceremonies of popular and martial character.[36]

This general overview of early Castilian history should not obscure the real difficulties we face in understanding the absence of anointing and crowning in Castile and the consequences for later Spanish history. As was the case in my *Annales* article, there are no fully satisfying explanations. Were these crownings and anointings or their absence willful acts or the result of circumstances? Obviously, Ferdinand III knew quite well what was at stake when he or his mother orchestrated the ceremonies of Valladolid; the military needs of the Reconquest, then at a critical juncture, and the need to appropriate ecclesiastical income may have dictated the nature of his initiations as king. In contrast, the conflictive minorities of Alfonso VIII and Alfonso XI may have precluded ceremonial events, marking the beginning of the reign. In the absence of royal memoirs or kingly instructions on these matters, we remain uncertain, for the extant material is not always a truthful guide to the past. Manuel Recuero Astray, for example, describes in lyrical terms the imperial coronation of Alfonso VII in 1135. This notice is followed by an extensive quote from an ordo for the coronation of kings, published by Berganza. The author explicitly links the events of 1135 and the existence of a supposed long tradition of anointing and crowning in Spain. In fact, no such tradition existed, and the ordo cited by Berganza had no actual use in Castile.[37] What the evidence does show, however, is that as far as we can verify, the kings did not accept or look favorably on ceremonies of initiation managed by priests. In that liminal world between the right to the throne by birth and election and the actual exercise of royal power, the intermediaries to royal authority were certainly not ecclesiastics. That is indeed remarkable, and if, as Nieto Soria claims, sacrality was bestowed on the king of Castile directly by God, that is still more remarkable, for it points to the conflict between the Church and political authority as to who wielded power and how this power was to be wielded. If the rulers of Castile assumed a religious mantle at all, it was always secondary to their role as warriors. Both the ecclesiastical and royal chronicles emphasized the military duties and accomplishments of the monarch over his piety or religiosity.

Although in my previous work I did not establish a causal link between unsacred monarchy and the political difficulties faced by the kings of Castile in the late Middle Ages, it should be noted that a kingship legitimized by military success, Gothic blood, and naked force opened the way for challenges, some of them successful, to established authority. On one hand, those with dubious claim could capture the throne, as Sancho IV, Henry II, and Isabella I did; on the other hand, unsacred monarchy may have served as a foundation for a stronger and more lasting form of authority. A comparison with France is revealing. The smooth course of royal succession in France under the Capetians and Valois kings contrasts with the uncertainty and near chaos of that of Castile throughout most of the Middle Ages. Yet, paradoxically, as Lloyd Moote has pointed out, sacral kingship provided the very argument for regicide and for overthrowing an un-christian monarch.[38] In the early modern period, the

Spanish monarchy did not have the ceremonies, throne, crown, or sacral trappings common to the English and French representations and display of royal power. Yet, even though the kings of Spain were not sacred, there was no regicide nor even attempts on their lives. There was no aristocratic Fronde, as was the case in France, nor a Puritanical revolution, as in England, where kings were surrounded by exquisite sacral ceremonies and divine attributes. Nonetheless, in both England and France, the assassin's dagger (in the cases of Henry III and Henry IV of France) or the possibility of being brought up in front of parliament and executed for treasonous behavior (as with Charles I in England) remained a threat to royal pretensions of absolutism. In the end, a monarchy founded on the exercise of force and legitimized by victory in the battlefields of the Reconquest proved far more effective in its uses of power than a monarchy sanctified by the hands of priests.

The slow emergence of unsacred monarchy, though dating to the vagaries of the Reconquest and internecine conflicts among royal heirs, had its roots in a complex series of developments. A new awareness of the land as physical space at the local level was paralleled by a shift from tribute gathering (the *parias*) to the conquest (or, in the ideologically laden language of the period, reconquest and/or crusade) of Muslim lands. Primogeniture and royal inheritance of the realms undivided coincided with new ways of conceiving royal authority. Unsacred kingship falls, in many respects, in the same category as the shift in values that led Castilians to articulate new strategies of salvation, in the perception and plotting of charity in more functional ways. A king who was neither crowned nor anointed, or, far more important, who did not depend on these ceremonies, or on the sanction of the Church to be king, fitted perfectly with the new Castilian attitudes toward property and the material world.

The Workings of Power

The rise of ever more complex bureaucracies throughout the medieval West has long attracted the attention of historians.[39] These scholars have correctly pointed out the role administrative innovations played in the emergence of the nation-state. In terms of new techniques of government, Castile may appear to have lagged behind England—perhaps the best-organized and -run realm in the late Middle Ages—or even France. But in Castile a fairly centralized royal authority came into being earlier than in other parts of the West despite these supposed administrative shortcomings. By the mid–thirteenth century, the kings of Castile were well under way to establishing a unified system of law throughout the

Fig. 10 Walls of Avila
A section of the twelfth-century walls of Avila show the strength of municipal governments. The militias of Avila played an important role in supporting the Crown against noble opposition. (Photo by Scarlett Freund)

realm. Royal taxes were collected and had been for quite a while before 1200. Representative assemblies, the cortes, were up and running as early as 1188, long before similar developments took place in France or England.[40]

But what was the connection between nonsacral kingship and the growing laic character of royal administration? This is certainly not a book about Castile's institutional history, nor of the workings of its bureaucracy, but some explanation is necessary for the shortcomings of Castile's bureaucracies.[41] The kingdom of the castles and lions suffered from the absence of a permanent administrative center or royal capital. It did not have—though Compostela, Toledo, and, to a lesser extent, Las Huelgas in Burgos competed for the privilege—a sacral or national religious center playing the unifying and inspirational role Reims and Canterbury did for the French and English monarchies. No royal archives have survived—the royal documentary depository in Avila (an odd choice for the royal archives) burned in the mid–fourteenth century. Yet, Castile was administratively innovative in a variety of ways.

Language

Castile is remarkable in that by the 1240s all government business, official communications, and royal charters began to be written in the ver-

Fig. 11 Alcázar of Segovia
Built on the ruins of an older medieval fortification, the alcázar of Segovia, which towered over the town, was a symbol of the power of monarchs and secular rulers over the Church. (Photo by Scarlett Freund)

nacular. Legal treatises, literary works, the official royal chronicles, the ordinances of the cortes, royal accounts, and all other items related to the kingdom as a whole, to Castilian culture, or to the business of everyday life throughout urban centers and villages were written in Castilian. Where did all the scribes, clerks, and royal agents writing in Castilian come from? The answer is very simple. They were often university-trained, studying in the new universities founded in the late twelfth and early thirteenth centuries. They came from the ranks of the middling sorts—were members of either the vast lesser nobility of Castile or the children of merchants and prosperous artisans. They were the same individuals who generated the wills and property transactions that signal the shift in values in early thirteenth-century Castile. We know this as a fact because we can match the names and families of urban elites and long-distance merchants with many of the names of royal officials.

From the 1220s onward, Castilian royal administration and local government was run, to a large extent, by the "good men," the so-called *omnes buenos*. After 1256, these were the people we would identify as nonnoble knights. They attended the meetings of the cortes as their towns' procurators. They served in the royal household as permanent representatives of urban interests, and they transacted all their official and unofficial business in Castilian. Jews and Muslims also appear as royal agents, but the actual running of the realm was firmly in the hands of the middling sorts.[42] Even for Jews and Muslims, the language of administration was Castilian.

The Laicization of Government

Although clergymen, as was the case elsewhere in the medieval West, still played a role in government, it is remarkable how many laymen appear—whenever we can make small attempts to reconstruct the Castilian bureaucracy in the thirteenth century—in the extant documentation. Bishops and powerful abbots still confirmed all the great royal charters. Important ecclesiastics frequented the royal court and accompanied the Castilian kings in their wanderings among their different realms and in their journeys to an embattled frontier, but the everyday running of royal affairs was solidly in lay hands. The fiscal accounts of the late 1280s and 1290s, magisterially edited with a substantive and insightful introduction by Francisco Hernández, show the overwhelming presence of secular agents.[43] Tax collecting and tax farming, perhaps the two most direct exercises of royal power, were shared by lay Christians and Jews. The latter were completely dependent on the Crown for their survival and profit, and this gave the Castilian kings an unprecedented control over fiscal matters. Even if medieval tax collection was always a somewhat chaotic affair, it was always under the royal thumb. The number of high-placed Jews who were executed at a moment of royal displeasure (or more likely at a moment of royal fiscal need) is a grim reminder of the danger of lofty positions. But it is also a reminder of the intrusive nature of royal power on financial matters.

Islam and Lay Administration

Several administrative positions throughout the realm were of Muslim provenance. The names of these offices denoted their Arabic origin: *alcalde, almotacén, alguacil, alferez,* and others in the thirteenth century. They tell us, through this semantic borrowing, how much Castilian administrative practices owed to Andalusi institutions. Although every one of these positions had a counterpart in northern European bureaucracies, there was in Castile a long understanding of the secular character of Islamic institutions and governmental practices—or, at least, of the subordination of religion to the ruler's needs. Although religion was not erased, it was placed in the service of the Crown long before such practices became common throughout the West.

Hermandades

In the end, the middling sorts came to play a vital role in the governance of the realm. In times of crisis, royal minorities, civil conflicts resulting from the predatory behavior of the high nobility, urban elites and hidalgos (the lower nobility sharing values and political interests with the urban nonnoble elites) joined together to protect the Crown and defend their own privileges. In 1282, 1284, 1295, 1302, and most forcefully in 1315, leagues of cities, allied sometimes with lesser nobles, stood as defenders of royal interests, as shadow governments against disorder, and as protectors of royal prerogatives.[44] We know who the leaders of these *hermandades* were. Their names, cities of origin, and sometimes even their trades were listed in the ordinances that established the great *hermandad* of 1315. The 1310s were a particularly wicked period of Castilian history; Alfonso XI was just a small child and several groups of magnates fought for control of the regency.[45] The four representatives of Burgos were clearly members of the town's mercantile elite, holders of municipal and royal offices, and members of the familial clans that dominated Burgos's social and political life. Those of Avila can also be traced back to the municipal administration and elite families of the town. Ecclesiastics played no role in forging the *hermandades* that included members of the bourgeoisie. Clergymen did organize their own leagues, but they sought to protect solely ecclesiastical privileges.

Just as clergymen were excluded from the rituals of monarchy, their presence in the day-to-day running of the realm was limited by the forceful claims of the middling sorts. Ecclesiastical power was also held in check by royal insistence on the king's supremacy within the realm. The middling sorts carried their part of the bargain to the end. They rallied to the side of the Crown again and again during times of trouble, while promoting their place and role in the financial and political governance of the realm. As a reward for their support, the kings guaranteed them the exercise of their oligarchical power within Castile's towns and cities.

CONCLUSION

~≈~

BORN TOWARD the end of the twelfth century, Gonzalo de Berceo (1195?–1265?) articulated many aspects of the change in values in his numerous poetical works. His life and works summarized the taste for new things with which this book begins. Berceo, Gonzalo's birthplace, was a small town on the road between Santo Domingo de la Calzada, the site of a reported miracle and thus an important stop on the pilgrimage route to Compostela, and the great and ancient monastery of San Millán de la Cogolla. Berceo grew up close to the pilgrimage thoroughfare, the fabled Milky Way, and spent most of his life in the shadows of the Benedictine monastery of San Millán. Also within walking distance was the stronghold of Clavijo, where, according to legend, St. James, riding a white horse, made his first appearance to snatch an almost certain Christian defeat from the hands of the Muslims. Berceo was also not far from Logroño or Nájera, both of which were referenced above. Sebastián, the cleric whose will opens the introduction to this book, was Gonzalo's contemporary and, in some respects, neighbor. Martín de Agonçiello, the well-to-do Logroño merchant whose will I discuss in two chapters and the appendix, lived up the road from Santo Domingo de la Calzada less than a century after Berceo's death.

Gonzalo de Berceo is the first Castilian poet we know by name. His new poetical style, the *mester de clerecía*, embraced a lyrical and learned approach that contrasted vividly with the heroic themes of epic poetry. The anonymous *Poema de mío Cid* (1206), written a few years before Berceo embarked on his literary career, reflected the influence of an epic tradition more than a century old in medieval Europe. Berceo's mostly hagiographical works epitomized the new values and mental attitudes. In his poetry, an avaricious peasant illegally moves boundary marks to acquire more land. References to purgatory abound, including a voyage to the new liminal space between heaven and hell and salutary instructions on how to lessen the term of punishment of those condemned to suffer there. In the *Milagros de Nuestra Señora* the usual pejorative representations of Jews surface; passages discussing the new standards of charity and devotion to the Virgin appear in his other poems. Departing from his glorification of older saintly figures—San Millán, Santo Domingo de Silos, Santa Oria, San Lorenzo—Berceo's work embraced the Mother of Christ as a pivotal figure in the new religious sensibilities sweeping Castile in the first half of the thirteenth century. The obvious counterpart to Berceo's *Milagros de Nuestra Señora*, a collection of twenty-five miracles brought about by the intercession of the Virgin, was of course Alfonso X's *Cantigas de Santa María*. The new Marian sanctuaries built by Alfonso X and his successors at Villasirga, Guadalupe, and other locations manifested a similar veneration for the Virgin.[1]

It is not far-fetched to link village communities' concern with the boundaries delineating their landholdings and the ongoing shift in spiritual values. The intensity with which families in their wills sought to protect their patrimony from dispersal, while at the same time negotiating for salvation or reduced time in purgatory, formed part of an interconnected, overarching plan. When the Castilian kings rejected sacral kingship, adopting a hard-nosed material approach to bolster their own unassailable power, the engine driving this new laic form was the same as the one operating at the local level. All of these changes were articulated in Castilian. Castilian became the language of material transactions, of new spiritual concerns, of new boundary definitions. It was the language of administration and power and the language of salvation and charity. It was the language that the anonymous poet of the *Poema de mío Cid* deployed so deftly. It was the language of Berceo.

After tracing the shift in attitudes toward property and the material world, toward salvation and charity, and the shift in family structure and royal power, the question remains: what led to these changes, and why did they occur in the late twelfth and early thirteenth centuries? A single explanation cannot be given for this vast array of changes. The transformation in Castile's mental landscape and in the economy of salvation and almsgiving formed part of an even more complex change in the individual and collective self-awareness of Castilians. The shift in values that transformed the way Castilians understood the materiality of property and their own relation to the sacred has to be seen as an elaborately textured tapestry, with multiple strands and colors. Emerging from a combination of social, economic, and political developments, these "webs of significance" laid the foundation for a distinctive Castilian culture in the late twelfth and early thirteenth centuries.

In the previous chapters, I raised the issue of secularization—albeit always qualifying the use of the term—and deployed the less controversial notion of laicization to describe the shifts in Castilian mentality and values. Neither term is fully satisfactory in this context, for neither fully explains this deep structural transformation. Fortunately, we do not have to reduce what took place in Castile to one explanatory term; nor are we obliged to accept a single causal relationship between event and cultural shift. Multitiered explanations, all intimately related, provide an intricate cultural grid that allows us to situate and understand the world-shattering descent from heaven to earth that thoroughly transformed the values of medieval men and women and spurred a reordering of Castilian society.

The growing rift between the secular and the spiritual cannot account for the specific ways in which Castile's values and language were transformed in the late twelfth and early thirteenth centuries. I do not wish here to seek refuge, as an untold number of Iberian historians have done, in the Reconquest as the deus ex machina of Spanish history. The struggle against Islam had a significant impact on the peninsula's history, but the changes I have attempted to describe here took place in northern Castile, far from the battlefields of the south, and were more a response to local conditions (systems of land tenure, the rapacity of urban elites, demographic pressure on specific areas) than to the mighty affairs being settled in al-Andalus. Throughout, particularly in chapter 1, I have pointed to more obvious explanations. In Castile, the rise of a money economy by the early twelfth century, the formation of urban mercantile elites in the cities along the road to Compostela in the eleventh century and their rise to power in the late twelfth, the intrusion of urban capital into the countryside by the early thirteenth century, and the final acceptance of primogeniture among the elite and especially all by the royal family, contributed to changing attitudes toward property, salvation, and the relation between the spiritual and the secular. The documentary evidence found in wills and legal codes and the change from Latin to Castilian tell us, incontrovertibly, of new ways of imagining property, of seeking rights of way, of obtaining salvation; they indicate that a significant shift in *mentalité*, in broad cultural values, was in the making.

The way Castilians and medieval men and women in other parts of Europe saw themselves, forged new economic roles, and discovered new forms of expressing their feelings for God and community—all of them corollaries to the new conceptions of property—signaled a sea change in Castilian mentality and history. After the 1220s, wills became the primary vehicle for the settlement of property among relatives and friends and for the disposition of financial obligations, replacing what must have been intervivos arrangements of an earlier age. Simply put, people began to hold on to their property—now thought of as tangible—a great deal longer, often well beyond death.

In their wills and writings, individuals also began to take a personal stake in their own salvation, using property to secure posthumous redemption. All of these transformations affected the way families formed lineages and carved places for themselves within society. These adjustments to the family coincided, in turn, with the way Castilian kings began to legitimize their authority and with the way Castilians began to represent themselves, their lands, and the minorities living in their midst. But something else was entirely new as well.

The shift in values or mentality—the new notions of property, salvation, and charity; the taste for the new; the early stages of laicization or secularization—also had dire consequences for the religious minorities and the political stability of the realm. It gave the Castilian language its first steps along the road that, almost three hundred years later, would make it "the language of empire" and lead to Castile's political and linguistic hegemony within Iberia. New ways of imagining property and the building of contiguous estates disrupted village communities throughout the land and set the stage for harsher social distinctions, eventually sharpening class differences and, in extreme cases, turning peasants who owned or had rights to the land into landless journeymen. These changes led to rigid social hierarchies in the cities and to the undisputed and "undemocratic" rule of a few patrician lineages. These changes turned nobles dependent on royal largesse for their privileges into *ricos hombres* (magnates) who, from this time until the reign of Isabella and Ferdinand, would visit untold violence on the land and its people, eventually threatening the monarchy itself. And with these changes, Castile joined the rest of the West in the broad social and cultural transformations that slowly but inexorably propelled medieval men and women from heaven to earth and ushered their world into modernity.

APPENDIX

THIS APPENDIX is self-explanatory. It contains the summary of three wills drawn from the published documentation of the collegiate churches of Albelda and Logroño in the Rioja area. The three testaments are typical of most wills from the 1230s onward. The first was drawn by Sebastián, a cleric of the church of Santa María la Redonda in the Rioja (1230). The second is from a *racionero* (prebendary) of the church of Albelda (1331), and the last is from a merchant of Logroño (1347). All three individuals settled the bulk of their property on relatives and friends, with pious donations to the Church in exchange for masses, anniversaries, and so forth, coming second, and legacies to feed and clothe the poor running a distant third.

For example, in Sebastián's will contributions to the poor amounted to an annual rent of 6 *sueldos*, plus the one-time expense of 6 *sueldos* (*ss.*), 12 *dineros* (*ds.*), and 100 *cannas de cordat* (a measure of cloth). In the 1230s one *marevedí* comprised 15 *ss*. Thus, each of his friends received far more than the poor did collectively. His relatives received lands, vineyards, and houses. Each of these properties alone was far more valuable than the ensemble of pious or charitable bequests. I have arranged the testamentary dispositions into the three distinctive groups identified above. Bequests within each category are listed in no discernible order, revealing the last wishes of the testator who named his beneficiaries as they came to mind.

Will of Sebastián, cleric of Santa María la Redonda (dated August 1230, in Latin)

A. Donations to relatives and friends

1. To Martín and Sebastián	a cupboard
2. To his brother	land
After his brother's death, the land would pass to Sebastián's sons and nephews.	

156 APPENDIX

3. To his nephew Martín From this income, Martín would pay 2 *ss*. annually for an anniversary mass in memory of Sebastián's mother (see below).	two *obradas* (a land measure) of vineyard
4. To his nephew John	a vineyard
5. To his sister	a vineyard
6. To Fray Peter (a Franciscan friar)	a piece of cloth
7. To Don Marco (a layman)	1 *mr*.
8. To Don Vicente de Palazuelos (a layman)	1 *mr*.
9. To Pedro Llares (a layman)	1 *mr*.
10. To Julián (a layman)	2 *mrs*.
11. To Petro Blanco (a layman)	1/2 *mr*.
12. To Martín Blanc (a layman)	1 *mr*.
13. To Don Nicolás (a layman)	10 *ss*.
14. To the sacristan of Santa María la Redonda	1 *plumazo*?
15. To his relatives for clothing	amount not specified
16. To John (his nephew), John (the clerk), and Don Gonzalo (his brother-in-law)	a piece of cloth from Stamford to each
17. To Martín (his nephew)	all his clothes, a cape, 5 wine barrels
18. To Sebastián (his nephew)	all his books
19. To the sons of John the carpenter	20 *ss*. each
20. To the sick sons of John the carpenter	25 *ss*. each
21. To Doña Milia's sons	20 *ss*. each
22. To his sister Bruna	50 *mrs*.
23. To the canons of Santa María la Redonda	1 *mr*. each
24. To the deacons of Santa María la Redonda	1/2 *mr*. each
25. To the subdeacons of Santa María la Redonda	2 *ss*. each

26. To the acolytes of Santa María la Redonda	1 *ss.* each
27. To his sister	his bed and bedclothes
28. To Domingo de Ubago (a layman)	5 *ss.*
29. To Sancha	1 *mr.*
30. To Sanchuela	1 *mr.*
31. To his grandchildren	half a house, a pigeon coop, and lands

B. Pious donations

1. To Santa María la Redonda for masses for his soul and his parents' souls, canons to visit and bless their tombs with holy water	30 *ss.* annually
2. To the collegiate chapter of the church of Logroño for food for the canons or the church in return for an anniversary mass	45 *ss.* annually
3. To Santa María la Redonda for wine and wheat (for hosts) to be used at masses	15 *ss.* annually
4. To the monastery of St. Prudentius, taken from the income from four pieces of land to pay for an anniversary mass	5 *ss.* annually
5. To clergymen of St. Bartholomew for his soul	10 *ss.* annually
6. To pay for an anniversary mass in memory of his nephew Martín	6 *ss.* annually
7. Anniversary mass for Sebastián's mother (see above)	2 *ss.* annually
8. To Santa María la Redonda	one silver chalice
9. To Santa María de Roncesvalles	one large wine barrel

10. To the chapter of the church of Logroño to sing an anniversary mass for Sebastián and supply bread, wine, meat or fish, and "all that is necessary" for a funeral feast for the canons on the day of Sebastián's burial and the second and seventh days after his death	4 *mrs.* plus other unspecified funds
11. To members of the brotherhood of Santa María Magdalen	3 *mrs.*
12. To the brotherhood of Santa María de Madres	12 *ds.*
13. To the brotherhood of St. Theodosius	12 *ds.*

C. Legacies to feed and clothe the poor

1. To the hospital of Santa María de Rocamadour to feed the infirm	2 *ss.* annually
2. To the hospital of St. John "ultra Iberum" to feed the infirm	2 *ss.* annually
3. To the hospital of St. Egidius to feed the infirm	2 *ss.* annually
4. To the hospital of St. Lazarus to feed the lepers	12 *ds.*
5. To give bread to the poor over his tomb	6 *ss.*
6. To clothe the poor	100 *cannas de cordat*

Will of Pedro García, prebendary of the church of San Martín de Albelda (dated May 1331, in Castilian)

A. Donations to relatives and friends

1. To García Yuánez, the priest	his best shoes
2. To his nephews (see below)	a vineyard
3. To his nieces	a vineyard
4. To his nephew Sancho	a piece of a vineyard

B. Pious donations

1. To San Martín for his burial in the cloister	amount not specified
2. To San Martín: rent from land in Sant Sol to pay for two anniversary masses for his soul	4 *mrs.* annually
3. To San Martín: rent from land in Sant Sol to pay for two anniversary masses for Pedro's son, Lope	2 *mrs.* annually
4. To John García, chaplain, to pray for Pedro's soul	1 *mr.*
5. To Rodrigo, chaplain, to pray for Pedro's soul	1 *mr.*
6. Three meals for above-mentioned chaplains and candles for his soul	amount not specified
7. To the chapter of Albelda for 30 masses	30 *mrs.*
8. For one liter of oil for every lamp in the churches of Albelda, Morçuero, Palazuelos, and Boyo	amount not specified
9. To the friars of the Trinity	his crossbow
10. To the church of Albelda for an anniversary mass for his sister Sancha. The income was drawn from a vineyard that was bequeathed to his nephews.	2 *mrs.* annually
11. To the monastery of Santa Caterina	"a vase of bees"
12. To Santa María de Veraça	2 liters of oil

C. Legacies to feed and clothe the poor

1. To clothe 10 poor men and women with burlap	amount not specified
2. To feed 10 poor men and women with bread, meat, and wine, until they are satisfied ("a que ffarten")	amount not specified

Will of Martín Ortiz de Agonçiello, citizen of Logroño (dated September 1347, in Castilian)

A. Donations to relatives and friends

1. To his brothers and two sisters	200 *mrs.* each
2. To his mother	cattle worth 1,000 *mrs.*
3. To his wife, two sons, and two nephews (orphans)	rest of his livestock
4. To his mother, his wife, his two children, and two nephews	rest of the wheat stored at Agonçiello to be divided equally
5. To his wife, children, and nephews	lands, vineyards, and houses in Agonçiello
6. To his mother	1,000 *mrs.* of the money in the strongbox
7. To his wife, children, and nephews	rest of the money in the strongbox
8. To his mother	his own house
9. To his wife	wine cellar
10. To his wife and children	houses in the neighborhood of San Gil
11. To his mother, wife, and children	linen cloth

B. Pious donations

1. To the church of San Bartolomé for burial next to his father's tomb	amount not stated
2. To the priests of San Bartolomé for daily bread, wine, and candles for prayers for his soul until one year after his death	around 1.095 *ds.*

3. To the sacristan of San Bartolomé for the ringing of bells on the day of his burial	2 *mrs.*
4. To send one pilgrim on foot to Compostela, another to San Salvador of Oviedo, another to Santa María de Rocamadour "for his soul." Two pilgrims were to go on foot to Santa María de Cameno, "one for his soul and another for his brother's soul."	amount not stated
5. For the building of San Bartolomé "for his soul"	20 *mrs.*
6. To San Bartolomé, to be inscribed in the calendar (of prayers)	20 *mrs.*
7. To clerics of San Bartolomé for pittance	20 *mrs.*
8. To clerics of San Bartolomé for sixty masses for the soul of his father	amount not stated
9. To clerics of San Bartolomé for sixty masses for the soul of his brother	amount not stated
10. To clerics of San Bartolomé for ninety masses for his own soul	amount not stated
11. To clerics of San Bartolomé for fifty masses for his own soul	amount not stated
12. To the Franciscan friars of Logroño for pittance, to pray for his soul, and to sing 100 masses for his soul	20 *mrs.*
13. To Fray Fernando de Castro to offer 30 masses for his soul	amount not stated
14. To Martín Sánchez, priest in Agonçiello, to sing masses for his soul and his father's soul	10 *mrs.*
15. To church of San Bartolomé for ten masses for the soul of Elvira Sánchez, his sister-in-law	amount not stated
16. To the churches of the Trinity and of Santa Eulalia in Barcelona and to the church of Santa María de Roncesvalles, for his soul	2 *mrs.* each
17. To the Crusade, for the rescue of captives in the land of the Moors	2 *mrs.*

18. To the neighbors of the *mercado* (the market quarters) to pray for his soul	5 *mrs.*
19. Wheat stored in Agonçiello: for an anniversary mass in memory of his father.	30 *coçuelos*
20. To the church of San Bartolomé, for an anniversary for himself, another for his father's soul and prayers at their tombs	rents from a vineyard
21. To Doña Toda, his mother-in-law, to pray for her soul	100 *mrs.*
22. To John Pérez, his brother-in-law, to pray for his soul	50 *mrs.*
23. To the brotherhood of Santa Catalina (of which he was a member) to pray for his soul	15 *mrs.*
24. To the brotherhood of San Gregorio (of which he was a member) to pray for his soul	2 *mrs.*

C. Legacies to feed and clothe the poor

1. To give thirty *pobres envergoñados*, citizens of Logroño, bread, wine, meat, or fish on the day of his death	amount not stated
2. To clothe preselected poor in his neighborhood	100 *varas* of sackcloth

D. Other

1. To the scribe who redacted his will	10 *mrs.*
2. To the church of San Bartolomé	175 *mrs.* owed from when he served the church as *mayordomo* (steward)

NOTES

PREFACE AND ACKNOWLEDGMENTS

1. The first of these articles appeared in *Past & Present* 77 (1977): 3–33; the second in *Annales E.S.C.* 3 (1979): 548–65.

2. I had already hinted at a change of mind in my *Crisis and Continuity: Land and Town in Late Medieval Castile* (Philadelphia, 1994), ch. 10; and more directly in "La conquista de Sevilla: Una revisión de la cuestión," in *Sevilla 1248: Congreso internacional commemorativo del 750 aniversario de la conquista de Sevilla por Fernando III, rey de Castilla y León* (Madrid, 2000), 267–77.

3. Peter Linehan, "Religion, Nationalism, and National Identity in Medieval Spain and Portugal," in *Religion and National Identity*, ed. S. Mews (Oxford, 1982), 161–99. See also his monumental *History and the Historians of Medieval Spain* (Oxford, 1993), above all, chs. 7–18, to which I refer throughout this book.

4. Jacques Le Goff, *The Birth of Purgatory*, trans. Arthur Goldhammer (Chicago, 1984). For a full bibliography of Le Goff's work, see the enchanting collection of essays about him in *L'ogre historien: Autour de Jacques Le Goff*, ed. Jacques Revel and Jean-Claude Schmitt (Paris, 1998), 337–53. Above all, see "Du ciel sur la terre: La mutation des valeurs du XIIe au XIIIe siècle dans l'Occident médiéval," in *Man in History: Anthropology History Today* (Moscow, 1990), 25–47 (in Russian). This is a version of a paper given at Columbia University.

5. For a bibliography of works on the twelfth century, see the introduction to this book.

6. Any perusal of these works will show that Iberia appears only peripherally, as a place northern scholars at the vanguard of cultural change went to study arcane knowledge or to "recover" Greek science and philosophy.

7. This is most obvious in the long debate on the origins of Romanesque architecture and the work of historians of architecture and art who trace most of the artistic development in northern Iberia to the influence of northern European, mostly French masters. On Spanish art, see Joaquín Yarza, *Historia del arte hispánico, vol. 2, La edad media* (Madrid, 1980).

8. See José María Soto Rábanos, ed., *Pensamiento medieval hispano: Homenaje a Horacio Santiago Otero*, 2 vols. (Madrid, 1998); Adeline Rucquoi, "Education et société dans la péninsule ibérique médiévale," *Histoire de l'education* 69 (1996): 3–36; and her "Las rutas del saber: España en el siglo XII," *Cuadernos de historia de España*, 75 (1998–99): 41–58.

INTRODUCTION

1. In 1230 Castile 300 *mrs.*, an amount close to that disposed by the will, would have bought enough land for two or three families, or two or three average houses in a town such as Burgos. It was not a sizable sum of money. An oven sold for 7 *mrs.* that same year and some small farms sold for as low as 6 *mrs.* Vineyards, in contrast, were far more expensive. For prices, see *Documentación del monasterio de Las Huelgas de Burgos, 1116–1230*, in *Fuentes medievales castellano-leonesas*, vol. 30 ed. José Manuel Lizoaín Garrido, (Burgos, 1985), docs. 239, 241, 247.

2. *Colección diplomática de las colegiatas de Albelda y Logroño*, vol. 1, 924–1399, ed. Eliseo Saínz Ripa (Logroño, 1981), 49–52. See appendix for a breakdown of Sebastián's will.

3. See Carlos M. N. Eire, *From Madrid to Purgatory: The Art and Craft of Dying in Sixteenth-Century Spain* (New York, 1995), in which he examines wills that followed the same pattern as those that began to be drawn in early thirteenth-century Castile.

4. Le Goff, commenting on one of the chapters in this book, noted the pitfalls of using terms such as *mentalité*, which are so broad as to describe nothing at all. See also Georges Duby, "L'histoire des systèmes de valeurs," *History and Theory* 11 (1962): 15–25.

5. I do not discuss this last topic in this book but have dealt with it elsewhere. See my "Representación: Castilla, los castellanoe y el Nuevo Mundo a finales de la edad media y principios de la moderna," in *Historia a debate: Medieval* (Santiago de Compostela, 1995), 63–77.

6. This discussion should be placed within the historiographical context of the so-called twelfth-century Renaissance. The work of Le Goff and other historians of the late Middle Ages supplies a much needed backdrop for the transformation of Castilian values or mentalities. The long list of works that have clearly sketched the deep cultural and social changes that swept most of western medieval Europe from the eleventh to the thirteenth century begins with Charles Homer Haskins's seminal book, *The Renaissance of the Twelfth Century*, first published in 1927 and reprinted numerous times; and continues with Richard W. Southern, *The Making of the Middle Ages* (first published in 1953; reprinted, New Haven, 1992); Georges Duby, *The Age of the Cathedrals: Art and Society, 980–1420* (first published in 1976 as *Le temps des cathedrals: L'art et la société, 980–1420*; reprinted, Chicago, 1981); Colin Morris, *The Discovery of the Individual, 1050–1200* (New York, 1972); Jacques Le Goff, *Les intellectuels au moyen âge* (first published in 1957; reprinted, Paris, 1985); Charles M. Radding, *A World Made by Men: Cognition and Society, 400–1200* (Chapel Hill, 1985), as well as his book with William W. Clark, *Medieval Architecture, Medieval Learning: Builders and Masters in the Age of Romanesque and Gothic* (New Haven, 1992); and Giles Constable, *The Reformation of the Twelfth Century* (Cambridge, 1996).

7. As Adeline Rucquoi has argued, the nature of Iberian culture and its intellectual concerns were deeply influenced by Arab thought and thus altogether different from northern European cultural developments. Important in this re-

writing of Castilian and Spanish medieval culture are the articles collected in José María Soto Rábanos, ed., *Pensamiento medieval hispano: Homenaje a Horacio Santiago Otero*, 2 vols. (Madrid, 1998). Rucquoi, in her excellent synthesis of learning in the Iberian Peninsula, argues for the strength of cultural production. See her "Education et société dans la péninsule ibérique médiévale," *Histoire de l'education* 69 (1996): 3–36; and her "Las rutas del saber: España en el siglo XII," *Cuadernos de historia de España* 95 (1998–99): 41–58. Notwithstanding her considerable and successful effort to illustrate the vigor of Iberian culture in this period, these developments must be seen in comparison to what was taking place elsewhere. That is to say, on one hand, Castile's culture was far more vital than the neglect of textbooks and general works on medieval culture would lead us to believe; on the other hand, although there were no universities, several cathedral schools, most notably Toledo and Santiago de Compostela, provided a high level of education to Castilians. But we find no great philosophical works comparable to those produced in Chartres in the twelfth century.

8. See Alan D. Deyermond, *The Middle Ages* (London, 1971), 55–106.

9. The Almoravids had invaded the peninsula from North Africa in the eleventh century, checking Christian advances into al-Andalus after 1085.

10. For the history of Alfonso VII's reign, see Bernard F. Reilly, *The Contest of Christian and Muslim Spain, 1031–1157* (Cambridge, 1992), 99–230; also his *The Kingdom of León-Castile under King Alfonso VII, 1126–1157* (Philadelphia, 1998). The history of other peninsular kingdoms in this period is found in Thomas N. Bisson, *The Medieval Crown of Aragon: A Short History* (Oxford, 1986), 31–57.

11. See Jean Gautier-Dalché, *Historia urbana de León y Castilla en la edad media, siglos IX–XIII* (Madrid, 1979), 67–134.

12. On the road to Compostela and its impact on Castilian urban life, see Luis Vázquez de Parga, José María Lacarra, and Juan Uría Ríu, *Las peregrinaciones a Santiago de Compostela*, 3 vols. (Madrid, 1948–49), 1: 465–97; Luis García de Valdeavellano, *Orígenes de la burguesía en la España medieval* (Madrid, 1969), 103–76.

13. See notes 6 and 7.

14. The reign of Alfonso VIII and his life have been studied by Julio González in *El reino de Castilla en la época de Alfonso VIII*, 3 vols. (Madrid, 1960). It awaits a new and more up-to-date study. There is no comprehensive work that examines the role of the battle at Las Navas de Tolosa in the subsequent history of the peninsula. The geographical location of the battlefield is significant. Las Navas lies a few kilometers north of the mountain pass of Despeñaperros and the opening into Andalusia, an almost liminal space between Muslim and Christian realms. This was also close to an important battle in the war of independence against the French in the early nineteenth century.

15. On Ferdinand III, see Julio González's excellent study, in *Reinado y diplomas de Fernando III*, 3 vols (Córdoba, 1980–86). The first volume is a study of Ferdinand's rule; the other two are an edition of documents from his reign.

16. For the later history of Castile-León, see José Angel García de Cortázar, *La época medieval: Historia de España alfaguara*, vol. 2 (Madrid, 1973). See also

Teofilo F. Ruiz, *Crisis and Continuity: Land and Town in Late Medieval Castile* (Philadelphia, 1994).

17. See Joseph F. O'Callaghan, *A History of Medieval Spain* (Ithaca, 1975); Angus MacKay, *Spain in the Middle Ages: From Frontier to Empire, 1000–1500* (London, 1977); Luis García de Valdeavellano, *Historia de España: Desde los orígenes a la baja edad media*, 2d ed. 1 vol. in 2. (Madrid, 1952); Adeline Rucquoi, *Histoire médiévale de la péninsule ibérique* (Paris, 1993).

18. See Peter Linehan, *The Spanish Church and the Papacy in the Thirteenth Century* (Cambridge, 1971), and his delightful and incisive *The Ladies of Zamora* (University Park, 1997).

19. In a suggestive and engaging book, *The Power of Kings: Monarchy and Religion in Europe, 1589–1715* (New Haven, 1999), Paul Kléber Monod argues the contrary, that is, that the rational state was born out of a refashioned Christian self. It is a most compelling presentation of the question of how Europe (or at least its governments) became secular.

20. Joseph R. Strayer, "The Laicization of French and English Society," in *Medieval Statecraft and the Perspectives of History*, ed. John F. Benton and Thomas N. Bisson (Princeton, 1971), 251–65; Georges Lagarde, *La naissance de l'ésprit laïque au declin du moyen âge*, 6 vols. (St. Paul-trois-Chateaux, 1934–46).

CHAPTER 1

1. Among González's notable contributions, one must emphasize *El reino de Castilla en la época de Alfonso VIII*, 3 vols. (Madrid, 1960); *Repartimiento de Sevilla: Estudio y edición* (fascimile reedition, Seville, 1993); and *Reinado y diplomas de Fernando III*, 3 vols. (Córdoba, 1980–86).

2. J. González, *Reinado y diplomas de Fernando III*, 1: 11–15; Pete Linehan, *The Spanish Church and the Papacy in the Thirteenth Century* (Cambridge, 1971), ch. 1.

3. On the spread of the Gothic and the craftsmen who built these new churches and cathedrals, see the numerous articles in P. Navascués, ed., *Medievalismo y neomedievalismo en la arquitectura española: Las catedrales de Castilla y León*, vol. 1 (Avila, 1994); Rafael Cómez, *Los constructores de la España medieval* (Sevilla, 2001), 120–58; F. Chueca Goitia, *Historia de la arquitectura española: Edad antigua y edad media* (Madrid, 1965).

4. On the writing of new histories and political treatises, see Peter Linehan, *History and the Historians of Medieval Spain* (Oxford, 1993), chs. 10–13. For literature, see A. Valbuena Prat, *Historia de la literatura española*, 3 vols. (Barcelona, 1960); *Poema del mío Cid*, ed. Ian Michael (Madrid, 1987), 11–64.

5. J. González, *Reinado y diplomas de Fernando III*, 1: 15–37.

6. Luis García de Valdeavellano, *Orígenes de la burguesía en la España medieval* (Madrid, 1969), 85–217.

7. On the pilgrimage and the pilgrimage road, see Luis Vázquez de Parga, José María Lacarra, and Juan Uría Ríu, *Las peregrinaciones a Santiago de Compostela*, 3 vols. (first published in 1948–49; reprinted with additional bibliography in Pamplona, 1993), 1: 47–70, 171–99, 465–98.

8. See T. F. Ruiz, "The Economic Structure of the Area of Burgos, 1200–1350" and "Two Patrician Families in Late Medieval Burgos: The Sarracín and the Bonifaz," in *The City and the Realm: Burgos and Castile, 1080–1492* (London, 1992), chs. 3 and 6; also Ruiz, *Crisis and Continuity: Land and Town in Late Medieval Castile* (Philadelphia, 1994), 196–234. For towns south of the pilgrimage road that did not develop into large commercial centers in this period, see Angel Barrios García, *Estructuras agrarias y de poder en Castilla: El ejemplo de Avila, 1085–1320*, 2 vols. (Salamanca, 1983–84), 1: 128–217.

9. On the Bonifaz, see Ruiz, "Two Patrician Families in Late Medieval Burgos," 10–13; Luciano Huidobro y Serna, "Nuevos datos sobre el almirante don Ramón Bonifaz y sus descendientes," *Boletín de la Comisión de Monumentos de Burgos* 113 (1950): 265. In 1228, Ramón Bonifaz, together with his cousin Guiralt Almeric, built a house on the street of Sanct Llorent for the very considerable sum of at least 6,000 mrs. The document bound the two cousins not to give any part of the houses if they were to "marry in Spain." *Documentación del monasterio de Las Huelgas de Burgos, 1116–1230*, ed. José Manuel Lizoaín Garrido, in *Fuentes medievales castellano-leonesas*, vol. 30 (Burgos, 1985), 334–36.

10. See Jean Gautier-Dalché, *Historia urbana de León y Castilla en la edad media, siglos IX–XIII* (Madrid, 1979), 97–134, 400–459; also Charles E. Dufourcq and J. Gautier-Dalché, *L' Espagne chrétienne au moyen âge* (Paris, 1957), 67–89.

11. On the settlement of towns in the Bay of Biscay area, see Salvador de Moxó, *Repoblación y sociedad en la España cristiana medieval* (Madrid, 1979), 275–78. On trade, see Ruiz, "Castilian Merchants in England, 1248–1350," in *The City and the Realm*, ch. 9; also Wendy R. Childs, *Anglo-Castilian Trade in the Later Middle Ages* (Manchester, 1978). On the reorientation of the Castilian economy, see Olivia R. Constable, *Trade and Traders in Muslim Spain: The Commercial Realignment of the Iberian Peninsula, 900–1500* (Cambridge, 1994), 209–58.

12. Ruiz, *Crisis and Continuity*, 196–234, 272–82.

13. On the communal rebellions along the road to Compostela, see Reyna Pastor, *Resistencias y luchas campesinas en la época del crecimiento y consolidación de la formación feudal: Castilla y León, siglos X–XIII* (Madrid, 1980), 113–56; and her "Las primeras rebeliones burguesas en Castilla y León, siglo XII: Análisis histórico-social de una coyuntura," in *Conflictos sociales y estancamiento económico en la España medieval* (Barcelona, 1973), 13–101; H. Salvador Martínez, *La rebelión de los Burgos* (Madrid, 1992), 155–348; Bernard F. Reilly, *The Kingdom of León-Castile under Queen Urraca, 1109–1126* (Princeton, 1982), 110–15. For revolts north of the Pyrenees and the establishment of communes, see the descriptions in *Self and Society in Medieval France: The Memoirs of Abbot Guibert of Nogent*, ed. John F. Benton (New York, 1970), 167–90. Also Fritz Rörig, *The Medieval Town* (Berkeley, 1971), 15–29.

14. See Joseph F. O'Callaghan, *The Cortes of Castile-León, 1188–1350* (Philadelphia, 1989), 9–19. In fact, the gatherings of the royal curia did not become a cortes until representatives of the cities and towns of León and Castile were chosen and voted on levying taxes.

15. See James F. Powers, *A Society Organized for War: The Iberian Municipal Militias in the Central Middle Ages, 1000–1284* (Berkeley, 1988), 40–67. See also the thorough and pioneer series of studies by Carmela Pescador, "La caballería popular en León y Castilla," *Cuadernos de historia de España* 33–34 (1961): 101–238; 35–36 (1962): 56–201; 37–38 (1963): 88–198; 39–40 (1964): 169–260.

16. For charity and parliamentary representation, see chapter 6 and notes 13 and 14 above.

17. On the emergence of the bourgeoisie along the road to Compostela, see García de Valdeavellano, *Orígenes de la burguesía*; and my *Crisis and Continuity*, chs. 6–9.

18. For the monetary history of Castile, see James J. Todesca, "What Touches All: Coinage and Monetary Policy in León-Castile to 1230" (PhD thesis, Fordham University, 1996), chs. 9 and 10. This is indeed a formidable work, and one truly deserving publication. See also Octavio Gil Farrés, *Historia de la moneda española*, 2d ed. (Madrid, 1976); Jean Gautier-Dalché, "L'histoire monétaire de l'Espagne septentrionale et centrale du IXe au XIIe siècles: Quelques réflexions sur divers problèmes," *Anuario de estudios medievales* 6 (1969): 43–95; Luis García de Valdeavellano, "La moneda y la economía de cambio en la península ibérica durante los siglos IX, X y XI: Notas para la historia económica de España en la edad media," *Moneda y crédito: Revista de economía* 10 (1944): 26–43.

19. On the first cortes, see Francisco Hernández, "Las cortes de Toledo de 1207," in *Las cortes de Castilla y León en la edad media*, 2 vols. (Valladolid, 1988), 1: 221–63; Ruiz, *Crisis and Continuity*, chs. 7 and 8.

20. O'Callaghan, *The Cortes of Castile-León*, 18, 187–91; also Angus MacKay, "Las cortes de Castilla y León y la historia monetaria," in *Las cortes de Castilla y León en la edad media*, 1: 377–426. See also Thomas N. Bisson, *Conservation of Coinage: Monetary Exploitation and Its Restraint in France, Catalonia, and Aragon, c.* A.D. 1000–1225 (Oxford, 1979).

21. See a series of essays on this topic in *El arte del alguarismo*, ed. Betsabé Caunedo del Potro and Ricardo Córdoba de la Llave (Salamanca, 2000), 38–65. See also Alain Boreau, "La construction ontologique de la mesure du temps chez Robert Kilwardby, ca. 1210–1279," in *La rationalisation du temps au XIII siècle: Musique et mentalités*, ed. Marcel Pères (Grâne, 1998), 31–45; and his paper "Calendars and the Instrumentalization of Time in XIIIth Century Scholastic Thought," given at the Calendar Reform and Religious Reformation Conference, UCLA 24 January 2003.

22. Vázquez de Parga, Lacarra, and Uría Ríu, *Las peregrinaciones a Santiago de Compostela*, 1: 76–77; 2: 152.

23. For the Dominicans, whose history in Castile preceded that of the Franciscans and who were, unlike the latter, already very active in Castile before 1250, see Francisco García Serrano, *Preachers of the City: The Expansion of the Dominican Order in Castile, 1217–1348* (New Orleans, 1997), 23–94; Peter Linehan, "A Tale of Two Cities: Capitular Burgos and Mendicant Burgos in the Thirteenth Century," in *Church and City, 1000–1500: Essays in Honour of Christopher Brooke*, ed. David Abulafia et al. (Cambridge, 1992), 81–110; and his *Ladies of*

NOTES TO CHAPTER 1   169

Zamora (University Park, 1997), ch. 1. See also Ricardo García-Villoslada, ed., *Historia de la iglesia en España*, 5 vols. (Madrid, 1979–82), 2-2: 125–74.

24. See Linehan, *The Spanish Church and the Papacy*, 276–321. Also García-Villoslada, ed., *Historia de la iglesia en España*, 2-2: 329–31, 419–62.

25. Jacques Le Goff, *The Birth of Purgatory*, trans. Arthur Goldhammer (Chicago, 1984), 167–68, 289–333, 368. The 1230 will from Logroño already cited (see my introduction and appendix) is one of our earliest examples of dispersal of donations.

26. Ibid., 134.

27. See Ariel Guiance, *Los discursos sobre la muerte en la Castilla medieval, siglos VII–XV* (Valladolid, 1998), 218–28; Philippe Ariès, "Le purgatoire et la cosmologie de l'au-delà," *Annales E.S.C.* 1 (1983): 151–57; Jean Pierre Maussaut, "La vision de l'au-delà au moyen âge: A propos d'un ouvrage récent (Jacques Le Goff, *La naissance du purgatoire*)," *Le moyen âge* 91 (1985): 75–86; E. Megier, "Deux exemples de prepurgatoire chez les historiens: A propos de *La naissance du purgatoire* de Jacques Le Goff," *Cahiers de civilisation médiévale* 28 (1985): 45–62.

28. Guiance, *Los discursos sobre la muerte*, 219–21.

29. Ibid., 221–27.

30. Ibid., 223.

31. Gonzalo de Berceo, *Milagros de Nuestra Señora*, ed. Daniel Devoto, 7th ed. (Madrid, 1982), 54: "un huerto que valía de sueldos muchos pares" (a garden worth many pairs of *sueldos*).

32. Ibid., 54–58. Guiance, *Los discursos de la muerte*, 221–22.

33. Some examples of fifteenth-century wills can be found in *Un linaje abulense en el siglo XV: Doña María Dávila*, ed. Carmelo Luis López 4 vols. (Avila, 1997–98), 1: 140–41; 2: 115–18. See also María del Carmen Carlé, *Una sociedad del siglo XV: Los castellanos en sus testamentos* (Buenos Aires, 1993).

34. See William James Entwistle, *The Spanish Language, Together with Portuguese, Catalan, and Basque* (London, 1936; reprinted, 1962); Rafael Lapesa, *Historia de la lengua española*, 6th ed. (Madrid, 1965); Ramón Menéndez Pidal, *Orígenes del español: Estado lingüístico de la península ibérica hasta el siglo XI* (Madrid, 1950).

35. Alan D. Deyermond, *The Middle Ages* (London, 1971), 55–106.

36. One example will suffice. Ferrand Martínez was a royal scribe in Burgos in 1278. He also served as procurator for the cathedral chapter of the city, collected tithes for the Crown in 1293–94, served as representative of the municipal council of Burgos in 1295 and 1304, and became *merino* of the city late in life in 1313. See T. F. Ruiz, "Burgos: Society and Royal Power, 1250–1350" (Ph.D. diss., Princeton, 1974), 318–19.

37. See Joseph F. O'Callaghan, *The Learned King: The Reign of Alfonso X of Castile* (Philadelphia, 1993). O'Callaghan argues that the *Partidas* were, in fact, the law of the land (though not officially promulgated), p. 37. For the rebellion of the nobility in the early 1270s, see *The Learned King*, 214–33.

38. T. F. Ruiz, "The Transformation of the Castilian Municipalities: The Case of Burgos, 1248–1350," *Past & Present* 77 (1977): 3–33.

39. J. González, *Reinado y diplomas de Fernando III*, 2: 391–93.
40. Ibid., 2: 536–37.
41. *Documentos de los archivos catedralicio y diocesano de Salamanca, siglos XII–XIII*, ed. José Luis Martín et al. (Salamanca, 1977), 296–338.
42. For scribes, see my *Crisis and Continuity*, 190–92.
43. Linehan, *History and The Historians of Medieval Spain*, 350–58. See Lucas de Tuy, *Chronicon mundi*, ed. Andreas Schottus, in *Hispania illustrata*, 4 vols. (Frankfurt, 1608), 4: 1–116. There is a Spanish translation that contains some later interpolations and changes by Julio Puyol, ed., *Crónica de España* (Madrid, 1926). Rodrigo Ximénez de Rada, *Historia de rebus Hispanie*, ed. F. de Lorenzana, in *Opera* (Madrid, 1793; reprinted, Valencia, 1968), 1–208.
44. *Primera crónica general*, ed. Ramón Menéndez Pidal, 2 vols. (Madrid, 1956); *Poema de Fernán González*, ed. John Lihani (East Lansing, 1991).
45. For a full discussion of these topics, see my "Representación: Castilla, los castellanos y el Nuevo Mundo a finales de la edad media y principios de la moderna," *Historia a debate: Medieval* (Santiago de Compostela, 1995), 63–77.
46. On the submission of the Castilian Church to the Crown, see Linehan, *The Spanish Church and the Papacy*, 102–6, 186, 224, 240.
47. See my "Unsacred Monarchy: The Kings of Castile in the Late Middle Ages," in *Rites of Power: Symbolism, Ritual, and Politics since the Middle Ages*, ed. Sean Wilentz (Philadelphia, 1985), 109–44. Also Linehan, *History and the Historians of Medieval Spain*, 413–660.
48. See Américo Castro, *La realidad histórica*, 2d ed. (Mexico, 1962), 38–39.
49. For the reign of Alfonso X and his legal, literary, and scientific contributions, see O'Callaghan, *The Learned King*, 131–46; Robert I. Burns, ed., *Emperor of Culture: Alfonso X the Learned of Castile and the Thirteenth-Century Renaissance* (Philadelphia, 1990).

CHAPTER 2

1. *Colección diplomática de las colegiatas de Albelda y Logroño*, vol. 1, 924–1399, ed. Eliseo Saínz Ripa (Logroño, 1981), 269–73 (2 September 1347). This work is hereafter cited a *Albelda y Logroña*. For *envergoñados*, the deserving poor, see Linda Martz, *Poverty and Welfare in Habsburg Spain: The Example of Toledo* (Cambridge, 1983). See also appendix.
2. See Carlos M. N. Eire, *From Madrid to Purgatory: The Art and Craft of Dying in Sixteenth-Century Spain* (New York, 1995). For an example of later wills, similar to those summarized above, see the testament of Doña María de Velasco (6 March 1505) and Doña Ana de Mendoza (9 March 1559) in Manuel de Castro, *Real monasterio de Santa Clara de Palencia II: Apéndice documental* (Palencia, 1983), 20–30, 112–15.
3. This is a modern typology, which I make here to distinguish between specific categories. Medieval men and women saw charity as yet another way to seek salvation.
4. On Seville in the thirteenth century and the role of the Genoese, see Antonio Ballesteros y Beretta, *Sevilla en el siglo XIII* (Madrid, 1913); Miguel Angel

Ladero Quesada, *Historia de Sevilla*, vol. 2, *La ciudad medieval, 1248–1492* (Seville, 1976), 81–100, 126–30; and the excellent book by Antonio Collantes de Terán, *Sevilla en la baja edad media: La ciudad y sus hombres* (Seville, 1977), 214–18.

5. I owe a great debt to Cynthia Chamberlin and Gregory Milton for information on Seville and Santa Coloma respectively. For Seville and notarial culture, see Pilar Ostos and María Luisa Pardo, *Documentos y notarios de Sevilla en el siglo XIII*, Acta Notariarum Hispaniae, no. 4 (Madrid, 1989), 22–30, 34–48. As Chamberlin pointed out to me in an extensive written commentary on an earlier paper dealing with this topic, the word *notario* does not appear in Seville's documents until 1329. As she contends, scribes in Seville and Toledo performed all the functions of notaries, but there was something in the word that made it unacceptable. She suggests the association of *notario* with papal interference and the Castilian rejection of foreign intrusion, especially by the Church. On Santa Coloma, the topic of Milton's doctoral dissertation, see *Inventari dels protocols notarials de l'arxiu històric arxidiocesà de Tarragona*, ed. S. Ramon i Vinyes and M. Fuentes i Gasso (Barcelona, 1987). See also Robert I. Burns, *Jews in the Notarial Culture: Latinate Wills in Mediterranean Spain, 1250–1350* (Berkeley, 1996) and his extensive bibliography therein. Most of these works, however, explore notarial culture in Catalonia and other areas of the Crown of Aragon. For other parts of Europe, see Anne-Marie Landès-Mallet, *La famille en Rouergue au moyen âge, 1269–1345: Etude de la pratique notariale* (Rouen, 1985); *De scriptis notarorum, s. XI–XV*, Rubrica no. 3, Diplomàtica no. 1 (Barcelona, 1989). For the *Partidas*, see *Las siete partidas* ed. Robert I. Burns, trans. Samuel P. Scott, 5 vols. (Philadelphia, 2001), partida 3, title 18, laws 8, 54; title 19.

6. For a good example of the use of extensive medieval archival resources in the Mediterranean basin, see Daniel L. Smail, *Imaginary Cartographies: Possession and Identity in Late Medieval Marseille* (Ithaca, 1999), 20–29, 69–94. See also Samuel K. Cohn, *Death and Property in Siena, 1205–1800: Strategies for the Afterlife* (Baltimore, 1988).

7. The extant wills and donations come in toto from ecclesiastical holdings, retained because they included legacies of property or income that had been donated to a particular church or monastery, or that eventually became part of the ecclesiastical domain. As with most medieval sources, however, these probably represent only a fraction of a far larger documentation. For the use of wills as a source for medieval history, see W. K. Jordan, *Philanthropy in England, 1480–1660: A Study of the Changing Pattern of English Social Aspirations* (New York, 1959), 22; Joel T. Rosenthal, *The Purchase of Paradise: Gift Giving and the Aristocracy, 1307–1485* (London, 1972), 29, 81. See also María del Carmen Carlé, *Una sociedad del siglo XV: Los castellanos en sus testamentos* (Buenos Aires, 1993); Louis de Charrin, *Les testaments de la region de Montpellier au moyen âge* (Ambilly, 1961); Margarita Cantera y Montenegro, "Derecho y sociedad en la Rioja bajomedieval a través de los testamentos, siglos XIII–XV," *Hispania* 165 (1987): 33–82; Steven Epstein, *Wills and Wealth in Medieval Genoa, 1150–1250* (Cambridge, 1984); For further bibliography on these topics, see below.

8. See *Cartulario de San Millán de la Cogolla, 759–1076*, ed. Antonio Ubieta

Arteta (Valencia, 1976), 30 (c. 884), 411 (1076); *Documentación del monasterio de San Salvador de Oña, 1032–1284*, ed. Isabel Oceja Gonzalo in *Fuentes medievales castellano-leonesas (FMCL)*, vol. 3 (Burgos, 1983), 68–69 (29 June 1198).

9. *Documentación del monasterio de San Zoilo de Carrión 1047–1300*, ed. Julio A. Pérez Celada, in *FMCL*, vol. 100 (Palencia, 1986), 53–54 (30 October 1137).

10. Ibid., 168–69 (? March 1225).

11. See Michel Mollat, *Les pauvres au moyen âge* (Paris, 1978), 53; Rosenthal, *The Purchase of Paradise*, 10, 29.

12. For a rare use of the word *testamentum* in an earlier document, see a chart of Raimundo II, bishop of Palencia, regulating how the bishops of Palencia were to draw their testaments, in *Documentación de la catedral de Palencia, 1035–1247*, ed. Teresa Abajo Martín, in *FMCL*, vol. 103 (Palencia, 1986), 194–97 (20 May 1183).

13. In Aragón, there are many early examples of testaments and donations that combined gifts to monasteries and provisions for relatives. See, for instance, *Documentación medieval de Leire, siglos IX a XII*, ed. Angel J. Martín (Pamplona, 1983). See donation *post obitum*, 155–56 (1074); on 27 April 1085 Sancha Garcés combined donations to the monastery of Leire "pro remedio anime mee" with legacies to her children, 170–71. See also *Colección diplomática de la catedral de Huesca*, ed. Antonio Durán Gudiol, 2 vols. (Saragossa, 1965), 1: 19–20 (576?), 26–27 (922), 31 (14 April 1035); also *Colección diplomática de Irache*, ed. José María Lacarra, 2 vols. (Saragossa, 1965), 1: 63–64 (1 January 1071); 64–66 (6 August 1072).

14. *Cartulario de Santo Toribio de Liébana*, ed. Luis Sánchez Belda (Madrid, 1948), 6 (1 June 826), 53–55 (23 January 941). Work hereafter cited as *Liébana*.

15. *Albelda y Logroño*, 24 (c. 947).

16. *Documentación de la catedral de Burgos, 804–1183*, ed. José Manuel Garrido Garrido, in *FMCL*, vol. 13 (Burgos, 1983), 34–39 (1 December 1053).

17. The best example of the latter is the monastery of Las Huelgas in Burgos. Founded by Alfonso VIII and Queen Eleanor, the ruler of the monastery, the lady of Las Huelgas, was always a member of the royal family.

18. Donations could have, as indicated, myriad meanings, including the memorialization of the dead. This topic has been well studied for northern Europe in an earlier period. See Wendy Davies and Paul Fouracre, eds., *The Settlements of Disputes in Early Medieval Europe* (Cambridge, 1986), and for an earlier Iberian perspective, Adam J. Kosto, *Making Agreement in Medieval Catalonia: Power, Order, and the Written Word, 1000–1200* (New York: 2001).

19. See Barbara H. Rosenwein's excellent books, *Rhinoceros Bound: Cluny in the Tenth Century* (Philadelphia, 1982); *To Be the Neighbor of Saint Peter: The Social Meaning of Cluny's Property* (Ithaca, 1989), above all, 1–108; and *Negotiating Space: Power, Restraint, and Privileges of Immunity in Early Medieval Europe* (Ithaca, 1999). Also Stephen D. White, *Custom, Kinship, and Gifts to Saints: The Laudatio Parentum in Western France, 1050–1150* (Chapel Hill, 1988), chs. 3–5.

20. Justo Pérez de Urbel, *El condado de Castilla: Los 300 años en que se hizo Castilla*, 3 vols. (Madrid, 1969–70), 1: 309–15 lists the foundation dates of

monasteries in northern Castile from 759 through the late tenth century. Many of these monastic foundations predated the county's emergence as a political entity or the settlement of nobles in the area.

21. See Luis García de Valdeavellano, *Historia de España antigua y medieval*, 2 vols. (Madrid, 1988), 2: 81–121. This is a reediting of the author's work published in one volume in 1952 (see bibliography).

22. See Maureen C. Miller, "Donors, Their Gifts, and Religious Innovation in Medieval Verona," *Speculum* 66 (1991): 27–42; also her "Clerical Identity and Reform: Notarial Descriptions of the Secular Clergy in the Po Valley, 750–1200," *Revista di storia e litteratura religiosa* (1996): 311–32; "From Episcopal to Communal Palaces: Places and Power in Northern Italy, 1000–1250," *Journal of the Society of Architectural Historians* 54 (1995): 175–85. I am most grateful to Professor Miller for her comments when I presented part of this research at Stanford University in 1997. See also Cantera y Montenegro, "Derecho y sociedad en la Rioja bajomedieval a través de los testamentos."

23. Miller, "Donors, Their Gifts, and Religious Innovation in Medieval Verona," 33–37.

24. Examples of these types of donations can be found in *Documentación de la catedral de Burgos*, ed. Garrido Garrido, 155–56 (6 May 1107); *Fuentes para la historia de Castilla*, ed. Luciano Serrano, 3 vols. (Valladolid, 1906–10), 3: 336.

25. Rosenthal, *The Purchase of Paradise*, 11–15. Most of the early donations and wills in northern Castile contain such expressions as "pro remedio anima mee [sic], ut evadam portas inferni," and occasionally "pro extinguenda incendia gehenne ignis." *Fuentes*, ed. Serrano, 3: 108–10, 189–90.

26. Miller reports the fragmentation of donations and testamentary legacies in Verona as early as the mid–twelfth century. See "Donors, Their Gifts, and Religious Innovation in Medieval Verona," 35ff. See also Cohn *Death and Property in Siena*, for extreme fragmentation of pious legacies in the thirteenth and fourteenth centuries.

27. Two rare examples of donations to relatives before 1250 are found in the documentation of San Salvador de El Moral. *Fuentes*, ed. Serrano, 1: 31, 67–70. See also *Documentación del monasterio de San Zoilo de Carrión*, ed. Pérez Celada, 53–54 (30 October 1137). The donor, Elvira Téllez, gave all her property to the monastery except some lands that she kept until her death, at which point they reverted to the monastery. In return, she was to receive prayers for her soul and that of her parents.

28. For an example, see *Cartulario de San Millán de la Cogolla*, ed. Ubieta Arteta, 167 (1022).

29. One exception is the region of Aguilar de Campoo, where donations "for the remedy of my soul" in Castilian continued into the fourteenth century.

30. For the economic transformation that affected Castile in the thirteenth century, see my *Crisis and Continuity*, chs. 10 and 11. For the new language of royal donations see *Documentación de la catedral de Burgos, 1254–1293*, ed. F. Javier Pereda Llarena, in *FMCL*, vol. 16 (Burgos, 1984), 53–55 (1257); *Recueil des chartes de l'abbaye de Silos*, ed. Marius Ferotin (Paris, 1897), 200–201, 241–42. For the breakdown of confidence in the Church, I follow the remarks made

by Professor Giles Constable at a meeting of the Shelby Cullom Davis Seminar at Princeton University, October 1986.

31. For a good example of this dispersion of gifts, see *Archivo Histórico Nacional*, Clero collection, carpeta 227, no. 1 (18 June 1337) and below.

32. For some examples see *Albelda y Logroño*, 49–52, 208–9, 269–73; also *Documentación de la catedral de Burgos, 1294–1316*, ed. F. Javier Pereda Llarena, in *FMCL*, vol. 17 (Burgos, 1984), 363–70 (4 May 1316). Don Julián willed 1,000 *mrs.* for the release of captives in the hands of the Moors, but he requested that those rescued with his money be shown to his executors. If the monks of the Trinity refused this condition, they were to receive nothing. For the reserving of chaplaincies for relatives, see *Archivo de la Catedral de Burgos*, vol. 48, f. 319 (30 July 1333), Martín Ibáñez reserved such for men of his lineage. Also see below.

33. Santo Toribio's actual advocation dates from the twelfth century, but it incorporated a series of small monasteries in the region. Until the twelfth century, it was known as San Martín de Turieno, and most of the donations before 1100 were to San Martín. See *Liébana*, ix–xlix.

34. *Liébana*, 13–14 (13 January 843); 15–16 (15 May 852); 57–58 (22 January 945). As with the word *testamentum*, the description *ut omnia quinta dabo* also disappears from donations and wills by the twelfth century.

35. *Liébana*, 53–55 (23 January 941); 57–58 (22 January 945).

36. *Liébana*, 112–14 (30 December 1065).

37. *Liébana*, 127–28 (1 November 1125).

38. *Liébana*, 157 (1204).

39. *Liébana*, 166–67 (8 July 1220); 171–72 (4 March 1236).

40. *Liébana*, 233–34 (12 June 1292); 277–78 (27 March 1315). In the latter document, Gómez's relatives, after some arbitration or litigation, sold some properties to fulfill Gómez's last wishes.

CHAPTER 3

1. Archivo de la Catedral de Burgos (hereafter abbreviated ACB), vol. 40, f. 209 (23 April 1225). In addition, see the testament of Don Martín in vol. 48, f. 315 (10 August 1253) which also provides a careful inventory of property to be donated and gives the lion's share to relatives and friends.

2. ACB, vol. 48, f. 319 (30 July and 7 August 1333): "empero tengo por bien e mando que las den a ommes de mio linage, a los mas propincos que oviere y que sean para ello; e mientre ouiere ommes de mio linage que sean [blurred] estas capellanias que las non puedan auer otros ningunos; e quando fallesciere que non ouiere ommes de mio linage para auer estas cappellanias, que el cabildo que las de a cappellanes que sean de misa e de buena vida e ydoneos para ello."

3. This is one of very few wills in the late Middle Ages in which wool is mentioned as a fabric donated for clothing of the poor. See chapter 6.

4. ACB, vol. 49, f. 438 (23 July 1349).

5. Gonzalo Pérez had been active in the market for land in Aguilar de Campoo. In 1338, together with his brother Juan, he sold houses in the town for 1,500 *mrs*. This was a rather large sum for Aguilar de Campoo in this period and

one of the largest urban real estate transactions in the town for the thirteenth and fourteenth centuries. Archivo Histórico Nacional (hereafter AHN), Clero collection, carpeta. 1672, no. 11 (21 June 1338).

6. ACB, vol. 48, f. 319 (30 July and 7 August 1333): "E mando que lieven sobre mio cuerpo vn panno con oro bueno quando yo finare."

7. AHN, Clero, carp. 1662, no. 12 (9 July 1293).

8. This type of arrangement can be found in *Documentación de la catedral de Burgos, 1254–1293*, ed. F. Javier Pereda Llarena, in *Fuentes medievales castellano-leonesas* (hereafter *FMCL*), vol. 16 (Burgos, 1984), 95–96 (11 September 1264). A couple donated houses to the Hospital of the Emperor in return for a house and the promise that they would be fed for the rest of their lives. See also pp. 196–97 (19 September 1276), in which a canon donated property to the chapter in return for masses for himself and his parents and the right to remain in the houses for the rest of his life. In addition, AHN, Clero, carp. 225, no. 12 (3 May 1275); carp. 200, no. 7 (20 March 1304).

9. In this I follow Jacques Le Goff, Lester Little, and others on the relationship between spiritual changes and property. See, for example, Lester K. Little, "Evangelical Poverty, the New Money Economy, and Violence," in *Poverty in the Middle Ages*, ed. D. Flood (Werl, Westfalia, 1975); Jacques Le Goff, *Merchants et banquiers du moyen âge* (Paris, 1956); his *La bourse et la vie: Economie et religion au moyen âge* (Paris, 1986; new ed. 1997); and "Au moyen âge: Temps de l'église et temps du marchand," *Annales E.S.C.* 13 (1960): 417–33, translated as "Merchant's Time and Church's Time in the Middle Ages," in *Time, Work, and Culture*, trans. Arthur Goldhammer (Chicago, 1980) 29–42.

10. Janet Coleman, "Property and Poverty," in *The Cambridge History of Medieval Political Thought, c. 350—c. 1450*, ed. J. H. Burns (Cambridge, 1988), 608.

11. See my *Crisis and Continuity: Land and Town in Late Medieval Castile* (Philadelphia, 1994), 140–74. This chapter on the land market in Castile is an English version of an article originally published in Italian, "La formazione del mercato della terra nella Castiglia del basso medioevo," *Quaderni storici* 65 (1987): 423–52. This particular issue of the *Quaderni* was dedicated to the market for land and impersonal transactions in the medieval West.

12. Coleman, "Property and Poverty," 616–25, 631–43.

13. See Lester K. Little, *Religious Poverty and the Profit Economy in Medieval Europe* (Ithaca, 1978), 113–69.

14. For other towns, see María Asenjo González, *Espacio y sociedad en la Soria medieval: Siglos XIII–XV* (Soria, 1999), 437–61; and her *Segovia: La ciudad y su tierra a fines del medievo* (Segovia, 1986), 263–321; Angel Barrios García, *Estructuras agrarias y de poder en Castilla: El ejemplo de Avila, 1085–1320*, 2 vols. (Salamanca, 1983–84), 2: 133–259; Adeline Rucquoi, *Valladolid en la edad media*, 2 vols. (Valladolid, 1987), 1: 188–267.

15. On *fueros*, see E. N. van Kleffens, *Hispanic Law until the End of the Middle Ages* (Edinburgh, 1968); Luis García de Valdeavellano, *Curso de historia de las instituciones españolas: De los orígenes al final de la edad media* (Madrid, 1968), 327–29, 476–80; Alfonso García Gallo, *Manual de historia del derecho español*, 4th ed., 2 vols. (Madrid, 1971).

16. *Colección de fueros municipales y cartas pueblas*, ed. Tomás Muñoz y Romero (Madrid, 1847), 27–30.

17. Ibid., 37–42. The fuero was confirmed, with further elaborations and privileges, by succeeding counts and kings. The last confirmation was by Ferdinand III, king of Castile and León in 1234. On 20 May 1299, Ferdinand IV gave a modified Romance version of the fuero to the canons and clerics of Castrojeriz. It should be noted that the charter was rendered in Castilian even though it was granted to ecclesiastics. See chapter 1.

18. Ibid., 273–78. See also the fueros of Nájera (1076), 287 ff.; Logroño (1095), 334 ff.; Sepúlveda; and others.

19. The fuero of Cuenca has elicited a flood of scholarship. There is a recent translation into English by James F. Powers, *The Code of Cuenca: Municipal Law on the Twelfth-Century Castilian Frontier* (Philadelphia, 2000). See his introduction, 1–24, and a short bibliography dealing with the study of fueros, 233–37.

20. *Fuero de Cuenca (formas primitiva y sistemática: texto latino, texto castellano y adaptación del fuero de Iznatoraf)*, ed. Rafael de Ureña y Smenjaud (Madrid, 1935), i–clxxii, presents the traditional reading of the Cuenca fuero and traces the sources and manuscript history of the charter. See book 1, title 1, law 4; tit. 2, laws 1–5, 7–15, 18, 23; tit. 3, laws 7, 9; tit. 4 and 5; tit. 10, laws 1–4; bk. 4, tit. 1–13.

21. Ibid., bk. 4, tit. 7, laws 2–3 read: "Si el mancebo asoldado o el pastor o el boyarizo o el ortelano, a su sennor pusiere los cuernos matelo con la mujer, como fuero es" (Any servant caught in adultery with his employer's wife will be killed as well as the adulterous woman). Title 7, laws 3–4: "Si el mancebo asoldado yoguiere con la fija de su sennor, pierda la soldada que ouiere seruido, si el sennor lo pudiere provar con testigos e salga enemigos de todos los parientes de su sennor por siempre" (If a servant lies with the daughter of his employer, the servant loses all his salary and, if proven by the testimony of witnesses, the servant earns the sworn enmity of all the young woman's relatives forever). These restrictions extended to wet nurses as well, highlighting the close link between legitimacy, property, and sexuality.

22. Ibid., bk. 1, tit. 9 and 10. On weddings and wills (testamentos), see 249–87.

23. For Ferdinand III's reforms and granting of the fuero of Toledo, which essentially contained the *Fuero juzgo* to Córdoba and Seville, see Julio González, *Reinado y diplomas de Fernando III*, 3 vols. (Córdoba, 1980–86), 1: 413–18; also García Gallo, *Manual de historia del derecho español*, 1: 376–77, 392–93.

24. In this context, see the familiarity of Visigothic law on questions of wills with Roman practices in Alfonso García Gallo, "Del testamento romano al medieval: Las líneas de su evolución en España," in *Anuario de historia del derecho español* 47 (1977): 425–97; Manuel M. Pérez de Benavides, *El testamento visigótico: Una contribución al estudio del derecho romano vulgar* (Granada, 1975).

25. *Fuero juzgo en latín y castellano* (Madrid, 1815), bk. 2, tit. 5: 1–17, pp. 27–37 (Latin), 38–45 (Castilian).

26. Ibid., bk. 4 tit. 5, laws 1–7, pp. 76–78. See, for example, law 1: "Que los fijos ni los nietos non deven seer desheredados: 'Onde mandamos que si el padre

ó la madre, el avuelo ó el avuela quisier meiorar á alguno de los fijos ó de los nietos de su buena, non les pueda dar mas de la tercia parte de sus cosas de meioria; ni pueda dar á omne estranno de su buena.'" This sought to guarantee that property be evenly distributed among heirs and stay within the family.

27. Joseph F. O'Callaghan, *The Learned King: The Reign of Alfonso X of Castile* (Philadelphia, 1993), 32–36, 214–29.

28. See García Gallo, *Manual de historia del derecho español*, 1: 396–401.

29. *Fuero real*, ed. Gonzalo Martínez Diez, in *Leyes de Alfonso X*, vol. 2 (Avila, 1988), bk. 3, tit. 1, laws 1–14 (pp. 298–304). Book 3, title 2 deals with dowries.

30. Ibid., bk. 3, tit. 5, (pp. 297–401). Tit. 5, p. 320, reads "Todo omne que fiziere su manda, quier seyendo sano quier enferm, fágala por escripto de mano delgún excriuano de los públicos, o por otro escripto en que ponga so seello el que faze la manda."

31. Ibid., bk. 3, titl. 6, law 1 (p. 326): "Todo omne que ouiere fiios o nietos <o dente ayuso> de mujer de bendición, non puedamn heredar con ellos otros fiios que aya de barragana, mas del quinto de su auer muebles e raýz puédales dar lo que quisiere."

32. On the *Siete partidas* and their political and cultural context, see O'Callaghan, *The Learned King*, 17–37. See also *Las siete partidas*, ed. Robert I. Burns, trans. Samuel P. Scott, 5 vols. (Philadelphia, 2001), 1: ix–xlviii.

33. *Las siete partidas*, partida 1, title 13, law 6; tit. 14, law 1; tit. 21, laws 3, 4, 5; part. 2, tit. 17, laws 1, 2, in *Los Códigos españoles concordados y anotados*, ed. M. Rivadeneyra, 12 vols. (Madrid, 1847–51), 2: 224, 229–30, 296–98, 431–33. *Partida* 1, title 21 is of particular interest since it deals with the private property of ecclesiastics. Even there the pull of the material world overcame the close relation with the Church. Law 4 ordered that all the goods obtained by the clerics should go to the family.

34. See Peter Linehan, *The Spanish Church and the Papacy in the Thirteenth Century* (Cambridge, 1971), 222–50, 322–34; and his "The Church, the Economy, and the *Reconquista* in Early Fourteenth-Century Castile," in *Past and Present in Medieval Spain* (Aldershot, 1992), ch. 9. See also *Siete partidas*, 1: 57. Burns, in a note to partida 1, title 5, law 17; describes these rights as "but a small part of the extraordinary authority enjoyed by their predecessors [Alfonso X's] under the Visigothic domination." After looking at the Muslim presence in Iberia as one of the reasons for the peculiar royal rights over the Church, Burns concludes his note by stating that "The most singular thing of all was that no opposition or protest appears in any of the ecclesiastical writers of the time against a condition which threatened the integrity and very existence of their organization."

35. *Las siete partidas*, part. 2, tit. 17 and 18. Title 19, laws 4 through 8 deal exclusively with the captives'(and their heirs) property rights.

36. As I have already indicated and reiterate later, there is disagreement on whether the *Partidas* became the law of the land or not. See O'Callaghan's introductory remarks in *Las siete partidas*, 1: xxxil–xl; and *The Learned King*, 37. Because of the noble revolt of the 1270s and the successful opposition of Alfonso's own son, Sancho, to the *Partidas*' prescriptions on royal succession, I do

not think the law code was ever in force in Castile until its promulgation by Alfonso XI in 1348.

CHAPTER 4

1. See José A. García de Cortázar et al., *Organización del espacio en la España medieval: La corona de Castilla en los siglos VIII a XV* (Barcelona, 1985), 11–161.
2. See Joseph R. Strayer, "Pierre de Chalon and the Origins of the French Customs Service," in *Medieval Statecraft and the Perspectives of History*, ed. John F. Benton and Thomas N. Bisson (Princeton, 1971), 232–38. For customs stations in Castile, see my *Crisis and Continuity: Land and Town in Late Medieval Castile* (Philadelphia, 1994), ch. 7. See also my article "Fronteras: De la comunidad a la nación en la Castilla bajomedieval," *Anuario de estudios medievales* 27, 1 (1997): 23–41.
3. *Cartulario de San Millán de la Cogolla, 759–1076*, ed. Antonio Ubieto Arteta (Valencia, 1976), 186–87 (6 December 1028).
4. *Cartulario de Santo Toribio de Liébana*, ed. Luis Sánchez Belda (Madrid, 1948), 11–13 (25 January 831): "terciam uero porcionem ad Lone in barao; ibdem in Lone horreum, cortes, seneiras III, sibi exitis, gressum uel regressum." This work hereafter cited as *Liébana*. In 979, García Fernández, count of Castile, gave some grazing rights to the monastery of San Millán and the boundaries were not fully defined. *Cartulario de San Millán, de la Cogolla*, ed. Ubieto Arteta, 109–110: "quod est inter ambos rivos et per eodem lumbo ad medium vallem Grandem."
5. *Documentación del monasterio de San Salvador de Oña, 1032–1284*, ed. Isabel Oceja Gonzalo, in *Fuentes medievales castellano-leonesas* (hereafter *FMCL*), vol. 3 (Burgos, 1983), 53–54 (c. 1170).
6. *Documentación del monasterio de San Zoilo de Carrión, 1047–1300*, ed. Julio A. Pérez Celada, in *FMCL*, vol. 100 (Palencia, 1986), 109–12 (no date; the ms. is assigned to the late twelfth or early thirteenth century): "De prado de Xemeno dixerunt iam dicti homines quod, del sendero quod uadit de saldania ad Riuum Tortum contra gannines, debebant pascere homines de gannines et de Rio Torto."
7. For the fragmentation of mill rights and the careful inventory of hours assigned to peasants owning rights in a mill, see T. F. Ruiz, "Tecnología y división de propiedad: Los molinos de Burgos en la baja edad media," in *Sociedad y poder real en Castilla: Burgos en la baja edad media* (Barcelona, 1981), 71–93.
8. See Daniel L. Smail's insightful book, *Imaginary Cartographies: Possession and Identity in Late Medieval Marseille* (Ithaca, 1999). Also *Documentación del monasterio de San Zoilo de Carrión, 1047–1300*, ed. Pérez Celada, 117–19 (14 August 1203).
9. Julio González, *Reinado y diplomas de Fernando III*, 3 vols. (Córdoba, 1980–86), 3: 183–87 (20 June 1239). For other examples of setting of mojones, see 3: 187–89 (18 October 1239), 217 (10 March 1241), 218 (12 March 1241), 245–46 (22 March 1242), 354–55 (24 August 1249). Mojones are also men-

tioned in *Documentación de los archivos catedralicio y diocesano de Salamanca, siglos XII–XIII*, ed. José L. Martín et al. (Salamanca, 1977), 275–76 (1236); *Recueil des chartes de l'abbay e de Silos*, ed. Marius Ferotin (Paris, 1897), 203; *Fuentes para la historia de Castilla*, ed. Luciano Serrano, 3 vols. (Valladolid, 1906–10), 1: 144–45; 2: 107, 109. In the conflict between the monastery of San Pedro of Gumiel de Izán and the rural council of Gumiel, seventeen men of different villages acted as surveyors, placing twenty mojones in the boundaries between village and monastic lands. See Archivo Histórico Nacional (AHN), Clero, carp. 232, no. 9 (29 August 1255); also carp. 380, nos. 16 and 17 (1255); carp. 300, no. 2 (1287); carp. 225, no. 3 (1290); carp. 239, no. 17 (2 November 1290); carp. 233, no. 3 (6 June 1293).

10. *Documentación del Hospital del Rey de Burgos, 1136–1277*, ed. María del Carmen Palacín Gálvez and Luis Martínez García, in *FMCL*, vol. 43 (Burgos, 1990), 237 (1252), 242 (1253).

11. *Documentación de la catedral de Burgos, 1254–1293*, ed. F. Javier Pereda Llarena, in *FMCL*, vol. 16 (Burgos, 1984), 79–81 (4 March 1262). See also 119–23 (22 January 1267) for the agreement between the cathedral chapter of Burgos and the village council of Madrigal as one of the parties in the dispute, and the village council of Ruyales and the monastery of Covarrubias as the other, setting the limits for the use of *montes*. The number of witnesses and of those involved in setting the boundaries (almost the entire male population of the two villages) serves as testimony to the importance of defining one's jurisdiction. For other litigation over boundaries, see *Colección diplomática de San Salvador de Oña*, ed. Juan de Alamo, 2 vols. (Madrid: Consejo Superior de Investigaciones Científicas, 1950–51), 2: 738–39 (28 January 1275), 778–79 (26 April 1277), 814 (26 June 1279), AHN, Clero, carp. 232, no. 9 (29 August 1255; carp. 239, no. 17 (2 September 1290).

12. See *The Code of Cuenca: Municipal Law on the Twelfth-Century Castilian Frontier*, trans. with an introduction by James F. Powers (Philadelphia, 2000), 137–38: "Whoever crosses the markers on the field should pay sixty *menkales*. Those pecuniary penalties should be for the *alcaldi* and for the plaintiff; but responsible intermediaries enter and position themselves where they please."

13. *Documentación del monasterio de San Zoilo de Carrión*, ed. Pérez Celada, 168–69 (1225).

14. AHN, Clero, carp. 232, no. 9 (29 August 1255).

15. For example, in 1208, Doña Inés sold her property in Centollinos, Rojas, Quintana-Urría, and other locations to the monastery of San Salvador de Oña for the large sum of 1,000 *áureos* (gold coins). The short extant record of the transaction does not mention boundaries or give any indication of the extent of the land. *Documentación del monasterio de San Salvador de Oña*, ed. Oceja Gonzalo, 85–86: "et omnem hereditatem quam ibi habeo, in monte et in fonte, cum pratis, pascuis, riuis, molendinis, cum ingresso et regressu et cum omnibus directuris, que ad me ibi pertinent." In many respects, the language is not too different from some small transactions, but direct references to boundaries or to the physical extention of the land appeared almost exclusively in smaller transactions. For other large transactions in which boundaries are not mentioned, see Archivo de la

Catedral de Burgos (ACB), vol. 49, f. 65 (3 August 1285), a sale of lands and other rural property for 4,500 *mrs.*, and ACB, vol. 50, f. 49 (17 September 1285), a sale of lands for 1,000 *mrs.*

16. Gonzalo de Berceo, *Milagros de Nuestra Señora*, ed. Daniel Devoto, 7th ed. (Madrid: Castalia, 1982), 59-60.

17. On this topic, see David E. Vassberg, *Land and Society in Golden Age Castile* (Cambridge, 1984); Ruth Behar, *Santa María del Monte: The Presence of the Past in a Spanish Village* (Princeton, 1986).

18. AHN, Clero, carp. 225, no. 2 (9 May 1288); carp. 225, no. 3 (8 April 1290).

19. AHN, Clero, carp. 233, no. 12 (3 February 1301).

20. Radulfus Glaber, *Historiarum libri quinque*, ed. and trans. John France (Oxford, 1998), 89. I am grateful to Scott Bruce for this reference.

21. Ruiz, *Crisis and Continuity*, ch. 3.

22. See Carlos M. Reglero de la Fuente, *Los señoríos de los Montes de Torozos: De la repoblación al becerro de las behetrías, siglos X-XIV* (Valladolid, 1993), 30.

23. See *Libro Becerro de las behetrías: Estudio y texto crítico*, ed. Gonzalo Martínes Díez, 3 vols. (León, 1981), 2: 175-82.

24. *Documentación de la catedral de Palencia, 1035-1247*, ed. Teresa Abajo Martín, in *FMCL*, vol. 103 (Palencia, 1986), 95-97 (16 April 1146).

25. *Documentación del monasterio de San Zoilo de Carrión, 1047-1300*, ed. Pérez Celada, 184-87 (c. 1230 and 1234).

26. See my *Crisis and Continuity*, chs. 4, 5, and 8.

27. See, for example, María del Carmen Carlé, "Gran propiedad y grandes propietarios," *Cuadernos de historia de España* 57-58 (1976): 1-224.

28. See my "Two Patrician Families in Late Medieval Burgos: The Sarracín and the Bonifaz," in *The City and the Realm: Burgos and Castile, 1080-1492* (London, 1992), ch. 6; and *Crisis and Continuity*, ch. 5.

29. See note 17.

30. *Cartulario de San Millán de la Cogolla*, ed. Ubieto Arteta, 27, 28.

31. Luis Martínez García, "La concentración de la propiedad urbana burgalesa mediante la concesión de 'pasadas de tierra,' 1150-1250," in *La ciudad de Burgos: Actas del Congreso de Historia de Burgos* (León, 1985), 89-90.

32. *Documentación de la catedral de Burgos, 1184-1222*, ed. José Manuel Garrido Garrido, in *FMCL*, vol. 14 (Burgos, 1983), 152-53 (? August 1202).

33. ACB, vol. 70, no. 170 (? July 1212), published in *Documentación de la catedral de Burgos, 1184-1222*, ed. Garrido Garrido, 254-55 (? July 1212). The description of the property being exchanged is quite detailed, clearly indicating what other properties served as boundaries for the garden and the house.

34. *Fuero de Cuenca (formas primitiva y sistemática: texto latino, texto castellano y adaptación del fuero de Iznatoraf)*, ed. Rafael de Ureña y Smenjaud (Madrid, 1935), book 1, title 2, law 22 (pp. 150-51). The Romance or Castilian version is far more explicit than the original Latin: "Omnis hereditas que introitum, vel exitum non habuerit, sicut est ager, et vinea, alcaldes adiurati eant ad hereditatem, et qua parte ipsi uiderent quod minus dampni facient, ea parte detur via, et illa via sit stabilis." The Castilian version runs as follows: "Toda eredad que

non oviere entrada nin salida, asi como es canpo o vinna, los alcaldes jurados vayan a la eredad e por aquella parte que ellos vieren que menos dannos sera, den la entrada por aquella parte e aquella sea estable; e qual quier que la carrera que los alcaldes dieren, desfiziere o mudare o cerrare, peche diez mrs.; ca las carreras e los exidos que los alcaldes fizieren o dieren sean firmes e estables para siempre." Translated in *The Code of Cuenca*, 39: "The sworn *alcaldi* should visit all property that does not have an entrance or an exit to establish if it is a field of work, such as a vineyard. If so, they should make an access in the location that causes the least amount of harm, and this access should stand."

35. Julius Klein, *The Mesta: A Study in Spanish Economic History, 1273–1836* (Cambridge, 1920), 20–22.

36. *Documentación del monasterio de la Trinidad de Burgos, 1198–1400*, ed. L. García Aragón, in *FMCL*, vol. 28 (Burgos, 1985), 191–92 (1368), 225–26 (1373), 246–47 (1378).

37. See, for example, a protoinventory in *Cartulario de San Millán de la Cogolla*, ed. Ubieto Arteta, 58–59 (1 August 947), 171–73 (1024).

38. *Liébana*, 53–54 (23 January 941), 101–2 (11 June 1048). One can compare these two pre-1150 quasi inventories in Liébana with the careful description of 1271 on 204–6, detailing the properties owned by the monastery of Santo Toribio in several locations.

39. *Documentación del monasterio de San Zoilo de Carrión, 1047–1300*, ed. Pérez Celada, 131–32 (1213): "Hec est notitia de thesauro et de ornamento ecclesias Sancti Zoili. De albis paratis, XXXIIII; de cotidianis, XL; de casulis, XI; de stolis cum suis manipulis, XI; de manipulis minoribus, XXII." Clearly, this represents a careful itemizing of all the monastery's holdings. See also 184–85 (c. 1230), the *apeo* of the monastery's property in Villasarracino. Also *Documentación del monasterio de San Zoilo de Carrión, 1301–1400*, ed. Julio Pérez Celada, in *FMCL*, vol. 101 (Palencia, 1987), 274–79 (c. late fourteenth century).

40. *Documentación del monasterio de San Zoilo de Carrión, 1047–1300*, ed. Pérez Celada, 132–38 (1213): "in Uillaoueco habemus hereditatem ad unum iugum boum per annum sufficientem, et collacios qui debent dare pro offurcione unusquisque eorum sex panes, et omnes in unum duos tocinos et duas gallinas et duas canadielas de uino et una eminam de ceuada." Note the manner in which Castilian and a very corrupted Latin are mixed in the document. Other notable inventories can be found in the documentation of Santo Toribio de Liébana. Though inventories could be found in an earlier period, longer series, itemizing all the monasteries' properties, were compiled in 1271, 1302, 1307, and 1308. See *Liébana*, 204–6 (1271), 248–55 (12 January 1302), 255–56 (16 January 1302), 265 (11 May 1307), 265–68 (3 May 1308). Examples of other inventories or apeos can also be found in *Documentación del Hospital del Rey de Burgos*, ed. Palacín Gálvez and Martínez García, 283–84 (12 April 1255). This is really a list of taxes due.

41. See, for example, *Repartimiento de Sevilla*, ed. Julio González, 2 vols. (Madrid, 1951); *El libro del repartimiento de Jerez de la Frontera*, ed. Manuel González Jiménez and Antonio González Gómez (Cádiz, 1980); *Repartimiento de Murcia*, ed. Juan Torres Fontes (Madrid, 1960). The *Repartimientos* represent

the equivalent of the apeos examined at a regional level. As such, they itemized landed and urban property through recently conquered areas in the south.

42. Two historians who have utilized the *Cuadernos de contabilidad* to great profit are Hilario Casado Alonso, in his *La propiedad eclesiástica en la ciudad de Burgos en el siglo XV: El cabildo catedralicio* (Valladolid, 1980), 97–137; and Angus MacKay, *Money, Prices, and Politics in Fifteenth-Century Castile* (London, 1981).

43. ACB, *Cuadernos de contabilidad capitular* 1, f. 1–11. For example, the *Cuadernos* for June 1267 through May 1268 included lists of expenses for liturgical ends, houses owned and rented by the chapter, mills, gardens, major and minor sources of rent, urban land, income from purveyance, charities, receipts and expenses, meadows, and the income from the *tercios*. See *Documentación de la catedral de Burgos, 1254–1293*, ed. Pereda Llarena, 137. The *Cuadernos* have not been published and this is only a bibliographical reference. I have used the *Cuadernos* to establish the rents paid for mills before and after the plague. See my *Crisis and Continuity*, 321–22. For the mill rents in 1279 and 1280, see ACB, *Cuadernos de contabilidad capitular, Mayordomías*, vol. 1.

44. See the *Becerro de visitaciones de casas y heredades* (1303), in *Documentación medieval de la catedral de Avila*, ed. Angel Barrios García (Salamanca, 1981), 213–457. For the lands of the monastery of Santa María la Real de Aguilar de Campoo, see AHN, Clero, carp. 1665, no. 1 (c. early fourteenth century). Published with some mistakes and omissions in Carlos Merchán Fernández, *Sobre los orígenes del régimen señorial en Castilla: El abadengo de Aguilar de Campóo, 1020–1369* (Málaga, 1982), 243–68.

45. A fuller discussion of this topic can be found in my "Fronteras: De la comunidad a la nación en la Castilla bajomedieval." See also García de Cortázar et al., *Organización social del espacio en la España medieval*; Peter Sahlins, *Boundaries: The Making of France and Spain in the Pyrenees*(Berkeley, 1989); and note 51 below.

46. *Viajes de extranjeros por España y Portugal*, ed. José García Mercadal, 3 vols. (Madrid, 1952), 1: 263.

47. Ibid., 1: 272.

48. In the account of Philip II's voyage to Saragossa in the late sixteenth century written by one of the king's cross bowmen, Enrique Cock, the border between Castile and Aragon—two very distinct kingdoms until the eighteenth century—was described as a *raya* (a line) and marked by the ubiquitous mojones. See *Viajes de extranjeros*, 1: 1303–4. See also the account of Antoine de Lalaing, 1: 445 ff.

49. Benedict Anderson, *Imagined Communities: Reflections on the Origin and Spread of Nationalism*, rev. ed. (London, 1991), 19–22. See also the collection of articles on "physical space" and the construction of a French identity in *L'espace français* in the multivolume *Histoire de la France*, ed. Andre Burguière and Jacques Revel (Paris, 1989).

50. See, for example, the work of Jean Bodin, *Method for the Easy Comprehension of History*, trans. B. Reynolds (New York, 1969), 162ff.

51. Most political and institutional historians emphasize the embryonic charac-

ter of the nation-state in the thirteenth and fourteenth centuries. See Joseph R. Strayer, *On the Medieval Origins of the Modern State* (Princeton, 1970); Ernst H. Kantorowicz, *The King's Two Bodies: A Study in Medieval Political Theology* (Princeton, 1957).

52. See Jacob Burckhardt, *The Civilization of the Renaissance in Italy*, 2 vols. (New York, 1958), 1: 21–142.

53. See my essay "The Economic Structure of the Area of Burgos, 1200–1350," in *The City and the Realm*, ch. 3.

54. Here I follow the excellent article by María Asenjo González, "Actividad económica, aduanas y relaciones de poder en la frontera norte de Castilla en el reinado de los Reyes Católicos," *En la España medieval* 19 (1996): 275–309. See also Manuel Rojas Gabriel, *La frontera entre los reinos de Sevilla y Granada en el siglo XV, 1390–1481* (Cádiz, 1995), ch. 3.

55. Asenjo, "Actividad económica," 275–76; Rojas Gabriel, *La frontera*, 363–78.

56. Ariel Guiance, "To Die for Country, Land, or Faith in Castilian Medieval Thought," *Journal of Medieval History* 24 (1998): 313–32.

CHAPTER 5

1. See Diane Owen Hughes, "Toward Historical Ethnography: Notarial Records and Family History in the Middle Ages," *Historical Methods Newsletter* 7, 2 (1974): 61–70; and her "Urban Growth and Family Structure in Medieval Genoa," *Past & Present* 66 (1975): 3–28; Jean Gaudement, *Les communautés familiales* (Paris, 1963). Also Georges Duby, *The Chivalrous Society*, trans. C. Postan (London, 1977), above all, 59–80, "Lineage, Nobility, and Knighthood: The Mâconnais in the Twelfth Century Revision"; Jack Goody, *The Development of the Family and Marriage in Europe* (Cambridge, 1983); and his "Inheritance, Property, and Women: Some Comparative Considerations," in *Family and Inheritance: Rural Society in Western Europe, 1200–1800*, ed. Jack Goody, J. Thirsk, and E. P. Thompson (Cambridge, 1976); David Herlihy, *Medieval Households* (Cambridge, 1985).

2. See Herlihy's *Medieval Households*; also Jacques Heers, *Family Clans in the Middle Ages: A Study of Political and Social Structures in Urban Areas*, trans. B. Herbert (Amsterdam, 1977); Philippe Ariès and Georges Duby, eds., *A History of Private Life*, 5 vols. (Cambridge, 1988), vol. 2, *Revelations of the Medieval World*, 33–309; David Herlihy and Christiane Klapisch-Zuber, *The Tuscans and Their Families: A Study of the Florentine Catasto of 1427* (New Haven, 1984); Barbara Hanawalt, *The Ties That Bound: Peasants Families in Medieval England* (New York, 1986).

3. For Castile, see Reyna Pastor, "Historia de las familias en Castilla y León, siglos X–XIV, y su relación con la formación de los grandes dominios eclesiásticos," *Cuadernos de historia de España* 43–44 (1967): 88–118; Isabel Beceiro Pita and R. Córdoba de la Llave, *Parentesco, poder y mentalidad: La nobleza castellana, siglos XII–XV* (Madrid, 1990); and her "La consciencia de los antepasados y la gloria del linaje en la Castilla bajomedieval," in *Relaciones de poder,*

de producción y parentesco en la edad media y moderna (Madrid, 1990), 329–49; Pascual Martínez Sopena, "Parentesco y poder en León durante el siglo XI: La 'casata' de Alfonso Díaz," *Studia histórica: Historia medieval* 5 (1987): 33–87; David Reher, *Town and Country in Pre-Industrial Spain: Cuenca, 1550–1870* (Cambridge, 1990), 96–97, 111, 194 ff. See also Teofilo F. Ruiz, "The Peasantries of Iberia, 1400–1800," in *The Peasantries of Europe: From the Fourteenth to the Eighteenth Centuries*, ed. Tom Scott (London, 1998), 53–58. For the formation of entailments in the fourteenth century, see the classic and influential book by Bartolomé Clavero Arévalo, *Mayorazgo y propiedad feudal en Castilla, 1369–1863* (Madrid, 1974).

4. Hughes, "Toward Historical Ethnography," 61.

5. See Ruth Behar, *Santa María del Monte: The Presence of the Past in a Spanish Village* (Princeton, 1986), 68–121; T. F. Ruiz, *Spanish Society, 1400–1600* (London, 2001), 41–47.

6. T. F. Ruiz, "The Transformation of the Castilian Municipalities: The Case of Burgos, 1248–1350," *Past & Present* 77 (1977): 3–33.

7. For patterns of inhabitation in Avila, see T. F. Ruiz, *Crisis and Continuity: Land and Town in Late Medieval Castile* (Philadelphia, 1994), 277–80; *Becerro de visitaciones de casas y heredades*, in *Documentación medieval de la catedral de Avila*, ed. Angel Barrios García (Salamanca, 1981), 222–32.

8. Archivo de la Catedral de Burgos (ACB), *Cuadernos de contabilidad capitular, Mayordomísa*, 1332, 1347.

9. Archivo Historico Nacional (AHN), Clero collection, carpeta 1665, no. 1. For a detailed study of this document, see my *Crisis and Continuity*, ch. 4.

10. AHN, Clero, carp. 1665, no. 1. These individuals also worked or rented other lands in the village, reflecting their relative prosperity.

11. Ibid.

12. Joan Corominas, *Diccionario crítico etimológico de la lengua castellana*, 4 vols. (Berne, 1954), 3: 103. See also Corominas, *Diccionario de autoridades* (Madrid, 1726), 410.

13. See my "Two Patrician Families in Late Medieval Burgos: The Sarracín and the Bonifaz," in *The City and the Realm: Burgos and Castile, 1080–1492* (London, 1992), ch. 6. This is a revised and expanded translation of my "Prosopografía burgalesa, 1248–1350," which appeared in the *Boletín de la Institución Fernán González* 184 (1975): 476–99. See also *Crisis and Continuity*, 237–55.

14. See notes 1, 2, 3, and 13.

15. Adeline Rucquoi, *Valladolid en la edad media*, 2 vols. (Valladolid, 1987), 1: 116–44, 235–66; María Asenjo González, *Segovia: La ciudad y su tierra a fines del medievo* (Segovia, 1986), 82–86, 263–98; and her *Espacio y sociedad en la Soria medieval, siglos XIII–XV* (Soria, 1999), 137–48, 437–86; Angel Barrios García, *Estructuras agrarias y de poder en Castilla: El ejemplo de Avila, 1085–1320*, 2 vols. (Salamanca, 1983–84), 1: 173–217; 2: 133–86.

16. ACB, vol. 49, f. 31 (? May 1179).

17. ACB, vol. 49, f. 34 (? May 1180); vol. 49, f. 33 (? May 1181): The two brothers bought land in Villatoro in exchange for another piece of land (a *pas-*

sata) and 7 *mrs.*; vol. 49, f. 35 (? December 1186): the brothers bought a vineyard in Valdecardeña in exchange for land and 35 *mrs.*

18. *Documentación del monasterio de las Huelgas de Burgos, 1116–1230*, ed. José M. Lizoaín Garrido (Burgos, 1985), in *Fuentes medievales castellano-leonesas* (*FMCL*), vol. 30, 32–33 (? December 1187). Pedro Sarracín's name is next to last in the list of witnesses.

19. ACB, vol. 70, no. 186 (? May 1195); vol. 70, no. 16 (? September 1196). Published in *Documentación de la catedral de Burgos, 1184–1222*, ed. José Manuel Garrido Garrido (Burgos, 1983), in *FMCL*, vol. 14, 117 (1195); 122–23 (1196); 124 (1196).

20. ACB, vol. 70, no. 60 (? June 1195). Also *Documentación de la catedral de Burgos, 1184–1222*, ed. Garrido Garrido, 120–21 (1195). That year Juan Sánchez and his wife exchanged land and money for a right of entry and exit ("passatam terre in longo et alia in amplio, cum introitu et exitu, in casas Petri Serrazin, alcalde").

21. See my "Two Patrician Families," 3–4 n. 7.

22. Ibid., 4 n. 8.

23. ACB, vol. 70, no. 159 (? June 1212). Also *Documentación de la catedral de Burgos, 1184–1222*, ed. Garrido Garrido, 253 (1212). Three Muslims exchanged a garden with a canon for "una passatam de terra, cum intrada et exida, in casa domne Stephanie, uxoris Petri Sarraceni."

24. ACB, vol. 50, p. 1, f. 46 (? May 1225).

25. See my "Two Patrician Families," 4–7.

26. Ibid., 4.

27. Ibid., 5.

28. Ibid., 5–7.

29. Ibid., 7–10.

30. Ibid., 9–10.

31. See my *Crisis and Continuity*, chs. 7 and 8.

32. See Marie-Claude Gerbet, *Las noblezas españolas en la edad media: Siglos XI–XV* (Madrid, 1997), 15–117. This is the Spanish translation of her 1994 book in French. Also Isabel Beceiro Pita and Ricardo Córdoba de la Llave, *Parentesco, poder y mentalidad: La nobleza castellana, siglos XII–XV* (Madrid, 1990); María del Carmen Carlé, "Infanzones e hidalgos," *Cuadernos de historia de España* 33–34 (1961): 56–100; Máximo Diago Hernando, "Caballeros e hidalgos en la Extremadura castellana medieval, siglos XII–XV," *En la España medieval* 15 (1992): 31–62; María Isabel Pérez de Tudela y Velasco, *Infanzones y caballeros: Su proyección en la esfera nobiliaria castellano-leonesa, siglos IX–XI* (Madrid, 1979), 250–478; and the excellent books by Simon Barton, *The Aristocracy in Twelfth-Century León and Castile* (Cambridge, 1997); and by Margarita Torres Sevilla, *Linajes nobiliarios de León y Castilla: Siglos IX–XIII* (Salamanca, 1999). Recently, Simon R. Doubleday, *The Lara Family: Crown and Nobility in Medieval Spain* (Cambridge, 2001), provides an insightful look into the history of one of Castile's greatest noble families.

33. Barton, *The Aristocracy in Twelfth-Century León and Castile*, 3, 39–43.

34. Margarita Torres Sevilla has pointed out the differences between magnate rank and dispersed property among the Leonese aristocracy between the tenth and the beginnings of the twelfth century. Only after 1126 did the great lineages attempt to consolidate their holdings. In contrast, the lower nobility tended to keep their property fairly consolidated. Not to do so would have meant the dissolution of their power altogether. See Torres Sevilla, *Linajes nobiliarios*, 401–24, 508. Describing the large holdings of the magnates in *The Aristocracy in Twelfth-Century León and Castile*, emphasizes the links between noble power and royal largesse. See Barton chs. 3 and 4.

35. The best example of the high nobility's rebellious nature is the Lara family. See Doubleday, *The Lara Family*, 60–97. Also Torres Sevilla, *Linajes nobiliarios*, 223–36.

36. Doubleday, *The Lara Family*, 30.

37. Adam J. Kosto, "The *Liber Feudorum* of the Counts of Barcelona: The Cartulary as an Expression of Power," *Journal of Medieval History* 27 (2001): 1–22, notes the ambivalence between lineage and territoriality in late twelfth-century Catalonia.

38. For the rivalry between the Castros and Laras during the minority of Alfonso VIII, see Luis García de Valdeavellano, *Historia de España antigua y medieval*, 2 vols. (Madrid, 1988), 2: 554–61. Doubleday argues in *The Lara Family* that there was a shift (certainly among the Laras) in the late twelfth and early thirteenth centuries from fraternal partnership to the concentration of landholding in the hands of the eldest son.

39. See Salvador de Moxó, "De la nobleza vieja a la nobleza nueva: La transformación nobiliaria castellana en la baja edad media," *Cuadernos de historia* 3 (1969): 1–210; also his "La nobleza castellana en el siglo XIV," *Anuario de estudios medievales* 7 (1970–71): 493–511. See also Clavero Arévalo, *Mayorazgo y propiedad feudal en Castilla*.

40. See *Cortes de los antiguos reinos de León y Castilla*, 5 vols., vols. 1 and 2 (Madrid, 1861–63), 1: 55, 57–59, 63 (Valladolid, 1258), 68, 79 (*ayuntamiento* of Jerez de la Frontera, 1268).

41. See my *Spanish Society, 1400–1600*, ch. 3.

42. For a later example of this connection between land and family, see Pascual Martínez Sopena, *El estado señorial de Medina de Rioseco bajo el almirante Alfonso Enríquez, 1389–1430* (Valladolid, 1977), 54–133.

43. For primogeniture in the Iberian Peninsula, see Louis de Molina, *De primogeniorum Hispanorum origine, ac natura, libri quatuor, in hae postroma editione puriores ac emendatiores prodeuntes (Ludguni, 1588);* Clavero Arévalo, *Mayorazgo y propiedad feudal en Castilla*; Andrés Barrera González, *Casa, herencia y familia en la Cataluña rural: Lógica de la razón doméstica* (Madrid, 1990); María Cruz Cabeza Sánchez-Albornoz, *La tierra llana de Avila en los siglos XV y XVI* (Avila, 1985).

44. On royal succession in England and France, see Joseph R. Strayer, *On the Medieval Origins of the Modern State* (Princeton, 1970); Robert Fawtier, *The Capetian Kings of France* (New York, 1962); Andrew Lewis, *Royal Succession in Capetian France: Studies in Familial Order and the State* (Cambridge, 1981).

45. AHN, Clero, carp. 227, nos. 1 (18 June 1337) and 3 (12 August 1341).

46. It is important to note that different regions within Iberia had completely particular paths into the future. The Crown of Aragon was as different from Castile as France or England was from the realm of the castles and lions. This serves as a caution against dealing with the peninsula as a whole. For the Crown of Aragon, see Thomas N. Bisson, *The Medieval Crown of Aragon: A Short History* (Oxford, 1986), 56–57.

47. On the way Spanish medieval history is taught as an exception to the history of the so-called center, see T. F. Ruiz, "Centers and Peripheries: Writing and Teaching Medieval and Early Modern Spanish History," in *Actas del II Congreso Internacional Historia a Debate*, ed. Carlos Barros, 3 vols. (Santiago de Compostela, 2000), 3: 85–92.

48. For the individual histories of these different kingdoms, see García de Valdeavellano, *Historia de España antigua y medieval*, 2: 9–498; Joseph F. O'Callaghan, *A History of Medieval Spain* (Ithaca, 1975), 163–253.

49. For the institutional structures of both Muslim lands and the early Christian kingdoms, see Luis García de Valdeavellano's extraordinarily useful *Curso de historia de las instituciones españolas: De los orígines al final de la edad media* (Madrid, 1968), 217–676. Above all, 406–84, 660–69.

50. For the early history of Galicia and Asturias-León, see Roger Collins, *Early Medieval Spain: Unity in Diversity, 400–1000* (New York, 1983).

51. For the political history of this period, see again García de Valdeavellano, *Historia de España antigua y medieval*, 2: 549–607; O'Callaghan, *A History of Medieval Spain*, 331–57.

52. See T. F. Ruiz, "Unsacred Monarchy: The Kings of Castile in the Late Middle Ages," in *Rites of Power: Symbolism, Ritual, and Politics since the Middle Ages*, ed. Sean Wilentz (Philadelphia, 1985), 109–44.

53. Cited from the *Primera crónica general*, 2: 772–73, in Angus MacKay, *Spain in the Middle Ages: From Frontier to Empire, 1000–1500* (London, 1977), 58–59.

54. On these developments, see Joseph R. Strayer, "France: The Holy Land, the Chosen People, and the Most Christian King," in *Medieval Statecraft and the Perspectives of History*, ed. John F. Benton and Thomas N. Bisson (Princeton, 1971), 300–314; Ernst H. Kantorowicz, *The King's Two Bodies: A Study in Medieval Political Theology* (Princeton, 1957).

55. See Joseph F. O'Callaghan, *The Learned King: The Reign of Alfonso X of Castile* (Philadelphia, 1993), 73–5, 154–56. The infante Henry clearly expected to be king, and some of his contemporaries, the king of the Crown of Aragon among them, were willing to recognize his claims.

56. "The eldest son has precedence and superiority over his other brothers. Superiority, by reason of primogeniture, is a great mark of affection which God bestows upon the sons of kings by distinguishing them from their other brothers who are born after them; for he makes it plain that he gives preference to, and places above the others, him upon whom he desires to confer this honor, in order that they may obey him and protect him, as they do their father and their lord"; *Las siete partidas*, ed. Robert I. Burns, trans. Samuel P. Scott, 5 vols. (Philadelphia, 2001), 2: 366.

57. O'Callaghan, *The Learned King*, 236–40. O'Callaghan explores the different interpretations and points, correctly, to the fact that Alfonso was forced to admit Sancho as his heir. "In his will of November 1282 Alfonso X stated that he had reverted to the 'ancient law and law of reason according to the *fuero* of Spain' and had designated Sancho, who represented a closer and more direct line of succession than the children of Fernando de la Cerda."

58. Ibid., 264–67.

CHAPTER 6

The inspiration for this chapter came from two presentations to the Davis Center Seminar by Professor Peter Brown and by Dr. Judith Herrin. A short version of this chapter was presented to the Denys Hay Seminar in Medieval and Renaissance History of the Antiquary Program at the University of Edinburgh and a full version to the Davis Center at Princeton University. I greatly benefited from the many useful suggestions made in both seminars.

1. Sections of this chapter, though reaching somewhat different conclusions, have been borrowed with significant changes and additions from my recent article "The Business of Salvation: Property and Charity in Late Medieval Castile," in *On the Social Origins of Medieval Institutions: Essays in Honor of Joseph F. O'Callaghan* (Leiden, 1998), 63–89.

2. For patterns of wills in late medieval and early modern Castile, see Carlos M. N. Eire, *From Madrid to Purgatory: The Art and Craft of Dying in Sixteenth-Century Spain* (New York, 1995). Also María del Carmen Carlé, *Una sociedad del siglo XV: Los castellanos en sus testamentos* (Buenos Aires, 1993).

3. For the cultural meaning of gift-giving, see the influential work by Marcel Mauss, "Essai sur le don: Forme et raison de l'échange dans les sociétés archaiques," *L'année sociologique* 1 (1923–24): 30–186; Natalie Zenon Davis, *The Gift in Sixteenth-Century France* (Madison, 2000), 23–42.

4. For a discussion of these transformations in other parts of Europe, see Michel Mollat, *Les pauvres au moyen âge* (Paris, 1978); Lester K. Little, *Religious Poverty and the Profit Economy in Medieval Europe* (Ithaca, 1978); James W. Broadman, *Charity and Welfare: Hospitals and the Poor in Medieval Catalonia* (Philadelphia, 1998). In addition, this entire discussion is illuminated by the influential work of Jacques Chiffoleau, *La comptabilité de l'au-delà: Les hommes, la mort et la religion dans la région d'Avignon à la fin du moyen âge, vers 1320–vers 1480* (Rome, 1980); also Michel Vovelle, *La mort et l'Occident de 1300 à nous jours* (Paris, 1983); *Vision de la mort et de l'au-delà en Provence d'après les auteles des âmes du purgatoire, XVe–XXe siècles* (Paris, 1970); and Pierre Chanu, *La morte à Paris, 16e, 17e, 18e siècles* (Paris, 1978). See too the excellent books by Ariel Guiance, *Los discursos sobre la muerte en la Castilla medieval, siglos VII–XV* (Valladolid, 1998), 187–231; and Sharon Farmer, *Surviving Poverty in Medieval Paris: Gender, Ideology, and the Daily Lives of the Poor* (Ithaca, 2002).

5. Cristóbal Pérez de Herrera, *Amparo de pobres*, intro. Michel Cavillac (Madrid, 1975), 86–88; Domingo de Soto, *Deliberación en la causa de los pobres* (Madrid, 1965), 62–70. For a discussion on the debate over the poor in early

modern Spain, see Cavillac's introduction, i–clxxix. Also Linda Martz, *Poverty and Welfare in Habsburg Spain: The Example of Toledo* (Cambridge, 1983), 7–91.

6. Jean Pierre Gutton, *La société et les pauvres en Europe, XVIe–XVIIIe siècles* (Paris, 1974), 97–115; Catherine Lis and Hugo Soly, *Poverty and Capitalism in Pre-Industrial Europe*, trans. James Coonan (Sussex, 1979); Martz, *Poverty and Welfare in Habsburg Spain*, 1–91.

7. Pérez de Herrera, *Amparo de pobres*, intro. Cavillac, lxxiv–lxxix; Gutton, *La société et les pauvres en Europe*, 93–97.

8. See Adeline Rucquoi, *Valladolid en la edad media*, 2 vols. (Valladolid, 1987). Also John H. Elliott, *The Count-Duke of Olivares: The Statesman in an Age of Decline* (New Haven, 1986), 16; Ruth Behar, *Santa María del Monte: The Presence of the Past in a Spanish Village* (Princeton, 1986), 183–84.

9. On the late medieval Castilian crisis, see Julio Valdeón Baruque, "Aspectos de la crisis castellana en la primera mitad del siglo XIV," *Hispania* 111 (1969): 5–24; T. F. Ruiz, "Expansion et changement: La conquête de Séville et la société castillane, 1248–1350," *Annales E.S.C.* 3 (1979): 548–65; and my *Crisis and Continuity: Land and Town in Late Medieval Castile* (Philadelphia, 1994) and bibliography therein.

10. See my "Expansion et changement."

11. The bibliography on the history of poverty and charity in western Europe is quite extensive, and a few references will suffice. See Mollat, *Les pauvres au moyen âge*; *Etudes sur l'histoire de la pauvreté moyen âge–XVIe siècle*, ed. Michel Mollat, 2 vols. (Paris, 1974), and comprehensive bibliographies included in both works. For the Iberian Peninsula, above all, northern Castile, see the articles collected in *A pobreza e a assistência aos pobres na península ibérica durante a idade média: Actas das jornadas luso-espanholas de história medieval*, 2 vols. (Lisboa, 1973); hereafter cited as *A pobreza*. Also Carmen López Alonso, *Los rostros, la realidad de la pobreza en la sociedad castellana medieval, siglos XIII–XV* (Madrid, 1983); and her *La pobreza en la España medieval: Estudio histórico social* (Madrid, 1986); Antonio Rumeu de Armas, *Historia de la previsión social en España: Cofradías, gremios, hermandades, montepíos* (Madrid, 1944); Luis Martínez García, *La asistencia a los pobres en Burgos en la baja edad media: El hospital de Santa María la Real, 1341–1500* (Burgos, 1981). For the eastern kingdoms, see the recent and most useful synthesis by Broadman, *Charity and Welfare*. For the early modern period see Martz, *Poverty and Welfare in Habsburg Spain* and her extensive bibliography. See also my article "Poverty," forthcoming in a supplement to the *Dictionary of the Middle Ages*.

12. For antagonisms against the poor in other parts of Europe, see Michel Mollat, "Pauvres et assistés au moyen âge," in *A pobreza*, 1: 26–27; Frantisek Graus, "Au bas moyen âge: Pauvres des villes et pauvres de campagnes," *Annales E.S.C.* 16 (1961): 1056–57.

13. *Las siete partidas*, partida 1, title 23, laws 7–10, in *Los códigos españoles concordados y anotados*, ed. M. Rivadeneyra, 12 vols. (Madrid, 1847–51), 2: 310–12.

14. For rights of inheritance, *Fuero juzgo* bk. 4, tit. 1 and 2, in *Códigos*, 1:

132–37; *Fuero real*, bk. 3, tit. 6, law 10, in *Códigos*, 1: 382. See also partida 6, tit. 3, law 20, in *Códigos*, 4: 42. For attacks against the idle, parti. 2, tit. 20, law 4, in *Códigos*, 2: 463; *Cortes de los antiguos reinos de León y Castilla*, 5 vols. (Madrid, 1861–63), 1: 78; 2: 76, 92, 112. On the martial and noble character of Castilian society, see my "Une royaute sans sacre: La monarchie castillane du bas moyen âge," *Annales E.S.C.* 3 (1984): 429–53. For repressive measures in early modern Spain, see Martz, *Poverty and Welfare in Habsburg Spain*, 14–21, 27; William A. Christian Jr., *Local Religion in Sixteenth-Century Spain* (Princeton, 1981), 24.

15. *Recueil de chartes de l'abbaye de Silos*, ed. Marius Ferotin (Paris, 1897), 380, 389, 390–91, 403. In his testament, Martín Ibáñez, prior of the cathedral chapter of Burgos, left 200 *mrs.* to clothe *pobres envergoñados*. Archivo de la Catedral de Burgos (ACB), vol. 48, f. 319 (30 July 1333). See also note 24 below.

16. See Luis Martín, "La pobreza y los pobres en los textos literarios del siglo XIV," in *A pobreza*, 2: 601, 611–12, 614.

17. Juan Ruiz, *Libro de buen amor*, ed. María Brey Mariño, 2d ed. (Valencia, 1960), 269 (1590a–d), 282–83 (1650a–1660d).

18. *Libro de Apolonio*, ed. Pablo Cabañas, 4th ed. (Madrid, 1982), 59–61; Gonzalo de Berceo, *Milagros de Nuestra Señora*, ed. Daniel Devoto, 7th ed. (Madrid, 1982), milagro 5, 38–39.

19. See *Libro de Apolonio*, 132b; Berceo, *Milagros de Nuestra Señora*, 135c; *Vida de Santo Domingo de Silos*, ed. Teresa Labarta de Chaves (Madrid, 1982), 46d, 105c, 467a, 467c; Juan Manuel, *El Conde Lucanor*, ed. José Manuel Blecua (Madrid, 1969), exemplo 1; Ruiz, *Libro de buen amor*, 149a, 1308c, 1572a, 1590b. For the distinction between alms and rations—"Dad limosna, o raçión"—see 1651a.

20. *Poema de mío Cid*, ed. Ian Michael (Madrid, 1987), 709, 714, 720, 3253; Berceo, *Milagros de Nuestra Señora*, 224; Berceo, *Vida de San Millán*, ed. Brian Dutton (London, 1967), 200d. The reference to charity as food and drink is on 352d. See also *Libro de Apolonio*, 128a, 255a; Ruiz, *Libro de buen amor*, 379d, 1309a, 1322d, 1594b, 1599b, 1603b.

21. Joel T. Rosenthal, *The Purchase of Paradise: Gift Giving and the Aristocracy, 1307–1485* (London, 1972), 9.

22. *Documentación de la catedral de Burgos, 804–1183*, ed. José Manuel Garrido Garrido, in *Fuentes medievals castellano-leonesas* (*FMCL*), vol. 13 (Burgos, 1983), 155–56; *Fuentes para la historia de Castilla*, ed. Luciano Serrano, 3 vols. (Valladolid, 1906–10), 3: 336.

23. Rosenthal, *The Purchase of Paradise*, 11–15. Most of the early donations and wills in northern Castile contain such expressions as "pro remedio anima mee" [*sic*]," "ut evadam portas inferni," and, occasionally, "pro extinguenda incendia gehenne ignis." *Fuentes*, ed. Serrano, 3: 108–10, 189–90.

24. For institutionalized support for the poor in the Iberian Peninsula, mostly after 1350, see relevant articles in *A pobreza*. Outside Iberia, see Mollat, *Les pauvres au moyen âge*, 169–76. For a later period, see Natalie Z. Davis, "Poor Relief, Humanism, and Heresy: The Case of Lyons," *Studies in Medieval and Renaissance History* 5 (1968): 240: "The other major difference between the medieval

period and the sixteenth century in redistributing income to the poor is in administration."

25. For the wills of kings after 1350 that included provisions for feeding the poor. see Julio Valdeón, "Problemática para un estudio de los pobres y de la pobreza en Castilla a fines de la edad media," in *A pobreza*, 2: 911. In their respective wills, John I and Henry III ordered that six hundred poor be clothed the day of their (the king's) burial and fed for the next nine days. Yet neither of Alfonso X's two wills included any provisions for the poor. *Memorial histórico español*, 47 vols. (Madrid, 1851–1915), 2: 110–34.

26. See Jaume Aurell, *Els mercaders catalans al quatre-cents: Mutació de valors i procés d'aristocratització a Barcelona, 1370–1470* (Lleida, 1996); Jaume Aurell and Alfons Puigarnau, *La cultura del mercader en la Barcelona del siglo XV* (Barcelona, 1998).

27. ACB, vol. 48, f. 319 (30 July and 7 August 1333): "E mando a Iohan Rodríguez provea a donna Maria, la que biue conmigo, en toda su vida de comer e de beuer e de lo que ouiere mester de lo mio, e mando a esta donna Maria una carga de trigo".

28. *Colección diplomática de las colegiates de Albelda y Logroño*, vol. 1, 924–1399, ed. Elisea Saínz Ripa (Logroño, 1981), 208–9 (1 May 1331). Hereafter cited as *Albelda y Logroño*.

29. Ibid., 269–73 (2 September 1347).

30. For other wills, see ACB, vol. 48, f. 315 (10 August 1253); *Documentación de la catedral de Burgos, 1254–1293*, ed. F. Javier Pereda Llarena, in *FMCL*, vol. 16 (Burgos, 1984)/ The extensive testament on 174–79 (1267–74). itemizes debts and legacies very carefully. Garci de Campo, a member of the cathedral chapter of Burgos, was clearly a wealthy man, and his legacies reached a good number of relatives, friends, and ecclesiastical institutions. One of his legacies was to support Ferrando Tellez at a school for six years and included his copies of the *Decretum* and glosses on canonical works. To the poor he left just 30 *mrs*. The testament of Don Julián on 363–70 (4 May 1316) is also a lengthy document in which vast wealth was widely distributed among many different ecclesiastical institutions and philanthropies. Most of the actual real estate was given to relatives and friends. Of note is a legacy of 1,000 *mrs.* to the ransoming order of the Trinity to rescue Christians in Muslim captivity. Those rescued had to show themselves to the will's executors to bear witness of their freedom. That day, they would be fed and given a pair of shoes. One hundred of the poor were also to be clothed and fed with wine, bread, and meat. To the woman who lived with him as a concubine (*manceba*), he gave 200 *mrs.* ACB, vol. 15, p. 2, f. 489 (31 January 1319) is the testament of the Infante Don Juan, one of the regents for the young Alfonso XI; ACB, vol. 48, f. 319 (30 July and 7 August 1333) is the will of Martín Ibáñez discussed above. See also ACB, vol. 36, f. 36 (18 June 1348). For Santander, see the will of Marín Roiz, a barrel maker, in *Archivo de la catedral de Santander*, ed. Lorena Fernández González (Santander, 1994), 113–15 (21 August 1334). This meager will made some pious donations, no legacies for the poor, and most of his limited income (around 300 *mrs.*) went to his daughter and son. There are numerous other wills in the extant Castilian docu-

mentation but they all follow essentially the same pattern as those mentioned above.

31. *Archivo de la catedral de Santander*, ed. Fernández Gonzáles, 104–6 (20 July 1315).

32. Archivo Histórico Nacional (AHN), Clero collection, carpeta 1662, no. 2 (15 April 1289).

33. What and how much the poor were fed at these charitable feasts or in hospitals remained constant throughout the next centuries. Similar portions were served in fifteenth-century Burgos and in sixteenth-century Lyons. See Carlos Estepa Díez et al., *Burgos en la edad media* (Valladolid, 1984), 453; N. Z. Davis, "Poor Relief, Humanism, and Heresy," 244; Luis Martínez García, "La asistencia material en los hospitales de Burgos a fines de la edad media," in *Manger et boire au moyen âge: Actes du colloque de Nice*, 2 vols. (Nice, 1984), 1: 335–47. See also Teofilo F. Ruiz, *Spanish Society, 1400–1600* (London, 2001), 209–19.

34. AHN, Clero, carp. 226, no. 17 (20 August 1334); carp. 227, no. 2 (20 October 1334).

35. AHN, Clero, carp. 227, no. 7 (13 April 1344).

36. ACB, vol. 49, f. 438 (23 July 1349).

37. Most of the ideas in this section were developed from comments made on an early draft of this paper by Charles M. Radding and from the discussion of this topic when first presented to the Davis Center at Princeton University.

38. For the selection of a symbolic number of the poor to be fed at special occasions or the endowment of a specific number of hospital beds, see Mollat, *Les pauvres au moyen âge*, 66; Estepa Díez et al., *Burgos en la edad media*, 452–53; *Regularis concordia: Anglicae nationis monachorum sanctimonialiumque*, trans. Dom Thomas Symons (London, 1953), xxxvii, 61–62. For giving bread to the poor over the tomb of the donor, see *Albelda y Logroño*, 50; Carmen Battle, "La ayuda a los pobres en la parroquia de San Justo de Barcelona," in *A pobreza*, 1: 64. For feasting around tombs in early Christianity, see Judith Herrin, "Women and the Faith in Icons in Early Christianity," in *Culture, Ideology, and Politics*, ed. R. Samuel and G. Steadman Jones (London, 1983), 57–58. Also Christian, *Local Religion in Sixteenth-Century Spain*, 57. On the idea of "social asymmetry," I follow Peter Brown's comments on Michael W. Dols's paper to the Davis Center on 18 October 1985, "where the donor is to God as the poor is to the donor." On primitive forms of funeral feasts, see James G. Frazer, *The Golden Bough: A Study in Magic and Religion*, abridged ed. (New York, 1927), 147–61; Richard Huntington, *Celebration of Death: The Anthropology of Mortuary Rites* (Cambridge, 1979), 105–7.

39. See my *Spanish Society, 1400–1600*, ch. 9.

40. These distinctions went beyond earthly boundaries. In heaven, the angels ate *pan candeal*, the purest white wheat bread. Among the many agreements found in Castilian archives in which donations of property were made in return for maintenance for life, the quality of the bread, meat, and wine was often clearly spelled out. In Oña we find references to the *pan de señores* (bread of the lords); AHN, Clero, carp. 312, no. 18 (8 August 1345). In 1293, when Doña María de Sagentes made arrangements for her support with the abbot and monastery of

Santa María la Real, she insisted on two liters of wine daily "of that which the abbot drinks," and meat on Sundays, Tuesdays, and Thursdays; AHN, Clero, carp. 1662, no. 12 (9 August 1293).

41. T. F. Ruiz, "The Transformation of the Castilian Municipalities: The Case of Burgos, 1248–1350," *Past & Present* 77 (1977): 17–20.

42. Juan José García González, *Vida económica de los monasterios benedictinos en el siglo XIV* (Valladolid, 1972), 115–16, and his edition of the accounts of northern Castilian Benedictine monasteries (1338), 131 ff.

43. Ibid., 91–99.

44. I owe thanks to Miguel Santamaría Lancho for the information on Segovia. See his *La gestión económica del cabildo de Segovia* (Master's thesis, Universidad Complutense, Madrid, 1979); García González, *Vida económica*, 131ff.

45. Estepa Díez et al., 189–92, *Burgos en la edad media*, 446–61.

46. ACB, vol. 44, f. 178 (15 November 1312), f. 179 (20 April 1338), f. 180 (2 December 1366).

CHAPTER 7

I owe an immense debt of gratitude to Dr. Peter Linehan for his intellectual contribution and friendly support. His early suggestions to my *Annales* article and his research, which he generously shared with me, shaped the nature of this chapter. This chapter, with some changes, additions, and different aims, follows my "La formazione della monarchia non consacrata: Simboli e realità di pottere nella Castiglia medievale," in *Federico II e il mondo mediterraneo*, ed. Pierre Toubert and Agostino Paravicino Bagliani, 3 vols. (Palermo, 1995), 1: 230–47.

1. The bibliography on sacred kingship is extensive indeed, and the topic still fascinates medieval historians as attested by the numerous conferences on the theme over the last few years. Among the normative studies a few titles stand out: Marc Bloch, *The Royal Touch: Sacred Monarchy and Scrofula in England and France*, trans. F. E. Anderson (London, 1973); Ernst H. Kantorowicz, *The King's Two Bodies: A Study in Medieval Political Theology* (Princeton, 1957); Percy E. Schramm, *A History of the English Coronation*, trans. Leopold C. Wickham (Oxford, 1937). See also a recent work by Jacques Le Goff et al., *Le sacre royal à l'époque de Saint Louis* (Paris, 2001).

2. See, for example, Joseph R. Strayer, *On the Medieval Origins of the Modern State* (Princeton, 1970), 19–111.

3. T. F. Ruiz, "Une royaute sans sacre: La monarchie castillane du bas moyen âge," in *Annales E.S.C.* 3 (1984): 429–53. See, in particular, 430–33. This article appeared with minor revisions as "Unsacred Monarchy: The Kings of Castile in the Late Middle Ages," in *Rites of Power: Symbolism, Ritual, and Politics since the Middle Ages,* ed. Sean Wilentz (Philadelphia, 1985), 109–44. Recently Peter Linehan and Carlrichard Bruhl have questioned whether ritual anointment was present in the Asturian monarchy. Such attributions seemed to have been part of the mythical recreation of the past by medieval chroniclers and accepted without the critical examination by some recent historians.

4. On Sancho IV, see Peter Linehan, *History and Historians of Medieval Spain*

(Oxford, 1993), 446–85. See also Mercedes Gaibrois de Ballesteros, *Historia del reinado de Sancho IV de Castilla,* 3 vols. (Madrid, 1922–28). On the early Trastámaras, see Luis Suárez Fernández, *Nobleza y monarquia: Puntos de vista sobre la historia castellana del siglo XV,* 2d ed. (Valladolid, 1959). See also Ruiz, "Unsacred Monarchy" 109–10, 117.

5. Linehan, *History and the Historians of Medieval Spain,* 427–30, 586. See also his review of Nieto Soria's *Iglesia y poder en Castilla: El episcopado, 1250–1350* and *Fundamentos ideológicos del poder real en Castilla, siglos XIII–XVI,* in *Speculum* 65 (1990): 469–72.

6. See José Manuel Nieto Soria, "La monarquía bajomedieval castellana: Una realeza sagrada?" in *Homenaje al profesor Juan Torres Fontes* (Murcia, 1987), 1225–37; *Fundamentos ideológicos del poder real en Castilla, siglos XIII–XVI* (Madrid, 1988).

7. Angus MacKay has studied the messianic attributions of Fernando of Antequera and Fernando II, the Catholic King. See his "Don Fernando de Antequera y la Virgen Santa María," in *Homenaje al profesor Juan Torres Fontes,* 949–57. See also *The 'Libro de las profecías' of Christopher Columbus,* trans and commentary Delno C. West and August King (Gainsville, 1991), 41–77; Valerie I. J. Flint, *The Imaginary Landscape of Christopher Columbus* (Princeton, 1992), 149–214; Alain Milhou, "Le chauve-souris, le nouveau David et le roi cache: Trois images de l'empereur des derniers temps dans le monde ibérique: XIIIe–XVIIe siecles," *Melanges de la Casa de Velásquez* 18 (1982): 61–78.

8. Ruiz, "Unsacred Monarchy," 127 n. 53.

9. Nieto Soria, *Fundamentos ideológicos,* 63–64.

10. Nieto Soria, "La monarquia bajomedieval," 1228 n. 12. See Ruiz, "L'image du pouvoir a travers les sceaux de la monarchie castillane," in *Genese médiévale de l'etat moderne: La Castille et la Navarre, 1250–1370,* ed. Adeline Rucquoi (Valladolid, 1987), 217–27.

11. As I indicated above, Peter Linehan has already, in his superb and elegant study of Castilian ideology and historical fabrication, provided a witty and resounding critique of Nieto Soria's views. I have never been shy, and certainly not now, to defer on this point to my betters. If I am allowed a further disgression, I fear that what Professor Nieto Soria and others could not forgive were my closing remarks in my *Annales* article. They contained an indictment of Franco and of religion expressed in an affected and melodramatic ending, the last words of which were "malheureuse Castile, malheureuse l'Espagne." Perhaps these sentiments clashed with Nieto Soria's own particular view of what Spain was and ought to be. Nor did I intend to posit France and England as paradigms of sacral kingship, or Castile as an aberration. To the contrary, my aim was to point out that we err when we subscribe to such a narrow view of medieval life.

12. There is a Spanish translation of Lucas de Tuy's chronicle with some later additions. See Lucas de Tuy, *Crónica de España,* ed. Julio Puyol (Madrid, 1926). Latin version, *Chronicon mundi,* ed. Andreas Schottus, in *Hispania illustrata,* 4 vols. (Frankfurt, 1608); Rodrigo Ximénez de Rada, *Historia de rebus Hispanie sive historia gothica,* ed. Juan Fernández Valverde, *Corpus christianorum continuatio mediaevalis* 72 (Turnhout, Belgium, 1987); *Primera crónica general de*

España que mandó componer Alfonso el Sabio y se continuaba bajo Sancho IV en 1289, ed. Ramón Menéndez Pidal, 2 vols. (Madrid, 1955).

13. See Linehan's *History and the Historians of Medieval Spain.* Also his "The Toledo Forgeries c. 1150–1300," in *Falschungen im Mittlealter,* vol. 1 (Hannover, 1988), 643–74; and his "Ideología y liturgia en el reinado de Alfonso XI de Castilla," in *Genese médiévale de l'état moderne,* ed. Rucquoi, 229–244.

14. On the so-called Neo-Gothic revival in Asturias and León, see Luis García de Valdeavellano, *Historia de España: Desde los orígenes a la baja edad media,* 2d ed., 1 vol. In 2 (Madrid, 1952), 507–25; Percy E. Schramm, *Las insignias de la realeza en la edad media española,* trans. L. Vásquez de Parga (Madrid, 1960), 26–27, 32, 61–63.

15. García de Valdeavellano, *Historia de España,* 746. On Navarrese institutions, see also García de Valdeavellano, *Curso de historia de las instituciones españolas: De los orígenes al final de la edad media* (Madrid, 1968), 226–39, 380–88.

16. The story is told laconically by Rodrigo Ximénez de Rada in *Historia de rebus,* 169–70, and was later embellished and expanded by the composers of the *Primera crónica general,* 467–68.

17. For a brief but enlightened discussion of different theories of the origins of power, see Walter Ullmann, *A History of Political Thought: The Middle Ages* (Baltimore, 1968), 53ff. The motif of valor and its counterpart, cowardice, in myths of origin is examined by Paul Freedman in his "Cowardice, Heroism, and the Legendary Origins of Catalonia," *Past & Present* 121 (1988): 6–14.

18. A careful description of this period is found in García de Valdeavellano, *Historia de España,* 744–97; Joseph O'Callaghan, *A History of Medieval Spain* (Ithaca, 1975), 191–214.

19. On the pilgrimage and its importance on Castilian society see Luis García de Valdeavellano, *Orígenes de la burguesía en la España medieval* (Madrid, 1969). For Spain and, in particular, Castile's proximity to the rest of the medieval West in this period, see *Santiago, Saint-Denis, and Saint Peter: The Reception of the Roman Liturgy in León-Castile in 1080,* ed. Bernard F. Reilly (New York, 1985), above all, 101–20.

20. Linehan, "Toledo Forgeries," 646–47.

21. Bernard F. Reilly, *The Kingdom of León-Castile under King Alfonso VI, 1065–1109* (Princeton, 1988), 103–4.

22. Ximénez de Rada, *Historia de rebus,* 207–8; *Primera crónica general,* 2: 542–43. See also Ramón Menéndez Pidal, *La España del Cid,* 7th ed., 2 vols. (Madrid, 1969), 2: 237–51.

23. See many examples in Peter Linehan's *History and the Historians of Medieval Spain.* Also Ruiz, "Unsacred Monarchy," 127–32; my "Festivités, couleurs et symboles du pouvoir en Castille au XVe siècle: Les célébrations de mai 1428," *Annales E.S.C.* 3 (1991): 521–46; and my "Elite and Popular Culture in Late Fifteenth-Century Castilian Festivals: The Case of Jaén," in *City and Spectacle in Medieval Europe,* ed. Barbara A. Hanawalt and Kathryn L. Reyerson (Minneapolis, 1994) where festivals in fifteenth-century Castile were significant for the absence of ecclesiastics.

24. On the Reconquest, see Derek Lomax, *The Reconquest of Spain* (London, 1978); José María Lacarra et al., eds., *La reconquista española y la repoblación del país* (Saragossa, 1951).

25. *Primera crónica general*, 2: 772–73. English translation quoted in Angus MacKay, *Spain in the Middle Ages: From Frontier to Empire, 1000–1500* (London, 1977), 59. MacKay's superb interpretative history of medieval Iberia emphasizes the role of war and the gaining of booty in the making of Castile.

26. *Crónica de Alfonso X*, in *Crónicas de los reyes de Castilla*, ed. C. Rosell, vol. 1 (Madrid, 1953), 53.

27. Ibid., 3–4.

28. See Peter Linehan, *The Spanish Church and the Papacy in the Thirteenth Century* (Cambridge, 1971), and his other works cited throughout.

29. For the argument of the defense of the realm, see Joseph R. Strayer, "Defense of the Realm and Royal Power in France," in *Medieval Statecraft and the Perspectives of History*, ed. John F. Benton and Thomas N. Bisson (Princeton, 1971), 291–99.

30. The conflicting claims of Santiago de Compostela, León, Burgos, Seville, and, above all, Toledo are explored in detail in Linehan's *History and the Historians of Medieval Spain*.

31. Ruiz, "Unsacred Monarchy," 113 n. 18, 126 n. 49; also Linehan's *History and the Historians of Medieval Spain*.

32. Ximénez de Rada, *Historia de rebus*, 229: "Post hec rediens Legionem imposuit sibi imperii diadema, et uocatus fuit deinceps imperator." *Primera crónica general*, 2: 654.

33. See Ramón Menéndez Pidal, *El imperio hispánico y los cinco reinos* (Madrid, 1950).

34. Ximénez de Rada, *Historia de rebus*, 175–76; 225; 233; 281; 285–86. *Primera crónica general*, 2: 663, 668, 708–9, 713, 722–23.

35. For a narrative of the political history of the period, see García de Valdeavellano, *Historia de España*, 859–1071; O'Callaghan, *A History of Medieval Spain*, 191–330.

36. For the ceremonies of Ferdinand III, see Ruiz, "Unsacred Monarchy," 122–23.

37. Manuel Recuero Astray, *Alfonso VII, emperador: El imperio hispánico en el siglo XII* (León, 1979), 130–33 n. 100.

38. See A. Lloyd Moote, "Sacred Monarchy and Regicide in France, 1589–1793" (a paper given at an Early Modern Seminar at Princeton in 1997), and Paul Kléber Monod, *The Power of Kings: Monarchy and Religion in Europe, 1589–1715* (New Haven, 1999), 33–141.

39. See Joseph R. Strayer's numerous works on the administrative transformations that took place in late twelfth- and early thirteenth-century England and France, for example, *The Administration of Normandy under Saint Louis* (Cambridge, 1932); *Les gens de justice du Languedoc sous Phillippe le Bel* (Toulouse, 1970); and *The Reign of Philip the Fair* (Princeton, 1980).

40. See Joseph F. O'Callaghan, *The Cortes of Castile-León, 1188–1350* (Philadelphia, 1989), 9–19.

41. The best study of medieval Spanish (mostly Castilian) institutional history is the formidable book by the great García de Valdeavellano, *Curso de historia de las instituciones españolas*.

42. See my *The City and the Realm: Burgos and Castile, 1080–1492* (London, 1992), chs. 3, 4, 6, 7, 9, and 12.

43. Francisco Hernández, *Las rentas del rey: Sociedad y fisco en el reino castellano del siglo XIII* 2 vols. (Madrid, 1993).

44. See O'Callaghan, *The Cortes of Castile-León*, 24–31; Luis Suárez Fernández, "Evolución histórica de las hermandades castellanas," *Cuadernos de historia de España* 16 (1951): 6–78.

45. *Cortes de los antigues reinos de León y Castilla*, 5 vols., vols. 1 and 2 (Madrid, 1861–63), 1: 247–72 (1315).

CONCLUSION

1. For Berceo and his work, see the introduction and commentary found in *Gonzalo de Berceo: Obras completas*, ed. Brian Dutton, 2d ed. (London, 1984).

BIBLIOGRAPHY

PRIMARY SOURCES AND SOURCE COLLECTIONS

Archivo de la Catedral de Burgos (ACB)
Archivo Histórico Nacional (AHN)
Archivo Municipal de Burgos (AMB)
Archivo Municipal de Segovia (AMS)
Avila: Fuentes y archivos. Ed. Cándido M. Ajo González y Sáinz de Zuñiga. 2 vols. Madrid: Artes Gráficas Arges, 1967.
El becerro del monasterio de San Juan de Burgos. Burgos: Ayuntamiento de Burgos, 1950.
Biblioteca Nacional (BN)
Cartulario de San Millán de la Cogolla, 759–1076. Ed. Antonio Ubieto Arteta. Valencia: Instituto de Estudios Riojanos, 1976.
Cartulario de Santo Toribio de Liébana. Ed. Luis Sánchez Belda. Madrid: Archivo Histórico Nacional, 1948.
Cartulario real a la provincia de Alava, 1258–1500. Ed. Esperanza Iñurrieta Ambrosio. San Sebastián: Sociedad de Estudios Vascos, 1983.
The Code of Cuenca: Municipal Law on the Twelfth-Century Frontier. Trans. and intro. James F. Powers. Philadelphia: University of Pennsylvania Press, 2000.
Los códigos españoles concordados y anotados. Ed. M. Rivadeneyra. 12 vols. Madrid: Imprenta de la publicidad, 1847–51.
Colección de fueros municipales y cartas pueblas. Ed. Tomás Muñoz y Romero. Madrid: Imprenta de don José M. Alonso, 1847.
Colección diplomática calceatense: Archivo catedral, 1125–1397. Ed. C. López de Silanos and E. Saínz de Ripa. Logroño: Instituto de Estudios Riojanos, 1985.
Colección diplomática de Cuéllar. Ed. Antonio Ubieta Arteta. Segovia: Diputación Provincial de Segovia, 1961.
Colección diplomática de las colegiatas de Albelda y Logroño. Vol. 1, 924–1399. Ed. Eliseo Saínz Ripa. Logroño: Instituto de Estudios Riojanos, 1981.
Colección diplomática de San Salvador de Oña. Ed. Juan de Alamo. 2 vols. Madrid: Consejo Superior de Investigaciones Científicas; 1950–51.
Colección diplomática de Sepúlveda, 1076–1454. Ed. Emilio Sáez. Segovia; Diputación Provincial de Segovia, 1956.
Colección diplomática del concejo de Burgos, 884–1369. Ed. Emiliano González Diez. Burgos: Instituto de Estudios Castellanos, 1984.
Colección diplomática del concejo de Segura (Guipuzcoa), 1290–1500. Ed. Luis M. Díez de Salazar Fernández. San Sebastián: Sociedad de Estudios Vascos, 1985.
Colección documental de Alfonso XI. Ed. Esther González Crespo. Madrid: Universidad Complutense, 1985.

Colección documental del archivo municipal de Piedrahita, 1372-1549. Ed. L. López Carmelo. Avila: Excma. Diputación Provincial de Avila, 1987.
Colección documental del archivo municipal de Santander. Ed. Manuel Vaquerizo Gil and Pérez Bustamante, Rogelio. Santander: Ayuntamiento de Santander, 1977.
Cortes de los antiguos reinos de León y Castilla. 5 vols. Vols. 1 qnd 2. Madrid: Imprenta y esterotipia de M. Rivadeneyra, 1861-63.
Crónicas de los reyes de Castilla. Ed. C. Rosell. Vol. 1. Madrid: Biblioteca de Autores Españoles, 1953.
Cuentas y gastos (1292-1294) del rey D. Sancho IV el Bravo (1284-1295). Ed. Asunción López Dapena. Córdoba: Publicaciones del Monte de Piedad y Caja de Ahorros de Córdoba, 1984.
Desde Estella a Sevilla: Cuentas de un viaje (1352). Ed. María D. Sanchez Villar. Valencia: Instituto de Estudios Medievales, 1974.
Descripción histórica del obispado de Osma. Ed. José Loperráez Corvalán. Vol. 3, *Colección diplomática*. Madrid: Imprenta Real, 1788.
Die Juden im Christilichen Spanien. Ed. Fritz Y. Baer. 2 vols. Berlin: Akademieverlag, 1929-36. Reprint, Farnborough: Gregg, 1970.
Diplomatario andaluz de Alfonso X. Ed. Manuel González Jiménez. Seville: El Monte, Caja de Ahorros de Huelva y Sevilla, 1991.
Diplomatario de Salinas de Añana, 1194-1465. Ed. Santiago López Castillo. San Sebastián: Sociedad de Estudios Vascos, 1984.
Documentacion medieval de la catedral de Avila. Ed. Angel Barrios García. Salamanca: Universidad de Salamanca, 1981.
Documentación medieval de la catedral de Segovia, 1115-1300. Ed. Luis M. Villar García. Salamanca: Universidad de Salamanca, 1990.
Documentación medieval del archivo municipal de San Bartolomé de Pinares (Avila). Ed. Gregorio del Ser Quijano. Avila: Excma. Diputación Provincial de Avila, 1987.
Documentos de los archivos catedralicio y diocesano de Salamanca, siglos XII-XIII. Ed. José L. Martín et al. Salamanca: Universidad de Salamanca, 1977.
Documentos inéditos de Alfonso X el sabio y del infante su hijo Don Sancho. Ed. Juan M. del Estal. Alicante: Cirilo Industrias Gráficas, 1984.
Fuentes medievales castellano-leonesas. Ed. J. José García, F. Javier de la Peña, et al. Twenty-five volumes published of a projected 103. Burgos, Palencia: Ediciones J. M. Garrido Garrido, 1983- .
Fuentes para la historia de Castilla. Ed. Luciano Serrano. 3 vols. Valladolid: G. del Amo, 1906-10.
Fuero de Cuenca (formas primitiva y sistemática: texto latino, texto castellano y adaptación del fuero de Iznatoraf). Ed. Rafael de Ureña y Smenjaud. Madrid, Tipografia de Archives, 1935.
Fueros locales en el territorio de la provincia de Burgos. Ed. Gonzalo Martínez Díez. Burgos: Caja de Ahorros Municipal de Burgos, 1982.
Historia de la diócesis de Siguenza y de sus obispos. Ed. Toribio Minguella. 3 vols. Madrid: Imprenta de la Revista de Archivos, Bibliotecas y Museos, 1910-13.
Historia del reinado de Sancho IV de Castilla. Ed. Mercedes Gaibrois de Ba-

llesteros. 3 vols. Madrid: Tipografía de la Revista de Archivos, Bibliotecas y Museos, 1922–28.
Libro becerro de las behetrías: Estudio y texto crítico. Ed. Gonzalo Martínes Díez, 3 vols. León: Centro de Estudios e Investigaciones "San Isidoro," 1981.
El libro del repartimiento de Jerez de la Frontera. Ed. Manuel González Jiménez and Antonio González Gómez. Cádiz: Instituto de Estudios Gaditanos, 1980.
Memorial histórico español. 49 vols. Madrid: Real Academia de la Historia, 1851–1948.
Memorias de Fernando IV de Castilla. Antonio Benavides. 2 vols. Madrid: Imprenta de J. Rodríguez, 1960.
Palencia: Panorámica foral de la provincia. Ed. Justiniano Rodríguez Fernández. Palencia: Merino A. G., 1981.
Primera crónica general. Ed. Ramón Menéndez Pidal. 2 vols. Madrid: Nueva Biblioteca de Autores Españoles, 1956.
"Primitiva regla escrita de la Cofradía de Nuestra Señora de Gamonal." Julián García Sáinz de Baranda. *Boletín de la Comisión de Monumentos Artísticos de la Provincia de Burgos* 65 (1938): 158–64.
El real monasterio de las Huelgas y el Hospital del Rey. Ed. Antonio Rodríguez López. 2 vols. Burgos: Imprenta y Librería del Centro Católico, 1907.
Recueil des chartes de l'abbaye de Silos. Ed. Marius Ferotin. Paris: Imprimerie Nationale, 1897.
Repartimiento de Murcia. Ed. Juan Torres Fontes. Madrid: C.S.I.C., 1960.
Repartimiento de Sevilla. Ed. Julio González. 2 vols. Madrid: C.S.I.C., 1951.
Las siete partidas. Ed. Robert I. Burns. Trans. Samuel P. Scott. 5 vols. Philadelphia: University of Pennsylvania Press, 2001.
Texto cronológico de las tres 'Reglas,' por las que sucesivamente, rigió su vida corporativa esta Real Hermandad fundada por el rey Alfonso XI en la era de 1376 [año de Cristo de 1338]. Ed. Ismael García Rámila. Burgos: Imprenta Provincial, 1970.
Viajes de extranjeros por España y Portugal. Ed. José García Mercadal. 3 vols. Madrid: Aguilar, 1952.
Vida económica de los monasterios benedictinos en el siglo XIV. Juan José García González. Valladolid: Universidad de Valladolid, 1972.

SELECTED SECONDARY SOURCES

Abel, Wilhelm. *Agricultural Fluctuations in Europe: From the Thirteenth to the Twentieth Centuries.* London: Methuen, 1980.
Albarellos, Juan. *Efemerídades burgalesas: Apuntes históricos.* 2d ed. Burgos: Diario de Burgos, 1964.
Alfonso, María I. "Las sernas en León y Castilla: Contribución al estudio de las relaciones socio-económicas en el marco del señorío medieval." *Moneda y crédito* 129 (1974): 153–210.
Alvarez Borges, Ignacio. *El feudalismo castellano y el libro becerro de las behetrías: La merindad de Burgos.* León: Junta de Castilla y León, 1987.
Alvarez Palenzuela, Vicente A. *Monasterios cistercienses en Castilla, siglos XII–XIII.* Valladolid: Universidad de Valladolid, 1978.

Araluce Cuenca, José R. *El libro de los estados: Don Juan Manuel y la sociedad de su tiempo.* Madrid: Ediciones José Porrua Turanzos, 1976.

Ariz, Luis de. *Historia de las grandezas de la ciudad de Avila.* Alcalá de Henares: L. Martínez Grande, 1607.

Asenjo González, María. "'Labradores ricos': Nacimiento de una oligarquía rural en la Segovia del siglo XV." In *En la España medieval: Estudios en honor del profesor D. Angel Ferrari.* Madrid: Universidad Complutense, 1984.

———. *Segovia: La ciudad y su tierra a fines del medievo.* Segovia: Excma. Diputación Provincial de Segovia, 1986.

———. *Espacio y sociedad en la Soria medieval, siglos XIII–XV.* Soria: Diputación Provincial de Soria, 1999.

Aston, T. H., and C. H. E. Philpin, eds. *The Brenner Debate: Agrarian Class Structure and Economic Development in Pre-Industrial Europe.* Cambridge: Cambridge University Press, 1985.

Ayala Martínez, Carlos de. "La monarquía y Burgos durante el reinado de Alfonso X." *Cuadernos de historia medieval* 7 (1984): 9–63.

Baer, Fritz Y. *A History of the Jews in Christian Spain.* 2 vols. Philadelphia: Jewish Publication Society of America, 1961–66.

Ballesteros, Enrique. *Estudio histórico de Avila y su territorio.* Avila: Tipografía de M. Sarachaga, 1896.

Ballesteros y Beretta, Antonio. *Alfonso X, el sabio.* Barcelona: Salvat, 1963.

Barrios García, Angel. *La catedral de Avila en la edad media: Estructuras sociojurídica y ecónomica (Hipótesis y problemas).* Avila: El Diario de Avila, 1973.

———. *Estructuras agrarias y de poder en Castilla: El ejemplo de Avila, 1085–1320.* 2 vols. Salamanca: Universidad de Salamanca, 1983–84.

Barton, Simon. *The Aristocracy in Twelfth-Century León and Castile.* Cambridge: Cambridge University Press, 1997.

Basas Fernández, Manuel. *El consulado de Burgos en el siglo XVI.* Madrid: Escuela de Historia Moderna, 1963.

Behar, Ruth. *Santa María del Monte: The Presence of the Past in a Spanish Village.* Princeton: Princeton University Press, 1986.

Bilbao, Luis M., and E. Fernández Pinedo. "En torno al problema del poblamiento y la población vascongada en la edad media." In *III symposium de historia medieval del señorío de Viscaya.* Bilbao: Excma. Diputación Provincial de Viscaya, 1973.

Bisson, Thomas N. *The Medieval Crown of Aragon: A Short History.* Oxford: Oxford University Press, 1986.

———. *Tormented Voices: Power, Crisis, and Humanity in Rural Catalonia.* Cambridge: Harvard University Press, 1998.

Blanco, Flor. *Belorado en la baja edad media.* Madrid: Hijos de Santiago Rodríguez, 1973.

Bloch, Marc. *Feudal Society.* 2 vols. Chicago: University of Chicago Press, 1966.

Bolens, Lucie. *Les méthodes culturales au moyen âge d'apres les traités d'agronomie andalouse: Tradition et techniques.* Geneva: Droz, 1974.

———. *Agronomes andalous du moyen âge.* Geneva: Droz, 1981.

Bolos y Capdevila, María de, et al. *Geografía de España*. Barcelona: de Gasso Hnos. editores, 1969.
Bonachía Hernando, Juan A. *El concejo de Burgos en la baja edad media, 1345–1426*. Valladolid: Universidad de Valladolid, 1978.
———. *El señorío de Burgos durante la baja edad media, 1255–1508*. Salamanca: Biblioteca de Castilla y León, 1988.
Bonoudo de Magnani, Marta. "El monasterio de San Salvador de Oña: Economía agraria y sociedad rural." *Cuadernos de historia de España* 51–52 (1970): 42–122.
Braudel, Fernand. *The Mediterranean and the Mediterranean World in the Age of Phillip II*. 2 vols. New York: Harper-Torchbooks, 1975.
Bustamante Bricio, José. *La tierra y los valles de Mena: Biografía de un municipio*. Bilbao: Gráficos Ellacuria, 1971.
Cabero, Valentín. *El espacio geográfico castellano-leonés*. Valladolid: Ambito, 1982.
Cabrillana, Nicolás."La crisis del siglo XIV en Castilla: La peste negra en el obispado de Palencia." *Hispania* 28 (1968): 245–58.
———. "Los despoblados en Castilla la Vieja." *Hispania* 31 (1971): 485–550; 32 (1972): 5–60.
Camacho, Angel M. *Historia jurídica del cultivo y de la ganadería en España*. Madrid: Establecimiento tipográfico de J. Ratés, 1912.
Cantera Burgos, Francisco. "Documentos de compraventas hebráicos de la catedral de Calahorra." *Sefarad* 6 (1946): 37–62.
———. "La judería de Burgos." *Sefarad* 12 (1952): 59–104.
———. "Los judíos de Calahorra." *Sefarad* 15 (1955): 353–73.
Cantera Burgos, Francisco, and Huidobro, L. "Los judíos de Aguilar de Campóo." *Sefarad* 14 (1954): 353–73.
Carlé, María del Carmen. "El precio de la vida en Castilla del rey sabio al Emplazado." *Cuadernos de historia de España* 15 (1951): 32–156.
———. "Mercaderes en Castilla, 1252–1512." *Cuadernos de historia de España* 21–22 (1954): 146–328.
———. "Boni homines y hombres buenos." *Cuadernos de historia de España* 39–40 (1964): 133–68.
———. *Del concejo medieval castellano-leonés*. Buenos Aires: Instituto de Historia de España, 1968.
———. *La sociedad hispano medieval: La ciudad*. Buenos Aires: Celtia, 1984.
———. *Una sociedad del siglo XV: Los castellanos en sus testamentos*. Buenos Aires: Instituto de Historia de España, 1993.
Carremolino, José M. *Historia de Avila, su provincia y obispado*. 3 vols. Madrid: Librería Española, 1872–73.
Casado Alonso, Hilario. *La propiedad eclesiástica en la ciudad de Burgos en el siglo XV: El cabildo catedralicio*. Valladolid: Universidad de Valladolid, 1980.
———. *Señores, mercaderes y campesinos: La comarca de Burgos a fines de la edad media*. Valladolid: Junta de Castilla y León, 1987.
Casado Soto, José L. *Arquitectura naval en el Cantábrico durante el siglo XIII*. Santander: Bedia, 1976.

Casas Díez, Angel. *Villada en Tierra de Campos: Historia, economía y costumbres*. Palencia: Excma. Diputación Provincial de Palencia, 1976.
Castro, Américo. "Unos aranceles de aduanas del siglo XIII." *Revista de filología española* 8 (1921): 1–29, 325–56; 9 (1922): 266–76; 10 (1923): 113–36.
Childs, Wendy R. *Anglo-Castilian Trade in the Later Middle Ages*. Manchester: Rowman and Littlefield, 1978.
Cohn, Samuel K. *Death and Property in Siena, 1205–1800: Strategies for the Afterlife*. Baltimore: Johns Hopkins University Press, 1988.
Contreras, Juan de. *Historia de las corporaciones de menestrales en Segovia*. Segovia: Mauro Lozano, 1921.
Corral García, Esteban. *Las comunidades castellanas y la villa y tierra antigua de Cuéllar*. Salamanca: Imprenta Varona, 1978.
Davies, Wendy, and Paul Fouracre, eds. *The Settlements of Disputes in Early Medieval Europe*. Cambridge: Cambridge University Press, 1986.
Deyermond, Alan D. *The Middle Ages*. London: Barnes and Noble, 1971.
Díaz de Durana, José R. *Alava en la baja edad media: Crisis, recuperación y transformaciones socioeconómicas, 1250–1525*. Vitoria: Diputación Foral de Alava, 1986.
Díez Espinosa, José R. *Santa María de Palazuelos: Desarrollo, crisis y decadencia de un dominio monástico*. Valladolid: Diputación Provincial de Valladolid, 1982.
Dillard, Heath. *Daughters of the Reconquest: Women in Castilian Town Society, 1100–1300*. Cambridge: Cambridge University Press, 1984.
Doubleday, Simon R. *The Lara Family: Crown and Nobility in Medieval Spain*. Cambridge: Harvard University Press, 2001.
Duby, Georges. *Rural Economy and Country Life in the Medieval West*. Reprint. Columbia: University of South Carolina Press, 1990.
Dufourcq, Charles E., and J. Gautier-Dalché. *Histoire économique et sociale de l'Espagne chrétienne au moyen âge*. Paris: Armand Colin, 1976.
Eire, Carlos M. N. *From Madrid to Purgatory: The Art and Craft of Dying in Sixteenth-Century Spain*. New York: Cambridge University Press, 1995.
Elliott, John H. *Richelieu and Olivares*. Cambridge: Cambridge University Press, 1984.
———. *The Count-Duke of Olivares: The Statesman in an Age of Decline*. New Haven: Yale University Press, 1986.
Epstein, Steven. *Wills and Wealth in Medieval Genoa, 1150–1250*. Cambridge: Harvard University Press, 1984.
Esteban Recio, María A. *Palencia a fines de la edad media: Una ciudad de señorío episcopal*. Valladolid: Universidad de Valladolid, 1989.
Estepa Díez, Carlos. "El alfoz y las relaciones campo-ciudad en Castilla y León durante los siglos XII y XIII." *Studia historica* 2, 2 (1984): 7–26.
Estepa Díez, Carlos, et al. *Burgos en la edad media*. Valladolid: Junta de Castilla y León, 1984.
Faci, Javier. "Vocablos referentes al sector agrario en León y Castilla durante la alta edad media." *Moneda y crédito* 144 (1978): 69–87.
Ferotin, Marius. *Histoire de l'abbaye de Silos*. Paris: Leroux, 1897.

Ferrari Núñez, Angel. *Castilla dividida en dominios según el libro de las behetrías.* Madrid: Ograma, 1958.
Fisher, W. B., and H. Bowen-Jones. *Spain. A Geographical Background.* London: Chatto and Windus, 1958.
Freedman, Paul H. "The Enserfment Process in Medieval Catalonia: The Evidence from Ecclesiastical Sources." *Viator* 13 (1982): 225–44.
———. *The Diocese of Victorian Tradition and Regeneration in Medieval Catalonia.* New Brunswick: Rutgers University Press, 1983.
———. *The Origins of Peasant Servitude in Medieval Catalonia.* Cambridge: Cambridge University Press, 1991.
———. *Images of the Medieval Peasant.* Stanford: Stanford University Press, 1999.
Gacto Fernández, María T. *Estructura de la población de la extremadura leonesa en los siglos XII y XIII.* Salamanca: C.S.I.C., 1977.
García de Cortázar, José Angel. *El dominio del monasterio de San Millán de la Cogolla, siglos X a XIII: Introducción a la historia rural de Castilla altomedieval.* Salamanca: Universidad de Salamanca, 1969.
———. *La época medieval: Historia de España alfaguara.* Vol. 2. Madrid: Alianza Editorial, 1973.
———. "La economía rural medieval: Un esquema de análisis histórico de base regional." In *Actas de las I jornadas de metodología aplicadas a las ciencias históricas,* vol. 2. Santiago de Compostela: Universidad de Santiago de Compostela, 1975.
———. *La historia rural medieval: Un esquema de análisis estructural de sus contenidos a través del ejemplo hispanocristiano.* Santander: Universidad de Santander, 1978.
———. *La sociedad rural en la España medieval.* Madrid: Siglo XXI, 1988.
García de Cortázar, José A., et al. *Organización social del espacio en la España medieval: La corona de Castilla en los siglos VIII a XV.* Barcelona: Ariel, 1985.
García de Valdeavellano, Luis. *Historia de España: Desde los orígenes a la baja edad media.* 2d ed. 1 vol. in 2. Madrid: Revista de Occidente, 1952.
———. *Curso de historia de las instituciones españolas: De los orígenes al final de la edad media.* Madrid: Revista de Occidente, 1968.
———. *Orígenes de la burguesía en la España medieval.* Madrid: Espasa-Calpe, 1969.
García Fernández, Ernesto. *La Guardia en la baja edad media, 1350–1516.* Vitoria: Diputación Foral de Alava, 1985.
García Fernández, Jesús. *Organización del espacio y economía rural en la España atlántica.* Madrid: Siglo XXI, 1975.
———. *El clima en Castilla y León.* Valladolid: Ambito, 1986.
García González, Juan J. "Rentas de trabajo en San Salvador de Oña: Las sernas, 1011–1550." *Cuadernos burgaleses de historia medieval* 1 (1984): 119–94.
García Sahagún, Javier. *La organización del espacio agrario en Liébana durante la edad media.* Santander: Ediciones Tantín, 1986.
García Sáinz de Baranda, Julián. *La ciudad de Burgos y su concejo en la edad media.* 2 vols. Burgos: Tipografía de la editorial El Monte Carmelo, 1967.

García Sanz, Angel. *Desarrollo y crisis del antiguo régimen en Castilla la Vieja.* Madrid: Akal, 1986.

Gautier-Dalché, Jean. "Le domaine du monastere de Santo Toribio de Liébana: Formation, structure et modes d'explotation." *Anuario de estudios medievales* 2 (1965): 63–117.

———. "Moulin à eau, seigneurie, communaté rurale dans le nord de l'Espagne, IXe–XIIe siècles." In *Etudes de civilisation médiévales, IXe–XIIe siècles: Mélanges offerts à E. R. Labande.* Poitiers: C.E.S.C.M., 1974.

———. *Historia urbana de León y Castilla en la edad media, siglos IX–XIII.* Madrid: Siglo XXI, 1979.

Glick, Thomas F. *Irrigation and Society in Medieval Valencia.* Cambridge: Harvard University Press, 1970.

———. *Islamic and Christian Spain in the Early Middle Ages: Comparative Perspectives on Society and Cultural Formation.* Princeton: Princeton University Press, 1979.

González, Julio. *Alfonso IX.* 3 vols. Madrid: Consejo Superior de Investigaciones Científicas, 1944.

———. *El reino de Castilla en la época de Alfonso VIII.* 3 vols. Madrid: Consejo Superior de Investigaciones Científicas, 1960.

———. *Reinado y diplomas de Fernando III.* 3 vols. Córdoba: Publicaciones del Monte de Piedad y Caja de Ahorros de Córdoba, 1980–86.

González, Nazario. *Burgos: La ciudad marginal de Castilla.* Burgos: Imprenta de Aldecoa, 1958.

González Bartolomé, Mariano. "Riaza: Datos históricos y documentos." *Estudios segovianos* 27 (1957): 385–691.

González Díez, Emiliano. *El concejo burgalés, 884–1369: Marco histórico-institucional.* Burgos: Imprenta de Aldecoa, 1983.

González García, Manuel. *Salamanca: La repoblación y la ciudad en la baja edad media.* Salamanca: C.S.I.C., 1973.

———. *Salamanca en la baja edad media.* Salamanca: Universidad de Salamanca, 1982.

González Jiménez, Manuel. *La repoblación de la zona de Sevilla durante el siglo XIV.* Seville: Universidad de Sevilla, 1975.

———. *En torno a los orígenes de Andalucía.* 2d ed. Seville: Universidad de Sevilla, 1988.

González Mínguez, César. *Fernando IV de Castilla, 1295–1312: La guerra civil y el predominio de la nobleza.* Vitoria: Colegio Universitario de Alava, 1976.

Gual Camarena, Miguel. "Para un mapa de la industria textil hispana en la edad media." *Anuario de estudios medievales* 4 (1967): 109–68.

———. "El comercio de telas en el siglo XIII hispano." *Anuario de historia económica y social* 1 (1968): 85–106.

Guiance, Ariel. *Los discursos sobre la muerte en la Castilla medieval, siglos VII–XV.* Valladolid: Junta de Castilla y León, 1998.

———. "To Die for Country, Land, or Faith in Castilian Medieval Thought." *Journal of Medieval History* 24 (1998): 313–32.

Guiard Larrauri, Teófilo. *Historia de la noble villa de Bilbao.* Bilbao: Editora de la Gran Enciclopedia Vasca, 1971–74.

Hernández, Francisco. "Las cortes de Toledo de 1207." In *Las cortes de Castilla y León en la edad media*. 2 vols. Valladolid: Cortes de Castilla y León, 1988.
Herrera Nogal, Alfredo. *El concejo de la villa de Tardajos: Fueros de historia*. Burgos: Caja de Ahorros Municipal de Burgos, 1980.
Homans, George C. *English Villages of the Thirteenth Century*. Cambridge: Harvard University Press, 1941.
Huetz de Lemps, Alain. *Vignobles et vins du nord-ouest de l'Espagne*. Bordeaux: Bibliotèque de l'Ecole des Hautes Etudes Hispaniques, 1967.
Huidobro y Serna, Luciano. "Los moros de Burgos y su influencia en el arte." *Boletín de la Comisión de Monumentos de la Provincia de Burgos* 105 (1945): 222-25.
———. *Las peregrinaciones jacobeas*. 2 vols. Madrid: Instituto de España, 1950.
———. *Breve historia de la muy noble villa de Aguilar de Campóo*. Palencia: Excma. Diputación Provincial de Palencia, 1980.
La investigación de la historia hispánica del siglo XIV: Problemas y cuestiones. Barcelona: C.S.I.C., 1973.
Iradiel Murugarrén, Paulino. *Evolución de la industria textil castellana en los siglos XIII-XVI: Factores de desarrollo, organización y coste de la producción manufacturera en Cuenca*. Salamanca: Universidad de Salamanca, 1974.
Jimeno, Esther. "La población de Soria y su termino en 1270." *Boletín de la Real Academia de la Historia* 96-97 (1958): 207-74, 365-94.
Kantorowicz, Ernst H. *The King's Two Bodies. A Study in Medieval Political Theology*. Princeton: Princeton University Press, 1957. Reprint, 1981.
Klein, Julius. *The Mesta: A Study in Spanish Economic History, 1273-1836*. Cambridge: Harvard University Press, 1920.
Kosto, Adam J. *Making Agreement in Medieval Catalonia: Power, Order, and the Written Word, 1000-1200*. New York: Cambridge University Press, 2001.
Ladero Quesada, Miguel Angel. *Historia de Sevilla*. Vol. 2, *La ciudad medieval, 1248-1492*. Seville: Universidad de Sevilla, 1976.
———. "Las ferias de Castilla, siglos XII a XV." *Cuadernos de historia de España* 67-68 (1982): 269-315.
———. *El siglo XV en Castilla: Fuentes de renta y política fiscal*. Barcelona: Ariel, 1982.
Layna Serrano, Francisco. *Historia de la villa de Atienza*. Madrid: C.S.I.C., 1945.
Le Goff, Jacques. *Time, Work, and Culture in the Middle Ages*. Trans. Arthur Goldhammer. Chicago: University of Chicago Press, 1980.
———. *The Birth of Purgatory*. Trans. Arthur Goldhammer. Chicago: University of Chicago Press, 1984.
———. *La bourse et la vie: Economie et religion au moyen âge*. Paris: Hachette, 1986.
———. *Medieval Civilization, 400-1500*. Trans. Julia Barrow. Oxford: Blackwell, 1988.
———. *L'imaginaire medieval: Essais*. New ed. Paris: Gallimard, 1991.
———. *History and Memory*. Trans. Steven Rendell and E. Claman. New York: Columbia University Press, 1992.
———. *Intellectuals in the Middle Ages*. Trans. Teresa L. Fagan. Cambridge: Blackwell, 1993.

———. *Saint Louis*. Paris: Gallimard, 1996.
Le Goff, Jacques, with Monique Goullet. *Le sacre royal à l'époque de Saint Louis d'après le manuscrit latin dela BNF*. Paris: Gallimard, 2001.
León Tello, Pilar. *Judíos de Avila*. Avila: Excma. Diputación Provincial de Avila, 1963.
Linehan, Peter. *The Spanish Church and the Papacy in the Thirteenth Century*. Cambridge: Cambridge University Press, 1971.
———. *Spanish Church and Society, 1150–1300*. London: Variorum, 1983.
———. "The Toledo Forgeries c. 1150–c. 1300." In *Falschungen im Mittlealter*. Vol. 1. Hannover: Hahnsche Buckhandlung, 1988.
———. *Past and Present in Medieval Spain*. London: Variorum, 1992.
———. *History and the Historians of Medieval Spain*. Oxford: Clarendon Press, 1993.
———. *The Ladies of Zamora*. University Park: Pennsylvania University Press, 1997.
Lourie, Elena. "A Society Organized for War: Medieval Spain." *Past & Present* 35 (1966): 54–76.
Lucas, H. S. "The Great European Famine of 1315–17." *Speculum* 5 (1930): 343–77.
MacKay, Angus. *Spain in the Middle Ages: From Frontier to Empire 1000–1500*. London: Macmillan, 1977.
———. "Ciudad y campo en la Europa medieval." *Studia historica* 2, 2 (1984): 27–53.
Maravall, José A. *El concepto de España en la edad media*. 2d ed. Madrid: Instituto de Estudios Políticos, 1964.
Martín, José L. *Economía y sociedad en los reinos hispánicos de la baja edad media*. 2 vols. Barcelona: El Albir, 1983.
Martínez Cea, Juan C. *El campesinado castellano de la cuenca del Duero: Aproximaciones a su estudio durante los siglos XIII al XV*. Valladolid: Concejo General de Castilla y León, 1983.
Martínez Díez, Gonzalo. *Alava medieval*. 2 vols. Vitoria: Diputación Foral de Alava, 1974.
———. *Las comunidades de villa y tierra de la extremadura castellana*. Madrid: Editora Nacional, 1983.
Martínez García, Luis. "La concentración de la propiedad urbana burgalesa mediante la concesión de 'pasadas de tierra,' 1150–1250." In *La ciudad de Burgos: Actas del Congreso de Historia de Burgos*. Madrid: Junta de Castilla y León, 1985.
———. *El Hospital del Rey de Burgos: Un señorío medieval en la expansión y en la crisis, siglos XIII y XIV*. Burgos: Ediciones J. M. Garrido Garrido, 1986.
Martínez Moro, Jesús. *La tierra en la comunidad de Segovia: Un proyecto señorial urbano, 1088–1500*. Valladolid: Universidad de Valladolid, 1985.
Martínez Sopena, Pascual. *La tierra de Campos occidental: Poblamiento, poder y comunidad del siglo X al XIII*. Valladolid: Diputación Provincial de Valladolid, 1985.
Martz, Linda. *Poverty and Welfare in Habsburg Spain: The Example of Toledo*. Cambridge: Cambridge University Press, 1983.

Mayoral Fernández, José. *El municipio de Avila: Estudio histórico*. Avila: Diputación Provincial de Avila, 1958.

Menéndez Pidal, Gonzalo. *Los caminos en la historia de España*. Madrid: Ediciones Cultura Hispánica, 1951.

Merchán Fernández, Carlos. *Sobre los orígenes del régimen señorial en Castilla: El abadengo de Aguilar de Campóo, 1020–1369*. Málaga: Universidad de Málaga, 1982.

Merino Alvarez, Abelardo. *La sociedad abulense durante el siglo XVI: La nobleza*. Madrid: Imprenta del Patronato de Huérfanos, 1926.

Molénat, Jean Pierre. "Chemins et ponts du nord de la Castille au temps des Rois Catholiques." *Melanges de la Casa Velázquez* 7 (1971): 115–62.

Mollat, Michel. *Les pauvres au moyen âge*. Paris: Hachette, 1978.

Monod, Paul Kléber. *The Power of Kings: Monarchy and Religion in Europe, 1589–1715*. New Haven: Yale University Press, 1999.

Monsalvo Antón, José M. *Teoria y evolución de un conflicto social: El antisemitismo en la corona de Castilla en la baja edad media*. Madrid: Siglo XXI, 1985.

———. *El sistema concejil: El ejemplo del señorío medieval de Alba de Tormes y su concejo de villa y tierra*. Salamanca: Universidad de Salamanca, 1988.

———. "La participación política de los pecheros en los municipios castellanos de la baja edad media: Aspectos organizativos." *Studia historica* 7 (1989): 37–93.

Moreta Velayos, Salustiano. *El monasterio de San Pedro de Cardeña: Historia de un dominio monástico castellano, 902–1338*. Salamanca: Universidad de Salamanca, 1971.

———. *Rentas monásticas en Castilla: Problema de método*. Salamanca: Universidad de Salamanca, 1974.

Moxó, Salvador de. "De la nobleza vieja a la nobleza nueva: La transformación nobiliaria castellana en la baja edad media." *Cuadernos de historia* 3 (1969): 1–210.

———. "Los judíos castellanos en la primera mitad del siglo XIV." *Sefarad* 35 (1972): 72–103.

———. "Los señoríos: En torno a una problemática para el estudio del régimen señorial." *Hispania* 94 (1974): 185–236.

———. "Los señoríos: Estudio metodológico." In *Actas de las I jornadas de la metodología aplicadas de las ciencias históricas*, vol. 2. Santiago de Compostela: Universidad de Santiago de Compostela, 1975.

———. "Campesinos hacendados leoneses en el siglo XIV." In *León medieval: Doce estudios*. León: Instituto de Estudios Leoneses, 1978.

———. *Repoblación y sociedad en la España cristiana medieval*. Madrid: Rialp, 1979.

Nieto Soria, José M. *Las relaciones monarquía-episcopado castellano*. 2 vols. Madrid: Universidad Complutense, 1983.

———. *Iglesia y poder real en Castilla: El episcopado, 1250–1350*. Madrid: Universidad Complutense, 1988.

O'Callaghan, Joseph F. "The Cortes and Royal Taxation during the Reign of Alfonso X of Castile." *Traditio* 27 (1971): 379–98.

———. *A History of Medieval Spain*. Ithaca: Cornell University Press, 1975.
———. *The Cortes of Castile-León, 1188–1350*. Philadelphia: University of Pennsylvania Press, 1989.
———. "Image and Reality: The King Creates His Kingdom." In *Emperor of Culture: Alfonso X the Learned of Castile and His Thirteenth-Century Renaissance*. Ed. Robert I. Burns. Philadelphia: University of Pennsylvania Press, 1990.
———. *The Learned King: The Reign of Alfonso X of Castile*. Philadelphia: University of Pennsylvania Press, 1993.
Ortega Varcárcel, José. *La transformación de un espacio rural: Las montañas de Burgos*. Valladolid: Universidad de Valladolid, 1974.
Ortega y Rubio, *Historia de Valladolid*. 2 vols. Valladolid: Imprenta y Librería Nacional y Extranjera de Hijos de Rodríguez, 1881.
Pastor, Reyna. "La sal en Castilla y León: Un problema de la alimentación y del trabajo y una política fiscal, siglos X–XIII." *Cuadernos de historia de España* 37–38 (1963): 42–87.
———. *Conflictos sociales y estancamiento económico en la España medieval*. Barcelona: Ariel, 1973.
———. *Resistencias y luchas campesinas en la época del crecimiento y consolidación de la formación feudal: Castilla y León, siglos X–XIII*. Madrid: Siglo XXI, 1980.
Pastor Díaz de Garayo. *Salvatierra y la llanada oriental alavesa, siglos XIII–XV*. Vitoria: Diputación Foral de Alava, 1986.
Pérez Bustamante, Rogelio. *Sociedad, economía, fiscalidad y gobierno en las Asturias de Santillana, s. XIII–XV*. Santander: Estudio, 1979.
———. *Historia de la villa de Castro Urdiales*. Santander: Ayuntamiento de Santander, 1980.
Pérez de Urbel, Justo. *El condado de Castilla: Los 300 años en que se hizo Castilla*. 3 vols. Madrid: Editorial Siglo Ilustrado, 1969–70.
Pérez-Embid, Javier. *El Cister en Castilla y León: Monacato y dominios rurales, s. XII–XV*. Valladolid: Junta de Castilla y León, 1986.
Pescador, Carmela. "La caballería popular en León y Castilla." *Cuadernos de historia de España* 33–34 (1961): 101–238; 35–36 (1962): 56–201; 37–38 (1963): 88–198; 39–40 (1964): 169–260.
Phillips, Carla R. "Spanish Merchants and the Wool Trade in the Sixteenth Century." *Sixteenth Century Journal* 14 (1983): 259–82.
Powers, James F. *A Society Organized for War: The Iberian Municipal Militias in the Central Middle Ages, 1000–1284*. Berkeley: University of California Press, 1988.
Proctor, Evelyn S. "The Interpretation of Clause 3 of the Decrees of Leon." *English Historical Review* 85 (1970): 45–53.
Raftis, J. Ambrose. *Tenure and Mobility: Studies in the Social History of the Medieval English Village*. Toronto: Pontifical Institute of Mediaeval Studies, 1964.
———. *Warboys: Two Hundred Years in the Life of a Medieval English Village*. Toronto: Pontifical Institute of Mediaeval Studies, 1974.
Raftis, J. Ambrose, ed. *Pathways to Medieval Peasants*. Toronto: Pontifical Institute of Mediaeval Studies, 1981.

Razi, Zvi. *Life, Death, and Marriage in a Medieval Parish: Economy, Society, and Demography in Halesowen, 1270–1400.* Cambridge: Cambridge University Press, 1980.
Reilly, Bernard F. *The Kingdom of León-Castile under Queen Urraca, 1109–1126.* Princeton: Princeton University Press, 1982.
―――. *The Kingdom of León-Castile under King Alfonso VI, 1065–1109.* Princeton: Princeton University Press, 1988.
―――. *The Contest of Christian and Muslim Spain, 1031–1157.* Cambridge: Blackwell, 1992.
―――. *The Kingdom of León-Castile under King Alfonso VII, 1126–1157.* Philadelphia: University of Pennsylvania Press, 1998.
Reilly, Bernard F., ed. *Sant Denis and Saint Peter: The Reception of the Roman Liturgy in León-Castile in 1080.* New York: Fordham University Press, 1985.
Represa Rodríguez, Armando. "Notas para el estudio de la ciudad de Segovia en los siglos XII–XIV." *Estudios segovianos* 2 (1949): 273–319.
―――. "La tierra medieval de Segovia." *Estudios segovianos* 21 (1969): 227–44.
―――. "Origen y desarrollo urbano del Valladolid medieval, siglos X–XIII." In *Historia de Valladolid*, Vol. 2, *Valladolid medieval.* Ed. José M. Ruiz Asencio et al. Valladolid: Ateneo de Valladolid, 1980
Ringrose, David. *Transportation and Economic Stagnation in Spain, 1750–1850.* Durham: Duke University Press, 1970.
Rosenthal, Joel T. *The Purchase of Paradise: Gift Giving and the Aristocracy, 1307–1485.* London: Routledge and K. Paul, 1972.
Rosenwein, Barbara H. *Rhinoceros Bound: Cluny in the Tenth Century.* Philadelphia: University of Pennsylvania Press, 1982.
―――. *To Be the Neighbor of Saint Peter: The Social Meaning of Cluny's Property.* Ithaca: Cornell University Press, 1989.
―――. *Negotiating Space: Power, Restraint, and Privileges of Immunity in Early Medieval Europe.* Ithaca: Cornell University Press, 1999.
Rucquoi, Adeline. "Molinos et aceñas au coeur de la Castille septentrionale, XIe–XVe siècles." In *Les Espagnes médiévales: Aspects économiques et sociaux.* Nice: Faculté des Lettres et Sciences Humaines de Nice, 1983.
―――. *Valladolid en la edad media: La villa del Esgueva.* Valladolid: Ayuntamiento de Valladolid, 1983.
―――. *Valladolid en la edad media.* 2 vols. Valladolid: Junta de Castilla y León, 1987.
―――. *Histoire médiévale de la péninsule ibérique.* Paris: Editions de Seuil, 1993.
―――. "Education et société dans la péninsule ibérique médiévale." *Histoire de l'education* 69 (1996): 3–36.
―――. "Las rutas del saber: España en el siglo XII." *Cuadernos de historia de España*, 75 (1998–99): 41–58.
Ruiz, Teofilo F. "The Transformation of the Castilian Municipalities: The Case of Burgos, 1248–1350." *Past & Present* 77 (1977): 3–33. Most of my essays are collected in *The City and the Realm: Burgos and Castile, 1080–1492.* London: Variorum, 1992.
―――. "Expansion et changement: La conquête de Séville et la société castillane, 1248–1350." *Annales E.S.C.* 3 (1979): 548–65.

———. *Sociedad y poder real en Castilla: Burgos en la baja edad media.* Barcelona: Ariel, 1981.
———. "Una nota sobre la estructura y relaciones fiscales del Burgos bajo medieval." In *En la España medieval: Estudios en memoria del profesor D. Salvador de Moxó.* Vol. 2. Madrid: Universidad Complutense, 1982.
———. "Notas para el estudio de la mujer en el área del Burgos medieval." In *El pasado histórico de Castilla y León.* 3 vols. Burgos: Junta de Castilla y León, 1983.
———. "Une note sur la vie rurale dans la region d'Aguilar de Campóo." in *Les Espagnes médiévales: Aspects économiques et sociaux.* Nice: Faculté des Lettres et Sciences Humaines de Nice, 1983.
———. "La formazione del mercato della terra nella Castiglia del basso medioevo." *Quaderni storici* 65 (1987): 423–52.
———. "Festivités, couleurs et symboles du pouvoir en Castille au XVe siècle: Les célébrations de mai 1428." *Annales E.S.C.* 3 (1991): 521–46.
———. *Crisis and Continuity: Land and Town in Late Medieval Castile.* Philadelphia: University of Pennsylvania Press, 1994.
———. "The Peasantries of Iberia, 1400–1800." In *The Peasantries of Europe: From the Fourteenth to the Eighteenth Centuries.* Ed. Tom Scott. London: Longman, 1998.
———. *Spanish Society, 1400–1600.* London: Longman, 2001.
Ruiz Gómez, Francisco. *Las formas del poblamiento rural en la Bureba en la baja edad media: La villa de Oña.* 2 vols. Madrid: Universidad Complutense, 1988.
———. *Las aldeas castellanas en la edad media: Oña en los siglos XIV y XV.* Madrid: C.S.I.C., 1990.
Sáinz Díaz, Valentín. *Notas históricas sobre la villa de San Vicente de la Barquera.* Santander: Institución Cultural de Cantabria, 1973.
Salomon, Noël. *La vida rural castellana en tiempos de Felipe II.* Barcelona: Editorial Planeta, 1973.
Sánchez Albornoz, Claudio. "Las behetrías: La encomendación en Asturias, León y Castilla" and "Muchas páginas más sobre las behetrías." *Anuario de historia del derecho español* 4 (1928). Both articles are reproduced in his *Estudios sobre las instituciones medievales españolas.* Mexico: Universidad Nacional Autónoma de México, 1965.
———. *Despoblación y repoblación del valle del Duero.* Buenos Aires: Instituto de Historia, 1966.
Sangrador Vitores, Matías. *Historia de la muy noble y leal ciudada de Valladolid desde su más remota antigüedad hasta la muerte de Fernando VII.* 2 vols. Valladolid: Imprenta de D. M. Aparicio, 1851–54.
Sinues Ruiz, Atanasio. *El merino.* Saragossa: C.S.I.C., 1954.
Slicher van Bath, Bernard H. *The Agrarian History of Western Europe, A.D. 500–1850.* London: Arnold, 1963.
Smail, Daniel L. *Imaginary Cartographies: Possession and Identity in Late Medieval Marseille.* Ithaca: Cornell University Press, 1999.
Sobrequés i Callicó, Jaume. "La peste negra en la península ibérica." *Anuario de estudios medievales* 7 (1970–71): 67–102.

La sociedad vasca rural y urbana en le marco de la crisis de los siglos XIV y XV. Bilbao: Excma. Diputación Provincial de Vizcaya, 1975.

Soto Rábanos, José María, ed. *Pensamiento medieval hispano: Homenaje a Horacio Santiago Otero.* 2 vols. Madrid: Consejo Superior de Investigaciones Científicas, 1998.

Strayer, Joseph R. *On the Medieval Origins of the Modern State.* Princeton: Princeton University Press, 1970.

———. *Medieval Statecraft and the Perspectives of History.* Ed. John Fenton and Thomas N. Bisson. Princeton: Princeton University Press, 1971.

Ubieto Arteta, Agustín. *Notas sobre el patrimonio calceatense, siglos XII y XIII.* Logroño: Instituto de Estudios Riojanos, 1978.

Vaca Lorenzo, Angel. "La estructura económica de la Tierra de Campos a mediados del siglo XIV." *Publicaciones de la Institución Tello Téllez de Meneses* 39 (1977): 229–399; 42 (1979): 203–387.

Valdeón Baruque, Julio. "Aspectos de la crisis castellana en la primera mitad del siglo XIV." *Hispania* 111 (1969): 5–24.

———. "La crisis del siglo XIV en Castilla: Revisión del problema." *Revista de la Universidad de Madrid* 79 (1971): 161–84.

———. *Los conflictos sociales en el reino de Castilla en los siglos XIV y XV.* Madrid: Siglo XXI, 1975.

Vassberg, David E. *Land and Society in Golden Age Castile.* Cambridge: Cambridge University Press, 1984.

———. *The Village and the Outside World in Golden Age Castile: Mobility and Migration in Everday Rural Life.* Cambridge: Cambridge University Press, 1996.

Vázquez de Parga, Luis, José María Lacarra, and Juan Uría Ríu. *Las peregrinaciones a Santiago de Compostela.* 3 vols. Madrid: C.S.I.C., 1948–49.

Vergara y Martín, Gabriel M. *Estudio histórico de Avila y su territorio desde su repoblación hasta la muerte de Santa Teresa de Jesús.* Madrid: Hernández, 1896.

Verlinden, Charles. "Draps des Pays-bas et du Nord de la France en Espagne au XIVe siècle." *Le moyen âge* 7, 1–2 (1937):

———. "La grande peste de 1348 en Espagne: Contribution a l'étude de ses conséquences économiques et sociales." *Revue belge de philologie et d'histoire* 17 (1938): 103–46.

———. *El comercio de paños flamencos y brabanzones en España durante los siglos XIII y XIV.* Madrid: Cátedra de la Fundación del excmo. Sr. Conde de Cartagena, 1952.

Vicens Vives, Jaume. *Historia de España y América social y económica. Vol. 2, Baja edad media.* Barcelona: Editoria Vicens Vives, 1974.

Villar y Macías, Matías. *Historia de Salamanca.* 3 vols. Salamanca: Imprenta de Francisco Núñez Izquierdo, 1971.

Villegas, Luis R. *Sobre el urbanismo de Ciudad Real en la edad media.* Ciudad Real: Excmo. Ayuntamiento de Ciudad Real, 1984.

Villuga, Pero Juan. *Repertorio de todos los caminos de España.* Medina del Campo, 1546. Reprint, New York: Hispanic Society of New York, 1902.

Vitoria en la edad media: Actas del Ier Congreso de Estudios Históricos. Vitoria: Ayuntamiento de Vitoria, 1982.

Way, Ruth. *A Geography of Spain and Portugal.* London: Methuen, 1962.

INDEX

Note: Page numbers in *italics* refer to the illustrations.

acclamation, 134–35, 139–40
account books, 82–83
Agreda, 86
agriculture, 72–73
agro-towns, 20
Aguilar de Campoo, 127, 173n.29, 174n.5
al-Andalus, 6–7, 23, 105–6
alcázar, of Segovia, *148*
Alfonso de la Cerda, 108
Alfonso II, king of Portugal, 12
Alfonso VI, 139–41, 143
Alfonso VII, 5, 106, 139, 141, 143
Alfonso VIII, 7–8, 23, 41, 96, 106, 43–45
Alfonso IX, 8, 24, 106, 144
Alfonso X, 31, 35–36, 39, 70, 107–8, 125, 142–43, 188n.57, 191n.25; *Cantigas de Santa María*, 13, 152; legal reform, 63, 65–66, 108
Alfonso XI, 108, 117, 131, 135, 145, 150
Almohads, 5, 7–8, 106, 144
Almoravids, 141, 165n.9
almsgiving, 115–16, 119–20
alms (limosna), use of term, 119
Alvarus Pelagius, 137
Ameryc Picard, 16
apeo, 82, 92
arabic numbers, use of, 24
Aragon, 7, 30, 38, 44, 104, 144, 172n.13, 182n.48, 187n.46
architecture, *15*; Gothic, 12–13, *14*; Romanesque, *50*, 163n.7
archives, 31; ecclesiastical, 40, 49–53, 171n.7; royal, 147
aristocracy. *See* noble families
arithmetic, commercial, 24
Asenjo González, María, 86
Asturias, 6
Asturias-León, 81, 105
Augustinus Triumphus, 84

Austen, Jane, 87
authority, royal, 133, 146–47
Avila, 13, 20, 77, 83, 91, 94, 99, 147, *147*, 150

Barcelona, 123
Bartolus of Sasseferrato, 84
Barton, Simon, 99
Bay of Biscay, 85
Beceiro, Isabel, 99
Becerro de behetrías, 73, 83, 102
beggars, 117
Behar, Ruth, 115
Benedictine monks, 25, 49, 129–30
bequests: charitable, 3, 38, 47, 110–12, 120–24, 192n.33 (*See also* feeding and clothing the poor; "remedy of one's soul"; salvation, economy of); to family and kin, 38, 55–56, 122–23, 127, 173n.27 (*See also* inheritance); litigation over, 53
Berceo, town of, 151
Berenguela, 8, 106
Berganza, 145
Blázquez family (Avila), 77, 94, 99
Bloch, Marc, 29
Bonifaz family (Burgos), 16–20, 90, 94, 97, 99, 167n.9
Boreau, Alain, 24
boundaries, 67–73, 133, 151–52, 179n.11, 182n.48. *See also* property, consolidation of travelers and, 83–84
boundary markers *(mojones)*, 68–73, 85
bourgeoisie, 3–4, 16, 20–22, 25–26, 28–30, 93, 148, 150. *See also* Bonifaz family; Sarracín family
Brown, Peter, 188n, 192n.38
Bruhl, Carlrichard, 193n.3
bureaucracy, royal, 21, 146–47, 149–50

Burgos, 54–56, 70, 76, 78, 95–99, *97,* 126, 150, 169n.36, 191n.30; cathedral, 13, *14,* 54, 82–83, 90–91, 179n.11, 191n.30; commercial life, 16, 20; confraternities, 89–91; hospitals, 130–31; land transactions, 59, *59. See also* Bonifaz family; Mathe family; Sarracín family
Burgundy, 72
burial, 52

Cadden, Joan, 85
Cádiz, 82
Calahorra, 86
cañadas, 72, 80
Cantabria, 50
cantigas de amigo, 13
cantigas de escarnio, 13
capital, royal, 143, 147
caritas, 127–28
Carrión, 69–70, 74
Castile, 5–6, 34–36, 65–66, 81, 85, 133, 182n.48. *See also* Castile, Crown of; kings, of Castile history, 6–9, 139–46
Castile, counts of, 46, 60
Castile, Crown of, 108, 120; and Church, 36, 140–42, 145, 149–50; and royal succession, 104–9
Castilians, changing representation of, 35, 133
Castro family, 7, 101
Castrojeriz, 60
Castro-Urdiales, 85
Catalonia, 22, 39, 104, 144
Catharism, 25–26, 58
cathedral chapters, and inventories, 81, 83
cathedral schools, 12, 164n.7
Cavillac, Michel, 114
ceremonialization, use of term, 127
Chamberlin, Cynthia, 171n.5
charity, 112, 114–15, 118–25, 127–31. *See also* bequests; feeding and clothing the poor; poor; poverty
Charles V, 104
Chiffoleau, Jacques, 188n.4
children, as testators, 61–62
Christian-Muslim relations, 8, 141–42
chronicles, 34–36, 133, 138–46
Church, the, 9–10, 12, 22, 34, 58; and care of poor, 120, 129–31; and Crown of Castile, 36, 140–42, 145, 149–50; and inheritance rights, 62–63. *See also* spirituality
churches: Saints Emeterius and Celedonius, 40; San Martín de Albelda, 122; Santa Gadea of Burgos, 140; Santa María de Roncesvalles, 121; Santa María la Redonda, 121; Sant Fagunt de Tanarrio, 81; Santillana del Mar, 50. *See also* monasteries
Cid, the, 140
Cistercian monks, 12–13, 74, *75,* 96, *97,* 172n.17
clerics: and concubines, 122; and land transactions, 95, 98; as testators, 56, 59
clothing, 12, 57. *See also* feeding and clothing the poor
Cluny, monks of, 16, 140
Cock, Enrique, 182n.48
Codex Calixtinus, 16
Coleman, Janet, 58
commerce. *See* trade
commercial life, rise of, 16–24
competition, for donations, 48–49
Compostela. *See* Santiago de Compostela
conditions, in wills and donations, 48–49
confraternities, 89–91, 122
conspicuous consumption, 101–2, 129
Constable, Giles, 173n.30
Córdoba, 8, 106
Corominas, *Diccionario de autoridades,* 92–93
cortes, 21, 24, 117, 147, 167n.14
crime, 61, 63
Crusade, 126
Cuadernos de contabilidad (cathedral of Burgos), 82–83, 90–91
Cuenca, fuero of, 61–62, 70, 79–80, 176n.19
cultural production, xi
customhouses, 85–86

Dávila family (Segovia), 99
Davis, Natalie Z., 190n.24
Diego García de Campos, *Planeta,* 13
diet, 57, 121–22, 124–25, 130, 192n.40. *See also* feeding and clothing the poor
Domingo de Guzmán, Santo, 25
Domingo de Soto, *Deliberación en la causa de los pobres,* 113

Dominicans, 25–26
donations, 26–29, 38, 40–47, *42–43,* 48, 51, 110–12, 172n.18, 173n.26
donors, 29; Beila Beilaz (1076), 40; Diego López (1198), 41; García Ciclero (947), 44–45; Count Gómez González (1107), 119–20; Don Juan Galindo, 74; Doña María de Sagentes (1293), 57; Palea (1146), 74; Sisnando (884), 40; Tello Muñoz (1053), 45
Doubleday, Simon, 99, 101, 186n.38
dowries *(arras),* 88
Dueñas, 74, *75*

economy: monastic, 130; monetary, 16–24; of salvation, 110–12, 121–22, 127–32, 153
education, 12, 95
Eleanor, daughter of Henry II and Eleanor of Aquitaine, 8, 96
emperor, title of, 140–41
England, 20, 102–3, 114, 146–47
entailments *(mayorazgos),* 88, 108
envergoñados, 117
estates, construction of, 75–77, 93–94, 96, 101–2
Extremadura, 105, 144

familial clans, 92–94
family, 3, 88–89, 98; rural, 88, 91–92; urban, 88–91. *See also* inheritance; lineages; noble families; property
family and kin, bequests to, 38, 55–56, 122–23, 127, 173n.27
fashion, 12
feeding and clothing the poor, 111, 114–16, 119–29
Ferdinand (brother of Philip II), 104
Ferdinand II, 5, 7, 106, 144
Ferdinand III, 8, 12, 35–36, 69, 106–7, 143–45, 176n.17
Ferdinand IV, 125, 176n.17
Ferdinand de la Cerda, 108
Fernando III, 142
Flanders, 20
formulas, used in wills, 50–51. *See also* "remedy of one's soul"
Fourth Lateran Council, 12
France, 20, 102–3, 114, 145–47. *See also* pilgrims

Francis, Saint, 25
Franciscans, 25–26, 58
Franco, Francisco, 136
Frederick II Hohenstaufen, 134
French Revolution, 85
Frías, 103–4, 125
frontiers. *See* boundaries
Fuenterrabía, 85
fueros, 31, 60–65, 176n.17; of Castrojeriz, 60; of Cuenca, 61–62, 70, 79–80, 176n.19; *Fuero juzgo,* 62–63, 105; *Fuero real,* 63–65; of Palenzuela, 60

Galicia, 5–6, 105
García, king of Galicia, 139
García de Valdeavellano, Luis, 16
García Fernández, count of Castile, 60
genealogy, 93, 102
Gerbet, Marie-Claude, 99–100
gifts, 111–12
González, Julio, 12–13
Gonzalo de Berceo, 4, 13, 27–28, 151–52; *Milagros de Nuestra Señora,* 27–28, 70–71, 118–19, 151–52; *Vida de San Millán,* 119
"good men" *(omnes buenos),* 148–49
government, 64, 81, 120, 131, *147,* 149–50. *See also* Castile, Crown of; *names of rulers*
Granada, 143
Guiance, Ariel, 27, 86

Haro family, 101
Henry, son of Ferdinand III, 108
Henry I, 8, 106
Henry III, 85–86, 145, 191n.25
Henry IV, 142
Herlihy, David, 88
hermandades, 150
Hernández, Francisco, 149
Herrin, Judith, 188n
hidalgos, 150
hospitals, 69, 98, 122, 125–26, 130–31

iconography, royal, 136–38
ida contra los moros, 142. *See also* Reconquest
inheritance, 62–64, 103–4, 117; partible, 77, 88, 100, 105, 139. *See also* primogeniture

inventories, 80–83, 85
investment strategies, 56–58
Isabella I, 145
itemization. *See* inventories

James, Saint, *18*
James I, 12
Jerez de la Frontera, 82
Jews, 36, 93, 126, 149
Jimena, Queen, 68
John I, 191n.25
John II, 86
Juan Carlos, king of Spain, 134
Juan Ruiz, *Libro de buen amor,* 118–19
Julian of Toledo, *Prognosticon futuri saeculi libri tres,* 27
jurisdiction, and spatial concept of property, 67–68, 71–73

kings, of Castile, 36, 100–102, 133–34; coronation and anointment, 134–35, 143–45; peripatetic lifestyle, 143, 149; and primogeniture, 106–8; as warriors, 135, 139, 141–42, 144–45. *See also names of kings*
kings and kingship, 102–3; English, 145–46; French, 134, 145–46; martial aspect of, 135, 139, 141–42, 144–45; sacral, 136–38; unsacred, 133–46
kin networks, 92–94; rural, 91–92; urban, 88–91
Klapisch-Zuber, Christiane, 88
Kléber, Paul, 166n.19
knighting, of Castilian kings, 135

laborers, 23–24
laicization, 10, 36, 149, 152–53
landmarks. *See* boundary markers *(mojones)*
land surveyors, 69
land transactions, 78–79. *See also* rights of way
language, Arabic, 36
language, Castilian: and laicization, 29–30; literary use, 27–28, 36, 138; official use, 23, 30–31, 147–49; and shift in values, 31–34, 152, 154; use in wills and other documents, 3, 51–52, 69, 82
language, Hebrew, 36
language, Latin, 3, 29–34, *33,* 35–36, 40, 52, 138

Lara family, 7, 101, 186n.35, 186n.38
Laredo, 85
Las Navas de Tolosa, 8, 106–7, 141, 144, 165n.14
learning, 4
legacies, typology of, 121
legal codes, 60–66, 116–17. *See also* fueros; *Siete partidas, Las*
legal system, 146–47
Le Goff, Jacques, ix–x, 4, 22, 25–27, 58, 164n.4, 175n.9
León, 5–6, 8, 13, *15,* 24, 139, 144
Leon of Rosmithal, 83–84
Lex visigothorum, 49–50, 105. *See also* fueros
Liber abbaci, 24
Liber Sancti Jacobi, 16
Libro de Apolonio, 118–19
Liébana, 49–53, *51,* 81
lineages, 92–94, 99–100, 154; bourgeois, 94–99; noble, 99–102; and primogeniture, 102–9. *See also* marriage alliances
Linehan, Peter, ix, 12, 66, 136, 139–40, 193n.3, 194n.11
literacy, of bourgeoisie, 29–30
literature, Castilian, 4, 12–13, 34–36, 133, 136–37. *See also names of authors; titles of anonymous works*
litigation, over bequests, 53
Little, Lester, 25, 175n.9
living gifts. *See* donations; donors
Logroño, 3, 25, 37–38, 86
Lopez, Robert, 16
lordships *(señoríos),* 102
Lucas de Tuy, 13, 27–28, 139; *Chronicon mundi,* 34–35, 138; *Milagros de San Isidoro,* 27–28

MacKay, Angus, 194n.7
Madrid, 69, 143
Manuel, Don Juan, *Conde Lucanor,* 119
Manuel Recuero, 145
marriage alliances, 97, 99, 104, 106–7
Marseilles, 69
Marsilio de Padua, 84
Martínez family, 91–92
Martínez García, Luis, 78
Martz, Linda, 114
Mathe family (Burgos), 89–90
meals, ritual, 121–22, 124–25

measurement of property, 51. *See also* boundaries; property, spatial concept of
Medina Sidonia family, 101
mendicant orders, 25–26, 58
mentalité, use of term, 164n.4. *See also* values, shift in
merchants, 37–38; foreign, 16–20
Mesta, 80
mester de clerecía, 13, 151
middling sorts. *See* bourgeoisie
Miguéllez family, 91–92
Miguel Pérez, 77
Milky Way. *See* pilgrimage road
Miller, Maureen C., 46, 173 nn. 22 and 26
Milton, Gregory, 171n.5
mojones, 68–73, 85
Molina, 86
monasteries, 25, 46, 49, 81, 129–31, 142; Albelda, 44; Covarrubias, 70, 179n.11; Las Huelgas (Burgos), 12–13, 74, *75*, 96, *97*, 98, 172n.17; Salas, 98; San Miguel de Busto, 120; San Millán de la Cogolla, 40, 151; San Pedro de Arlanza, 35, 70; San Pedro de Cardeña, 130; San Pedro in Gumiel de Izán, 70–71, 178n.9; San Quirce, 45; San Salvador de Oña, 41, 130, 179n.15; Santa María de Aguilar de Campoo, 57, 83, 91, 124; Santa María de Nájera, 68; Santa María in Fresnillo de las Dueñas, 71; Santo Domingo de Silos, 117, 130; Santo Toribio (San Martín de Turieno), 49–53, 81, 174n.33; San Vicente, 126; San Zoilo de Carrión, 41, 68–70, 74, 81–82
monastic foundations, 172n.20
money, 23–24, 95, 164n.1
moneylending, 125–26
Moote, Lloyd, 145
Murcia, 82, 143
Muslims, 8, 36, 93, 105, 149–50. *See also* Christian-Muslim relations; Reconquest

negotiation, in wills, 52, 56–58. *See also* reciprocity
Nieto Soria, José Manuel, 86, 136–38, 145, 194n.11
nobility, and royal power, 100–102
noble families, 45–46, 73, 93–94, 103, 107–8, 186n.34; Castro family, 7, 101; Lara family, 7, 101, 186 nn. 35 and 38. *See also* lineages
notarial culture, 30–31, 38, 171n.5. *See also* scribes
notario, use of term, 171n.5
novelty, taste for *(gusto de novedades)*, 13

officeholding, 94–95; ecclesiastical, 94–95, 98; municipal, 94–96, 98
Olivares, count-duke of, 115
Oña, 68
orientalism, use of term, x
origin myth, royal, 139

Palencia, 74
Palenzuela, fuero of, 60
pantheon, royal, 143–44
patria, concept of, 86
peasants, 91–92; artful, 71; idle, 117
Pérez de Herrera, Cristóbal, 113
periphery, x–xi, 163n.6, 187n.47
Peter of John Olivi, *On contracts*, 24
Petronila of Aragon, 104
Philip II, 104, 182n.48
pilgrimage, *18*, 126
pilgrimage road, 3, 7, 12, *14–15*, 16, 21, 27, *97*, 121–23, 151. *See also* Santiago de Compostela
pilgrims, 6; French *(francos)*, 16, 21, 140
Poema de Fernán González, 4, 35
Poema de mío Cid, 4, 13, 24, 151–52
poor, 116–17, 120, 127–28; charitable bequests for, 3, 38, 47, 110–12, 120–24, 192n.33; feeding and clothing, 111, 114–16, 119–29. *See also* poverty
ports, of Castile, 85
poverty, 26; debate on, 113–15; taxonomy of, 116–18; voluntary *vs.* involuntary, 127–28. *See also* charity
power, 73; and concept of property, 79–80, 94–95; royal, 100–102, 133–35, 146–47. *See also* kings and kingship; sovereignty
Primera crónica general, 35, 138–42
primogeniture, 102–9, 146
property, 61–63, 79, 93, 98; consolidation of, 73–77, *75*, 88, 101–2, 186n.34; spatial concept of, 9, 67, 71–73, 79–80, 83–86
property exchange, wills as, 53–56

protowills, 40–41; Don Alvaro (1225), 41; Elvira Téllez (1137), 41
puertos secos, 86
purgatory, 26–29

Quintanilla Muniocisla, 79

Radulfus Glaber, *Histories,* 72
Raimundo II, bishop of Palencia, 172n.12
Ramón Berenguer IV, 104
Real Hermandad of the Santísimo y Santiago, 89–90, *90*
rebellions: bourgeois, 21; royal, 108
reciprocity; of charity, 118, 128; in donations, 45, 48, 51, 80–81. *See also* salvation, economy of
Reconquest, 6–7, 66, 100, 140–42, 144, 146, 153
Regularis concordia, 128
Reilly, Bernard, 140
religion. *See* Christian-Muslim relations; Church, the; Jews; Muslims; spirituality
religious beliefs: devotion to Virgin Mary, 13, 151–52; purgatory, 26–29
religious images, and kingship, 136–38
"remedy of one's soul," 40, *42–43,* 46, 48–49, 119–20, 190n.23
remembrança, use of term, 82
Renaissance, twelfth-century, 164n.6
Repartimientos, 82
rex Dei Gratiae, 136–38
ricos hombres, use of term, 107–8, 154
rights of way, 77–80
Rioja, 122–23
ritual, use of term, 127
Rodrigo Ximénez de Rada, 34–35, 139–40, 143; *Historia de rebus Hispanie sive historia gothica,* 138
Rosenwein, Barbara, 45
royal family, 100, 107; and monastic foundations, 46, 48, 172n.17. *See also* kings, of Castile
royal gifts, as basis for nobles' power, 100–101
Rucquoi, Adeline, 6, 164n.7

Salamanca, 13, 27, 34
salvation, economy of, 110–12, 121–22, 127–32, 153
Sancho (Infante), 39

Sancho (heir of Alfonso X), 188n.57
Sancho the Great, 139
Sancho II, 139
Sancho III, 5, 7, 106, 143
Sancho IV, 71, 108, 135, 139, 143, 145
Sancho VI, 7
San Sebastián, 85
Santamaría Lancho, Miguel, 193n.44
Santander, 85
Santiago de Compostela, 6, *17–19,* 25, 105
San Vicente de la Barquera, 85
Sarracín family (Burgos), 16, 76–77, 94–99, *97*
scholars, traveling, 6
scribes, 2, 10, 30–32, 34, 37, 39–40, 48, 64, 148, 169n.36; use of Castilian language, 32–34
seals, royal, 137–38
secularization, 10, 152–53
Segovia, 13, 69, 99, 130, *148*
self-representation, 133
Seville, 8, 30, 38–39, 82, 106, 143
Siete partidas, Las, 39, 63–66, 108, 116–17, 177 nn. 33 and 36, 187n.56
silversmiths, *17*
Smail, Daniel, 69
Smith, Colin, 4
social class; and charity, 118–19, 128–29; and donations, 46–47. *See also* bourgeoisie; lineages; noble families
social mobility, 20, 94–99
sovereignty, and territory, 83–86
spirituality, 25–26, 121
Strayer, Joseph R., 10
structural changes, 21
sumptuary laws, 101–2, 129

taxation, 147, 149
territoriality, 83–86, 106–7
testamentum, use of term, 44, 49–50, 52, 172n.12
testators, 29, 56, 59, 61–62, 115; Diego Gutiérrez (1220), 52; Doña Elvira Alfonso (1289), 124–25; Ferrant Pérez (1334 and 1344), 125–26; García Gónzalez (1204), 51–52; Garci de Campo, 191n.30; Gómez Pérez de la Lama (1292), 52–53; Gonzalo Pérez (1349), 55, 126–27, 174n.5; Iohana

INDEX 221

Peres (1315), 123–24; Don Juan (Infante) (1319), 191n.30; Juan Peregrin (1225), 54; Don Julián (1316), 191n.30; Marín Roiz (1334), 191n.30; Don Martín Ibáñez (1333), 54–55; Martín Ortiz de Agonciello (1347), 37–38, 123, 151; Pedro Díaz (1236), 52; Pedro García (1331), 122–23; Pedro Ibáñez, 122; Sancha Alfonso (1337), 103–4; Sebastián (1230), 1–3, 121–22, 151; Sindino, 50
testimony, recorded in Castilian language, 32–33
time measurement, 24
Toledo, 5, 105, 139–41
Torres Sevilla, Margarita, 99, 186n.34
trade, 16–20, 37–38; maritime, 20; and social mobility, 96. *See also* bourgeoisie; urban centers
travel accounts, 83–84
Treaty of Cazola (1179), 7
tribute *(parias)*, 100, 146

universities, 4, 12, 164n.7
urban centers, 6, 20, 25–26, 32, 79
urban leagues, 150
urban militias, 21, *147*
urban oligarchs, 75

Valencia, 104
Valladolid, 115
Vallarta, 68
Valpuesta, 98

values, shift in, 3–5, 21–23, 31–34, 58, 101–2, 110–12, 114–15, 146, 151–54
Verona, 46–47
Vezdemarván, 41
Vida de Santo Domingo de Silos, 119
villages: Castrillo, 68; Estudos de Baño, 71; Fontoria de Val de Aradores, 71; Gallejones de Zamanzas, *78*; Gañinas (Gannines), 68; Ganiz (Geniz), 44; Madrigal, 179n.11; Melgar de Suso, 60; Montejo, 71; Nogal de las Huertas, 69; Piedraportún (Per Apertum), 91; Prado, 76, 96; Ruyales, 179n.11; Saint Quirze, 71; San Felices, 41; Trespaderne, 68; Valdecardeña, 76, 96; Varenciella de Río Pisuerga, 124; Villatoro, 76–77, 95–96
Virgin Mary, devotion to, 13, 151–52
Visigoths, 49–50, 105, 140
Vitoria, 86

Waldensianism, 25–26, 58
White, Stephen, 45
wills, 1–3, 5, 38, 61–62, 64, 110–12, 191n.25; from Burgos, 121–24; from Logroño, 121–24; post-1220, 40–41, *42–43*, 48–49, 153–54; pre-1220, 40–41, *42–43*. *See also* bequests; donations; donors; protowills; *testamentum;* testators
witnessing, of legal documents, 96
women, 61, 91, 103–4, 123–25
wool, 126, 174n.3

Ximénez de Rada, 13